DMU 0715870 01 4

CW00969384

Disability Discrimination

Other titles available from Law Society Publishing:

Age Discrimination: A Guide to the New Law
General Editor: Shaman Kapoor

Drafting Employment Contracts (2nd edn)
Gillian Howard

Employment Law Handbook (5th edn)
Henry Scrope, Daniel Barnett and Keira Gore

Equality Act 2010
General Editor: Michael Duggan

Lexcel People Management Toolkit
The Law Society

Managing People in a Legal Business
General Editor: Jill Andrew

Mental Health Tribunals
Philip Fennell, Penny Letts and Jonathan Wilson

Titles fom Law Society Publishing can be ordered from all good bookshops or direct (telephone 0870 850 1422, email **lawsociety@prolog.uk.com** or visit our online shop at **bookshop.lawsociety.org.uk**).

DISABILITY DISCRIMINATION

Law and Case Management

Karen Jackson and Lydia Banerjee

The Law Society

All rights reserved. No part of this publication may be reproduced in any material form, whether by photocopying, scanning, downloading onto computer or otherwise without the written permission of the Law Society except in accordance with the provisions of the Copyright, Designs and Patents Act 1988. Applications should be addressed in the first instance, in writing, to Law Society Publishing. Any unauthorised or restricted act in relation to this publication may result in civil proceedings and/or criminal prosecution.

The authors have asserted the right under the Copyright, Designs and Patents Act 1988 to be identified as authors of this work.

Whilst all reasonable care has been taken in the preparation of this publication, neither the publisher nor the authors can accept any responsibility for any loss occasioned to any person acting or refraining from action as a result of relying upon its contents.

The views expressed in this publication should be taken as those of the authors only unless it is specifically indicated that the Law Society has given its endorsement.

© The Law Society 2013

Crown copyright material is reproduced with the permission of the Controller of Her Majesty's Stationery Office

ISBN-13: 978-1-907698-60-6

Published in 2013 by the Law Society
113 Chancery Lane, London WC2A 1PL

Typeset by Columns Design XML Ltd, Reading
Printed by Hobbs the Printers Ltd, Totton, Hants

The paper used for the text pages of this book is FSC® certified. FSC (the Forest Stewardship Council®) is an international network to promote responsible management of the world's forests.

This book is dedicated to three very important men in my life, without whom this book would not have been possible: my husband, Christopher; Dr Jayan Parameshwar, Consultant Cardiologist at Papworth Hospital; and my donor – **Karen Jackson**

This book is dedicated to my husband, Vikram; my family, both Carters and Banerjees; and to the many friends and colleagues at Littleton Chambers and beyond who inspire me and keep me going – **Lydia Banerjee**

This book is also dedicated to the many clients we have had the honour of representing and the invaluable lessons we have learned from their cases

DE MONTFORT UNIVERSITY LIBRARY

Fund: 110	Date: 22|12|5
Sequence	
Class	344.10287
Suffix	JAC

Contents

Foreword		xiii
Preface		xiv
Table of cases		xvii
Table of statutes		xx
Table of statutory instruments		xxii
Abbreviations		xxiii

Introduction to disability discrimination law xxv

PART 1: DISABILITY DISCRIMINATION: THE LAW

1 The definition of disability **3**

1.1	The elements of the definition	3
1.2	Specified conditions	9
1.3	Variable conditions	11
1.4	Past disabilities	13
1.5	The effect of medical treatment and prostheses	13
1.6	The material time for assessing disability	14
1.7	Conclusion	16

2 Direct disability discrimination, associative discrimination and discrimination by perception **17**

2.1	Direct disability discrimination	17
2.2	Associative discrimination	24
2.3	Perception discrimination	25
2.4	Other aspects of direct discrimination	27
2.5	Conclusion	29

3 Section 15 discrimination arising from disability **30**

3.1	Brief background	30
3.2	Section 15	32
3.3	Some early cases	37

3.4   Relationship with indirect discrimination   39
3.5   Overlap with the reasonable adjustments duty   39
3.6   Conclusion   40

4   Reasonable adjustments   **41**

4.1   Background   41
4.2   The breadth of the duty   42
4.3   The three requirements   43
4.4   The required steps   47
4.5   Substantial disadvantage   50
4.6   The comparison with non-disabled people   50
4.7   Reasonableness   51
4.8   Knowledge   55
4.9   Employer duty to consult   56
4.10   Reasonable adjustments around sick pay   57
4.11   Disability leave   59
4.12   Reasonable adjustments and dismissals   59
4.13   No justification   60
4.14   Conclusion   60

5   Indirect disability discrimination   **61**

5.1   Indirect disability discrimination   61
5.2   The s.19 definition   62
5.3   Conclusion   66

**6   Other prohibited conduct: harassment, victimisation and other
       unlawful acts**   **67**

6.1   Harassment   67
6.2   Victimisation   73
6.3   Liability for discriminatory acts   76
6.4   Conclusion   78

7   Other legal aspects of disability in the workplace   **79**

7.1   Recruitment and promotion   79
7.2   Obtaining medical records   82
7.3   Adjustments to policies during employment   85
7.4   Contractual provisions around sickness and disability   87
7.5   Pay arrangements   88
7.6   Conclusion   91

8   Termination of employment   **93**

8.1   Reasonable adjustments and termination   93

8.2   Discriminatory dismissals   94
8.3   Redundancy   94
8.4   Capability   95
8.5   Ill health retirement   99
8.6   Payments on account of disability   99
8.7   Conclusion   100

9   Mental health disabilities   101

9.1   Attitudes and sensitive management   101
9.2   Case management issues   103
9.3   Conclusion   108

PART 2: CASE STUDY

10   Managing disability in the workplace: case study   111

10.1   Recruitment and interview   111
10.2   Reasonable adjustments   112
10.3   Knowledge   113
10.4   New management   114
10.5   Obtaining medical records   116
10.6   Sick pay   117
10.7   Medical evidence   117
10.8   Managing a return to work   118
10.9   Vicarious liability   119
10.10 Harassment   119
10.11 Dismissal   120
10.12 Conclusion   121

PART 3: LITIGATION CASE MANAGEMENT

11   The tribunal process   125

11.1   Overview of this Part   125
11.2   Steps before the tribunal process   126
11.3   Adjustments before tribunal proceedings   126
11.4   Overview of the tribunal process   127

12   Bringing a claim   129

12.1   Purpose of the ET1   129
12.2   Timing of the ET1   129
12.3   The ET1 form   130
12.4   Heading   131

12.5   Content   131
12.6   Conclusion   137

13   Responding to a claim   **138**

13.1   Purpose of the ET3   138
13.2   Timing of the ET3   138
13.3   The ET3 form   139
13.4   Heading   139
13.5   Content   139
13.6   Conclusion   146

14   Settlement   **147**

14.1   Benefits of settlement   147
14.2   Compromise agreement   148
14.3   ACAS   149
14.4   Judicial mediation   150
14.5   Independent mediation   150
14.6   Consent order   151
14.7   Conclusion   151

15   The process for determining disability   **152**

15.1   Overview of the process for determining disability   152
15.2   Impact statement   153
15.3   Other evidence the parties may adduce   154
15.4   Medical evidence   155
15.5   Conclusion   160

16   Preparation for a hearing   **161**

16.1   Process overview   161
16.2   Case management discussion   163
16.3   Schedule of loss   163
16.4   Disclosure   164
16.5   Preparation of the bundle   165
16.6   Witness statements   167
16.7   Other orders   168
16.8   Conclusion   170

17   The hearing   **171**

17.1   Running order   171
17.2   Adjustments to the hearing process   174
17.3   Adjournments   174
17.4   Remedies   176

17.5 The review process 181
17.6 The appeal process 181
17.7 Costs 182
17.8 Conclusion 182

APPENDICES

A Case study: sample correspondence **183**

A1 Summary of rights under the Access to Medical Reports Act 1988 185
A2 Letter to employee requesting consent for medical report or access to medical records 187
A3 Employee consent to obtaining medical records/report 188
A4 Letter to request medical assessment 189
A5 Employee consent to attending medical assessment 190
A6 Letter to medical adviser requesting assessment 192

B Litigation case management: sample documents **195**

B1 Sample grounds of complaint 197
B2 Sample grounds of resistance 202
B3 Impact statement 207
B4 Joint letter of instruction 210
B5 Schedule of loss 215
B6 Scott Schedule 217

C Statutory and guidance material **221**

C1 Equality Act 2010 (extracts) 223
C2 Equality and Human Rights Commission: Equality Act 2010 Code of Practice (extracts) 239
C3 Office for Disability Issues: Equality Act 2010 Guidance (extracts) 264
C4 Access to Medical Reports Act 1988 272
C5 Employment Rights Act 1996 (extracts) 277
C6 Income Tax (Earnings and Pensions) Act 2003 (extracts) 286

D Other reference material **289**

D1 Online resource list 291

Index 293

Foreword

No one asked to be disabled. So if you are, you are entitled to be treated fairly, to be given equal access to work opportunities and to expect reasonable adjustments to be made so that you can play a full role. When that doesn't happen, your complaints must be acted upon and, as a last resort, enforced through the law.

This book looks in two directions. It is primarily written for employers, to show you how to provide fair treatment for disabled workers. It is also written so that disabled people can see how employers and fellow employees are required by law to behave towards you. It's complicated. Any book which aims to change behaviour has to explain the current legal framework. From the outset in 1995, disability law has proceeded hand in hand with soft law: guidance, codes, examples. And that's how the book works. Loads of practical examples and proportionate citing of legal cases guide us through the many problems in our way.

Litigation is daunting. According to the authors it is a lottery. What all of us involved in enforcement of the law aim to achieve is an environment where resort to the tribunal means a failure in sensible resolution of disputes. Making working life fair for people with disabilities ought to be a day-to-day ambition, and not simply an exercise in litigation avoidance. If employers and workmates understand the responsibilities we all owe, complaints will be rare and their solution more likely to be amicable.

These two highly experienced lawyers have written a book about illness and disability from the inside, and with a wealth of experience representing employees, employers and the third sector. Understanding disabilities and enforcing rights is made easy here because they both describe how the system works and how it can be made to work better. The reshaping of the law in the Equality Act 2010 is an ongoing endeavour, to be used in a focused way and, we hope, only in the last resort.

Judge Jeremy McMullen QC
Employment Appeal Tribunal
Salisbury Square
London EC4Y 8JX

5 March 2013

Preface

The idea for this book came from a desire to give a wide range of users – solicitors, HR and occupational health professionals, employees and business managers – a practical book on managing disability in the workplace. Our main aim is to provide not a definitive work on disability law but an overview of the law (**Part 1**), a case study illustrating how the law is applied in practice (**Part 2**), a guide to managing litigation around disability (**Part 3**) and templates and sample documents ready to adapt for use (**Appendices A** and **B**). Our other aim is to bring together in one volume the relevant extracts from statute, statutory and other guidance, so that most users will need nothing more than this book to manage a wide range of situations (**Appendix C**). The book is divided into parts so that you can just dive in where you need to.

We have attempted to make this a lively read. It's not always easy to avoid too much legalese, especially when explaining complex legal provisions and cases, but we've tried to bring it to life for you. Key cases and examples are highlighted in text boxes.

It has been hard to know where the limits of this book should end. We simply don't have enough space for a definitive guide to tribunal proceedings, for example. We hope we have given you the core elements and documents. We have also provided a list in **Appendix D** of online links taking you to further resources. Finally, we will be providing quarterly updates via the Law Society website **www.lawsociety.org.uk/disabilitydiscriminationbook** to keep pace with the law in this area as it changes.

Our case study in **Part 2** focuses on two mental health disabilities. There are reasons for this. First, physical disabilities are often easier to manage in practice, both in the workplace and in tribunal proceedings. Mental health disabilities give rise to a number of specific tricky issues which we have flagged up for you. Secondly, mental health illness is the primary reason for long-term sickness absence. The CBI calls it the biggest risk to business in the 21st century. We know that our society has much to do to tackle the stigma around mental health. It must stay at the top of the agenda. One in four people suffer depression in their lifetime. This has a big impact on the workplace. Of the 190 million working days lost to illness last year, 25 per cent of this is long term and mental health illness is the largest single cause. Early intervention and proactive management are key to avoiding the long-term sick and disabled falling out of work and into long-term benefits. Those with long-term disabilities have a key contribution to make to work and to society.

Sickness costs the UK economy £17 billion a year. With sensitive, constructive management of disabilities in the workplace, a real contribution can be made by employers giving disabled people real opportunities. With dialogue and understanding, employers and employees can work together to avoid costly litigation.

We hope this book meets our aims and that you will find it a useful companion. We have certainly enjoyed writing it and hope you share our enthusiasm for it.

Karen Jackson and Lydia Banerjee
March 2013

Table of cases

Abadeh v. British Telecommunications plc [2001] IRLR 23, EAT 1.5
Aderemi v. London and South Eastern Railway Ltd (2012) UKEAT/0316/12 .... 1.1.4
Ahmed v. Metroline Travel Ltd [2011] Eq LR 464, EAT 1.1.4
Aitken v. Commissioner of Police of the Metropolis [2011] EWCA Civ 582 .... 2.3
Amnesty International v. Ahmed [2009] ICR 1450, EAT 2.1.7
Andreou v. Lord Chancellor's Department [2002] EWCA Civ 1192 .... 17.3
Archibald v. Fife Council [2004] UKHL 32 .... 4, 4.2, 4.3.1, 4.7.2.1, 8.1, 8.3
Ashton & Ashton v. Burbage and District Constitutional Club (2012)
    UKEAT/0496/11; UKEAT/0497/11, EAT 17.3
Aspden v. Webbs Poultry and Meat Group (Holdings) Ltd [1996] IRLR 521,
    QBD 7.5.3
Associacion Nacional de Grandes Empresas de Disribucion v. Federation de
    Associacions Sindicales (Case C-78/11), 21 June 2012, ECJ 7.5.4
Austin v. Samuel Grant (North East) Ltd (2011) ET/2503956/11 .... 2.3
Briscoe v. Lubrizol Ltd (No.2) [2002] EWCA Civ 508 .... 7.5.3
British Airways plc v. Starmer [2005] IRLR 863, EAT 4.3.1
British Home Stores Ltd v. Burchell [1980] ICR 303, EAT 8.4.2
Chacon Navas v. Eurest Colectividades [2006] IRLR 706, ECJ 1.1
Chief Constable of Lothian and Borders Police v. Cumming [2010] IRLR 109,
    EAT 1.1.2, 1.1.4
Chief Constable of South Yorkshire v. Jelic [2010] IRLR 744, EAT 4.2
Chief Constable of West Yorkshire Police v. Khan [2001] UKHL 48 .... 2.1.7
Clark v. TDG Ltd (t/a Novacold) [1999] ICR 951, CA 3.1.1, 3.1.2, 3.1.4, 4.12, 8.1
Cordell v. Foreign and Commonwealth Office [2012] ICR 280, EAT 4.7.2.2
Cosgrove v. Caesar and Howie [2001] IRLR 653, EAT 4.9
Da'Bell v. National Society for the Prevention of Cruelty to Children [2010]
    IRLR 19, EAT 17.4.3.2
De Keyser v. Wilson [2001] IRLR 324, EAT 9.2.1, 15.4
Dundee City Council v. Sharp (2011) UKEATS/0009/11 .... 8.4.1
Eagle Place Services Ltd v. Rudd [2010] IRLR 486, EAT 2.1.3, 3.2.1
East Lindsey DC v. Daubney [1977] ICR 566, EAT 8.4.1
EBR Attridge Law LLP v. Coleman [2010] ICR 242, EAT 2.2, 6.1.4
Edmund Nuttall Ltd v. Butterfield [2006] ICR 77, EAT 1.2.2
Environment Agency v. Rowan [2008] ICR 218, EAT 4.4, 4.7.2.2
Eweida v. British Airways plc [2010] EWCA Civ 80 .... 5.2.3
Fareham College Corp v. Walters [2009] IRLR 991, EAT 4.6
First West Yorkshire Ltd (t/a First Leeds) v. Haigh [2008] IRLR 182, EAT 8.5
Foster v. Leeds Teaching Hospital NHS Trust [2007] IRLR 579, EAT 4.7.1
Fowler v. Waltham Forest LBC (2007) UKEAT/0116/09 .... 7.5.2
Garricks (Caterers) Ltd v. Nolan [1980] IRLR 259, EAT 8.1
GCHQ v. Bacchus [2012] All ER (D) 151 (Aug), EAT 15.4

Ginn v. Tesco Stores [2005] All ER (D) 259 (Oct), EAT 1.1.2
Goodwin v. Patent Office [1999] IRLR 4, EAT 1.1.1, 1.1.2
Hammersmith & Fulham LBC v. Farnsworth [2000] IRLR 691, EAT 2.1.6
Hartman v. South Essex Mental Health and Community Care NHS Trust
    [2005] EWCA Civ 6 .... 4.8
High Quality Lifestyles Ltd v. Watts [2006] IRLR 850, EAT 2.1.1
Hinsley v. Chief Constable of West Mercia Constabulary (2010)
    UKEAT/0200/10 .... 4.7.2.1
HJ Heinz Co Ltd v. Kenrick [2000] IRLR 144, EAT 2.1.6
HMRC v. Stringer [2009] UKHL 31 .... 7.5.4
Horner v. Hasted (Inspector of Taxes) [1995] STC 766, ChD 8.6
Hudson v. Home Office (2009) ET/2301061/09 .... 6.2.2
Hudson v. Post Office (1998) ET3100773/98 .... 1.1.2
J v. DLA Piper UK LLP [2010] IRLR 936; [2010] ICR 1052, EAT 1.1.1, 2.3, 9.2.1
Jessemey v. Rowstock Ltd (2011) ET/2701156/11 .... 6.2.5
Kapadia v. Lambeth LBC [2000] IRLR 699, CA 1.5
Lewisham LBC v. Malcolm [2008] UKHL 43 .... Intro, 3.1.1, 3.1.2, 3.1.3, 3.1.4, 3.6
Lloyd v. BCQ Ltd (2010) UKEAT/0148/12/1211; UKEAT/0239/12 .... 7.5.3
Logan v. Celyn House (2012) UKEAT/0069/12 .... 8.2
McAdie v. Royal Bank of Scotland [2007] EWCA Civ 806 .... 8.4.4
McGraw v. London Ambulance Service NHS Trust (2011) ET/3301865/11 .... 3.3
Martin v. Devonshires Solicitors [2011] ICR 352, EAT 6.2.4.3
Meikle v. Nottinghamshire CC [2004] EWCA Civ 859 .... 4.10, 7.5.2
Millar v. IRC [2006] IRLR 112, CS, Scot 1.1.1
Ministry of Defence v. Hay [2008] ICR 1247, EAT 1.1.2
Morgan v. Staffordshire University [2002] ICR 475, EAT 9.2.1
Newcastle upon Tyne Hospitals NHS Foundation Trust v. Bagley [2012] Eq
    LR 634, EAT 4.3.1, 4.10, 7.5.2
NHS Leeds v. Larner [2012] EWCA Civ 1034 .... 7.5.4
Nottingham City Transport Ltd v. Harvey [2013] Eq LR 4, EAT 4.3.1
O'Hanlon v. Commissioners of the Inland Revenue [2007] EWCA Civ 283 ...... 4.7.2.2,
                                                                         4.10, 7.5.2
O'Hanlon v. Revenue and Customs Commissioners [2006] ICR 1579, EAT 7.5.2
O'Neill v. Governors of St Thomas More Roman Catholic Voluntarily Aided
    Upper School [14997] ICR 33, EAT 2.1.4
Patel v. Oldham MBC; Patel v. Governing Body of Rushcroft Primary School
    [2010] ICR 603, EAT 1.1.3, 1.3.3
Paterson v. Commissioner of Police of the Metropolis [2007] IRLR 763,
    EAT 1.1.4
Power v. Panasonic UK Ltd [2003] IRLR 151, EAT 1.2.2, App.B4
Project Management Institute v. Latif [2007] IRLR 579, EAT 4.7.1
Rhys-Harper v. Relaxation Group plc; D'Souza v. Lambeth LBC; Jones v. 3M
    Healthcare Ltd [2003] UKHL 33 .... 6.2.5
Richmond Adult Community College v. McDougall [2008] EWCA Civ 4 .... 1.6
Roberts v. North-West Ambulance Service [2012] Eq LR 196, EAT 4.3.1
Rowstock Ltd v. Jessemey (2012) UKEAT/0112/12 .... 6.2.5
Royal Bank of Scotland v. Ashton [2011] ICR 632, EAT 4.4
Royal Bank of Scotland plc v. Morris [2012] Eq LR 406, EAT 9.2.1
Rugamer v. Sony Music Entertainment UK Ltd [2001] ICR 381, EAT 9.2.1
Salford NHS Primary Care Trust v. Smith [2011] Eq LR 1119, EAT .. 4.7.2.2, 4.11, 4.12
SCA Packaging v. Boyle [2009] UKHL 37 .... 1.1.3, 1.3.1, 1.3.2, App.B4
Sheffield City Council v. Norouzi [2011] IRLR 897, EAT 6.1.7
Singh v. University Hospital NHS Trust (2002) UKEAT/1409/01 .... 17.4.3.9

Slack v. Weldcare Ltd (2008) ET/2603076/08 .... 6.1.6
Stockton-on-Tees Borough Council v. Aylott [2010] EWCA Civ 910.. 2.1.3, 2.1.4, 4.12, 8.1
Stuckey v. Daido Industrial Bearings Europe Ltd (2008) ET/0700302/08 .... 6.1.6
Taiwo v. Olaigbe (2012) ET/2389629/11 .... 6.2.5
Tameside Hospital NHS Foundation Trust v. Mylott (2010)
    UKEAT/0399/10/1304 .... 8.5
Tarbuck v. Sainsbury Supermarkets Ltd [2006] IRLR 664, EAT 4.9
Taylor v. OCS Group Ltd [2006] EWCA Civ 702 .... 8.2
Teinaz v. Wandsworth LBC [2002] EWCA Civ 1040 .... 17.3
Tudor v. Spen Corner Veterinary Centre (2005) ET/2404211/05 .... 2.1.1
Vento v. Chief Constable of West Yorkshire Police [2002] EWCA Civ 1871 ..... 17.4.3.2
Wilcox v. Birmingham CAB Services Ltd [2011] Eq LR 810, EAT 4.8
Williams v. Ystrad Mynach College (2011) ET/1600019/11 .... 3.3
Woodcock v. Cumbria Primary Care Trust [2012] EWCA Civ 330 .... 3.2.5
Woodrup v. Southwark LBC [2002] EWCA Civ 1716 .... 1.1.1
Yorkshire Housing Ltd v. Cuerden (2010) UKEAT/0397/09 .... 4.3.1, 4.7.2.1

Table of statutes

Access to Medical Reports Act
   1988 .... 7.2, 7.2.1, 7.2.2, 7.4, App.A1,
          App.A2, App.A3, App.A4,
          App.A5, **App.C2**

Data Protection Act 1998.......... App.A3,
          App.B1, App.B2

Disability Discrimination Act
   1995 ..... Intro, 1.1.1, 1.1.4, 2.1.2, 2.2,
          3.1.2, 3.1.3, 4.1, 4.2, 4.5,
          4.9, 4.12, 5.1.1, 9.2.1
   s.3A 3.1.1, 3.1.4, 4.10
   s.3B 6.1.1

Disabled Persons (Employment)
   Act 1944 .... Intro

Employment Rights Act 1996...... App.B1
   ss.86–91 .... 7.5.8, **App.C5**
   s.98 .... 12.5.2, **App.C5**
      (2)(a) 8.4
      (3)(a) 8.4
   ss.112–117 .... 17.4.4.2
   s.118 .... **App.C5**
   ss.119–123 .... 17.4.3.1, **App.C5**
   ss.124–126 .... **App.C5**

Equality Act 2010.... 1.1.4, 2.1.2, 2.2, 2.3,
          3.2.3, 4.1, 4.9, 4.10, 5.2.2,
          6.2.2, 8.6, 9.2.1, 10.3,
          App.B4, App.D1
   s.6 .... 1, 1.1, 2.1.5, 9.2.1, 12.5.3,
          App.B4, **App.C1**
      (3) 5.2.4
   s.13 .. 2.1.1, 2.1.3, 12.5.2, 12.5.5.1,
          13.5.6.1, App.B1, **App.C1**
      (1) 2.4.3
      (3) 2.4.1
   s.14 .... **App.C1**
      (1) 2.4.4
      (3) 2.4.4

s.15 .... 2.3, 3, 3.1.1, 3.1.2, 3.1.3,
          3.1.4, 3.2.1, 3.2.2, 3.2.4,
          3.2.6, 3.3, 3.4, 3.5, 3.6,
          4.3.1, 5, 5.1.1, 6.2.3, 8.2,
          8.4.6, 12.5.5.2, 13.5.6.2,
          App.B1, **App.C1**
s.19 ..... 3.4, 5.2, 12.5.5.3, 13.5.6.3,
          App.C1
s.20 .... 8.1, 12.5.5.4, 13.5.6.4,
          App.B1, **App.C1**
   (2)–(7) 4.3
   (9) 4.3.2, 4.7.2.1
   (11) 4.3.3
   (12) 4.3.2
s.21 ..... 12.5.5.4, 13.5.6.4, App.B1,
          App.C1
s.23 .... **App.C1**
   (1), (2) 2.1.3
s.24 .... 2.4.3, **App.C1**
s.26 .. 6.1.1, 6.1.2, 12.5.2, 12.5.5.5,
          13.5.6.5, App.B1, **App.C1**
   (1)(b) 6.1.3, 6.1.6
   (4) 6.1.6
s.27 .... 6.2.1, 12.5.5.6, 13.5.6.6,
          App.B1, **App.C1**
   (2) 12.5.5.6
   (d) 12.5.5.6, App.B1,
          App.B2
s.39 .... **App.C1**
   (2) 7.1.3
s.60 .... 7.1.1, **App.C1**
s.108 .... 6.2.5, **App.C1**
s.109 .... 6.3.2, **App.C1**
   (1), (3) 6.3.1
s.110 .... 6.3.2, **App.C1**
   (3) 6.3.2
s.111 .... 6.3.3, **App.C1**
s.112 .... 6.3.4, **App.C1**
s.123 .... **App.C1**
s.124 .... **App.C1**
s.138 .... 16.4

Equality Act 2010 – *continued*
    s.147(3)(a)–(f) 14.2
    s.212(1) 1.1.2, 4.5, 6.2.3
    Sched.1 .... **App.C1**
      Part 1 .... 1.1, App.B4
        para.1(1), (2) 2.4.2
        para.2 .... 1.1.3
          (2) 1.3.1
        para.3(1) 1.2.1
        para.5 .... 1.5, App.B4
        para.6 .... 12.5.3
          (1) 1.2.1
          (4) 1.1.1

        para.8 .... 1.3.2
        para.9 .... 1.4
    Sched.8
      Part 3, para.20 ..... 4.8, **App.C1**

Income Tax (Earnings and
    Pensions) Act 2003
      s.403 .... 8.63, **App.C6**
      ss.404, 404A, 405 .... **App.C6**
      s.406 .... 8.6, **App.C6**

Sex Discrimination Act 1975.......... 4.3.1

Table of statutory instruments and European legislation

Council Directive 2000/78/EC (Establishing a general framework for equal
  treatment in employment and occupation) .... Intro, 1.1, 2.1.2, App.D1
Disability Discrimination Act 1995 (Amendment) Regulations 2003, SI
  2003/1673 .... 6.1.1
Disability Discrimination (Exemption for Small Employers) Order 1998, SI
  1998/2618 .... Intro
Disability Discrimination (Meaning of Disability) Regulations 1996, SI
  1996/1455 .... Intro
Employment Tribunals (Constitution and Rules of Procedure) Regulations
  2004, SI 2004/1861
    Sched.1 (Employment Tribunal Rules of Procedure)
      rule 10 .... 16.4, 16.7
      rule 11 .... 16.1, 16.4
      rules 33–36 .... 17.5
      rule 40 .... 17.7
Equality Act 2010 (Disability) Regulations 2010, SI 2010/2128...... Intro, 1.2.1, App.D1
    reg.3 .... 1.2.2
    reg.4 .... 1.2.2, App.B4
Transfer of Undertakings (Protection of Employment) Regulations 2006.............. 12.3

Abbreviations

ACAS	The Advisory, Conciliation and Arbitration Service
ADR	alternative dispute resolution
AMRA 1988	Access to Medical Reports Act 1988
CMD	Case management discussion
DCM	Diagnostic and Statistical Manual of Mental Disorders
DDA 1995	Disability Discrimination Act 1995
EAT	Employment Appeal Tribunal
EHRC	Equality and Human Rights Commission
ERA 1996	Employment Rights Act 1996
ET	Employment Tribunal
ET1	Employment Tribunals Claim Form
ET3	Employment Tribunals Response Form
FCO	Foreign and Commonwealth Office
ICD	World Health Organization's International Statistical Classification of Diseases
ODI	Office for Disability Issues (now under Government Equalities Office)
PCP	provision, criterion or practice
PHI	permanent health insurance
PHR	pre-hearing review
PIB	permanent injury benefit
PIP	performance improvement plan
PSL	professional support lawyer
SSP	statutory sick pay
TUPE	Transfer of Undertakings (Protection of Employment) Regulations 2006

Introduction to disability discrimination law

BRIEF HISTORY

This book is not intended to be an academic study of the law of disability discrimination. We have provided this brief history to set the current law in proper context. It is neither comprehensive nor detailed but we trust that it provides some background to the rest of the book as it examines the current legal position.

In the beginning ...

Those suffering disabilities have been confined to the fringes throughout history. How a society treats its most vulnerable is said to be the very measure of civilisation. It is no coincidence that protection for those suffering disabilities is late to arrive and provision that they be treated as equals as opposed to the mere provision of financial aid, later still.

In the employment field the first piece of legislation in England and Wales, the jurisdiction addressed in this book, was the Disabled Persons (Employment) Act 1944. The legislation sought to impose on employers with over 20 employees a quota of at least three per cent of disabled employees within the organisation. The requirement was inadequately enforced and prosecutions were rare. The main impact was to provide some protection in terms of dismissals where the dismissal of a disabled person would bring the employer under the quota.

Disability Discrimination Act 1995

The first really significant piece of domestic legislation in the employment field was over 50 years later in the form of the Disability Discrimination Act (DDA) 1995. DDA 1995 repealed the Disabled Persons (Employment) Act 1944 and created for the first time a general framework to seek to challenge disability discrimination. The DDA introduced a legal definition of disability that had to be satisfied in order to obtain the legislative protection offered. At that time the protection offered was a duty on employers to make reasonable adjustments, protection from disability-related discrimination and protection from victimisation. The legislation applied only to employers with over 20 employees.

Subsequent amendments to DDA 1995

DDA 1995 was amended regularly to gradually increase the protection offered. Significant amendments included:

- the gradual removal of the exemption for small employers (Disability Discrimination (Exemption for Small Employers) Order 1998, SI 1998/2618, Disability Discrimination Act 1995 (Amendment) Regulations 2003, SI 2003/ 1673);
- the inclusion of previously excluded occupations such as police, barristers and partners in firms (Disability Discrimination Act 1995 (Amendment) Regulations 2003;
- the introduction of express protection from direct discrimination and harassment (Disability Discrimination Act 1995 (Amendment) Regulations 2003;
- an increase in the scope of the definition of disability by the automatic inclusion of some conditions and the removal of the need for clinical recognition with mental impairments (DDA 2005); and
- the introduction of express protection from direct discrimination and harassment (Disability Discrimination Act 1995 (Amendment) Regulations 2003.

European influence

In more recent years disability discrimination has been heavily influenced by European legislation. Members of the European Union are required by the EU Equal Treatment Framework Directive (Council Directive 2000/78/EC Establishing a general framework for equal treatment in employment and occupation) to prevent discrimination in the circumstances prescribed by the Directive. For our purposes we need only note that this includes disability. For the most part the requirements of the Directive were already satisfied by DDA 1995 but some amendment was needed. One such amendment was the introduction of direct discrimination, noted above, which was in response to the requirement from the Directive to provide express protection from direct discrimination.

If there is a dispute over the interpretation of domestic legislation that enacts the Directive's requirements then ambiguity will be resolved by reference to the Directive. It is important to note that the Directive does not define disability and it is possible that decisions of the European Court of Justice (ECJ) may in future require further amendment or expansion to the protection now offered in the UK.

Guidance, codes of practice and secondary legislation

No history of disability discrimination law in this country would be complete without consideration of the supporting legislation and guidance. These sources supplement the primary provisions and provide guidance to the courts and tribunals interpreting individual cases. Following the introduction of the Equality Act 2010, the sources set out below have been replaced by an Equality Act 2010 equivalent: see below for details.

The Disability Regulations

DDA 1995 provided the power to issue statutory instruments. This was exercised in the Disability Discrimination (Meaning of Disability) Regulations 1996, SI 1996/1455 to exclude a number of conditions from the definition of disability. This included conditions such as alcohol or drug addiction, tattoos, exhibitionism and a tendency to set fires.

The Office for Disability Issues Guidance

DDA 1995 also provided the power to issue statutory guidance which was exercised to issue 'Guidance on matters to be taken into account in determining questions relating to the definition of disability' (2006).

Codes of Practice

In addition, different bodies have exercised a power to issue Codes of Practice since 1999 when the Disability Rights Commission (DRC) was created. Codes issued by the DRC included the Code of Practice: Employment and Occupation (2004) and Code of Practice: Trade Organisations and Qualifications Bodies (2004). From 1 October 2007 the DRC was replaced by the Equality and Human Rights Commission (EHRC)which issued the Code of Practice: Trade Organisations, Qualifications Bodies and General Qualifications Bodies (2008).

THE CURRENT POSITION

The Equality Act 2010 has now completely repealed DDA 1995 although many of the former provisions can be found within the discrimination framework of the Equality Act 2010. The previous legislation continues to apply where the discriminatory acts complained of took place wholly before 1 October 2010. Given the time limits applicable to tribunal disability discrimination claims it is likely that cases governed by DDA 1995 are now concluded or in the final stages and therefore this book will focus solely on the provisions of the Equality Act 2010 .

To complete this brief overview it is helpful at this point to note the key changes introduced by the Equality Act 2010. These include:

- the replacement of disability-related discrimination with discrimination arising from a disability (see **Chapter 3**). Disability-related discrimination had

INTRODUCTION TO DISABILITY DISCRIMINATION LAW

been delivered a fatal blow by the House of Lords decision in *Lewisham LBC* v. *Malcolm* [2008] UKHL 43 and required legislative revival if it was to remain a cause of action;

- the introduction of indirect discrimination for disability cases, which is explored further in **Chapter 5**; and
- the new definition of direct discrimination that opens the door to the potential for claims based on a person's association with a disabled person or a perception that a person has a disability. These issues are discussed in more detail at **2.2** and **2.3** respectively.

Alongside the Equality Act 2010, the previous code of practice is now replaced by the Statutory Code of Practice on Employment (Equality and Human Rights Commission, January 2011). The previous statutory guidance has now been replaced with the 'Guidance on matters to be taken into account in determining questions relating to the definition of disability' (Office for Disability Issues, 2011). There remains a power to issue secondary legislation which has been exercised to issue the Equality Act 2010 (Disability) Regulations 2010, SI 2010/2128 which revoked and replaced the Disability Discrimination (Meaning of Disability) Regulations 1996.

This book sets out the current state of the law under the Equality Act 2010, the Code, the Disability Regulations and the Guidance. We begin with the central question of what amounts to a disability for the purposes of the legislative protection.

PART 1

Disability discrimination: the law

CHAPTER 1

The definition of disability

This chapter looks at one of the most difficult areas of disability discrimination law: the definition of disability. Illness does not equate to disability unless the specific requirements of the Equality Act 2010, s.6 definition are met (**1.1**). Certain conditions qualify automatically as disabilities and are spared the requirement to show all of the elements; others are specifically excluded by the legislation (**1.2**). It is never going to be easy to assess conditions which are variable, fluctuating, progressive or cumulative: in this chapter we consider the cases which are instructive in this regard (**1.3**). We also consider the effect of past disabilities (**1.4**). Two further aspects of the definition of disability present their own challenges. They are the effect of medical treatment and prostheses (**1.5**) and the material time for assessing disability (**1.6**). This area has seen many cases over the last 15 or so years as the law has developed. We provide you with outline facts and propositions from the key cases on the definition so that you can understand how the definition can be met in practice.

1.1 THE ELEMENTS OF THE DEFINITION

Disability is defined by the Equality Act 2010, s.6 as follows:

(1)   A person (P) has a disability if–

    (a)   P has a physical or mental impairment, and
    (b)   the impairment has a substantial and long-term adverse effect on P's ability to carry out normal day-to-day activities.

This apparently straightforward definition is anything but simple. It is however supplemented by:

• guidance in the Equality Act 2010, Sched.1, Part 1, Determination of disability;

- the *Equality Act 2010 Guidance – Guidance on matters to be taken into account in determining questions relating to the definition of disability* (ODI, 2010) ('the Guidance');
- the use of examples in the Equality Act 2010 Statutory Code of Practice on Employment ('the Code'); and
- a significant body of case law which has developed around the definition.

The definition comprises four elements, each of which must be satisfied if the threshold of disability is to be met. It is for a claimant to prove that they have a disability within the meaning of the Equality Act 2010 and if the claimant falls down on any of the elements their claim will fail.

The elements are that:

(a)   there must be a physical or mental impairment;
(b)   the impairment must have a substantial adverse effect;
(c)   the impairment must be long term; and,
(d)   there must be an effect on normal day-to-day activities.

In this chapter we examine each of the elements in order to determine when the definition is met.

It should be noted that the fact that an individual is suffering from illness is not conclusive of disability. There is a tendency for people to equate illness with disability. The threshold of demonstrating disability is a much higher hurdle than demonstrating that someone is suffering from sickness. The European Court of Justice (ECJ) specifically gave an opinion on this point in the case of *Chacon Navas* v. *Eurest Colectividades* [2006] IRLR 706 (ECJ). The ECJ held that sickness alone is not covered by Council Directive 2000/78/EC of 27 November 2000 establishing a general framework for equal treatment in employment and occupation ('the Directive').

1.1.1   Physical or mental impairment

There must be a physical or mental impairment. An individual could have both.

The cause of the impairment is irrelevant unless the claim comprises an element of personal injury which is being pleaded in the tribunal (Sched.1, para.6(4)) in which case medical evidence will be required to assist the tribunal in determining this point (*Millar* v. *Inland Revenue Commissioners* [2006] IRLR 112 (Court of Session, Scotland) (**Chapter 15**)).

It is not a requirement of the Equality Act 2010 that there is a clinically well-recognised condition. This was previously a requirement under the Disability Discrimination Act (DDA) 1995 which has now been repealed. It is no longer necessary that an impairment is classified in the International Classification of Diseases (ICD) or the Diagnostic and Statistical Manual of Mental Disorders (DCM). References in older cases to this requirement are no longer relevant although, as a matter of practice, in many cases it will prove useful and could be key to a tribunal's determination.

It is for the tribunal, not doctors, to determine whether an impairment is a disability under the Equality Act 2010 (*Goodwin* v. *Patent Office* [1999] IRLR 4 (EAT)). However, medical evidence may be crucial in establishing the effects of an impairment, without treatment (*Woodrup* v. *London Borough of Southwark* [2002] EWCA Civ 1716). For more on the role of medical evidence in disability discrimination proceedings in the tribunals, see **Chapter 15**.

An impairment might be the cause or the effect. It is sometimes helpful for a tribunal to consider first whether the claimant's ability to carry out normal day-to-day activities has been affected on a long-term basis (**1.1.2**, **1.1.3**, **1.1.4**). If it finds that the claimant's ability has been affected in this way then in most cases it will be appropriate to draw an inference that the claimant suffers from an impairment. In *J* v. *DLA Piper UK LLP* [2010] IRLR 936 (EAT), the Employment Appeal Tribunal (EAT) noted that this approach can be helpful in some cases but it does not permit a tribunal to ignore the question of whether or not there is an impairment. This may be particularly relevant where there is no clinical diagnosis to identify the impairment.

Some examples of impairments which the tribunals have held to amount to disabilities include diabetes-related conditions, cerebral palsy, dyslexia, depression and epilepsy. Each case, however, unless the condition is an automatic disability, will turn on its own facts. A condition must meet the remaining elements of the definition.

1.1.2   Substantial adverse effect

Tribunals take a *functional* approach to disability (*Ministry of Defence* v. *Hay* [2008] ICR 1247 (EAT)). The emphasis is on the *impact* on individuals of their disability not the condition itself. For example, those suffering from depression will not automatically be disabled by the fact of a diagnosis of depression. They will have to demonstrate that the impact of the condition on their normal day-to-day activities is substantial and long term.

'Adverse effect' is given its common-sense meaning. 'Substantial' is defined by the Equality Act 2010, s.212(1) as meaning 'more than minor or trivial'. 'Substantial' goes beyond the normal differences in capability between individuals.

Further guidance is available in the Code and the Guidance as follows:

- Appendix 1 to the Code at p.287, paras.8–10 addresses 'What is a "substantial" adverse effect?'.
- The Guidance cites examples of substantial adverse effect at paras.B1–B10.

The case law is perhaps most useful in helping to determine whether an effect is substantial. This can be difficult. Tribunals may require a claimant to provide an impact statement setting out the impact of the impairment (**15.2**) in order to assist the tribunal in determining whether the effect of a condition is substantial.

Goodwin v. Patent Office [1999] IRLR 4 (EAT)

Mr Goodwin suffered from paranoid schizophrenia. The tribunal assessed that since he could perform normal domestic activities, get himself to work and work to a satisfactory standard this meant that there was no impact from his impairment on his normal day-to-day activities. This decision was overturned by the EAT. The fact that he could not interact with his colleagues at work because of auditory hallucinations and 'thought broadcasting' (when he thought others could hear his thoughts) meant that his normal day-to-day activities *were* impaired. The first tribunal had erred in focusing on what he *could* do.

In the words of Mr Justice Morison:

> The focus of attention required by the Act is on the things that the applicant either cannot do or can only do with difficulty, rather than the things the person can do. (para.35)

The burden is on the claimant to demonstrate that they are substantially affected by their impairment. Proving that an effect is substantial is no easy task. In *Hudson* v. *Post Office* (1998) ET3100773/98 a tribunal held that a man who worked as a driver and who lost the use of an eye was not disabled because his remaining eye could compensate for the loss of the other.

Chief Constable of Lothian and Borders Police v. Cumming [2010] IRLR 109 (EAT)

Ms Cumming failed to persuade a tribunal that the effect on her of her condition of mild left-sided amblyopia, a sight condition, was substantial. She was held not to be disabled. In this case, Ms Cumming brought a claim against the police for disability discrimination. They did not allow her to become a police constable because she had failed the basic sight requirement. On the evidence of the consultant ophthalmic surgeon, her sight impairment was not substantial. The only disadvantage which Ms Cumming suffered as a result of her sight condition was that she could not go forward with her chosen profession. Being afforded general participation in or access to professional life is not a normal day-to-day activity, nor was being prevented access an adverse effect.

In *Ginn* v. *Tesco Stores* [2005] All ER (D) 259 (Oct) (EAT), the EAT said the correct approach to the effect of two illnesses was to add up the component parts and see whether together they amount to more than the individual parts taken separately. The effect of Mrs Ginn's combined conditions of rhinitis and vertigo was enough to render her disabled. Taken separately they may not have.

A claimant may be unable to do something because of pain, fatigue or social embarrassment. It might be that, although able to do an activity, it takes the person much longer to do it. The tribunal needs as much information as possible in relation to what the claimant can and cannot do in order to determine whether the individual is disabled.

The fact that a person can carry out activities does not mean that his or her ability to carry them out has not been impaired. In fact many people with disabilities compensate for the fact of their disability and would say that they are not affected when they clearly are. The challenge to those representing claimants is to really explore and set out the impact of the impairment on their client's ability to perform the activity. This may involve explaining the adaptations which the client has made in order to enable him or her to carry out the activity.

1.1.3 Long term

'Long term' is defined by the Equality Act 2010, Sched.1, Part 1, para,2 as follows:

(1) The effect of an impairment is long-term if–

    (a) it has lasted for at least 12 months,
    (b) it is likely to last for at least 12 months, or
    (c) it is likely to last for the rest of the life of the person affected.

The material time for assessing whether a disability is long term is the time at which the discrimination is alleged to have occurred. For more detail on this see **1.6**. For rules relating to progressive conditions see **1.3.2**.

Following the House of Lords decision in *SCA Packaging* v. *Boyle* [2009] UKHL 37, 'likely' means 'could well happen'. The House of Lords examined the intention of Parliament in applying the word 'likely' to the definition of long term and concluded that it did not mean 'more likely than not'. It will suffice that a condition is likely to last 12 months or longer if there is a possibility that it could happen. The fact that there is a more than reasonable chance that it will last 12 months will be conclusive of the point, although this is an area which will be open to dispute between the parties and one which ultimately may have to be decided by a tribunal. The claimant is not required to demonstrate that there is a more than 50 per cent chance the impairment will last 12 months, but there must be a substantial probability. In the view of the authors, this probably equates to at least a 30 per cent chance.

A series of consecutive short-term conditions is capable of amounting to a long-term impairment if the subsequent conditions arise from one initial impairment and are therefore related, *and* if the short-term conditions cumulatively meet the 12-month hurdle (*Patel* v. *(1) Oldham Metropolitan Borough Council and (2) The Governing Body of Rushcroft Primary School* [2010] ICR 603 (EAT) (**1.3.3**)).

1.1.4 Normal day-to-day activities

Normal day-to-day activities are normal daily activities such as walking, shopping and carrying groceries, and taking care of personal hygiene, showering and bathing. They also include social interaction, talking on the telephone and doing housework. They are the things we all do every day which are a normal part of human existence.

Normal day-to-day activities also include normal work activities and irregular activities which are normal in the course of a job (*Paterson* v. *Commissioner of Police of the Metropolis* [2007] IRLR 763 (EAT) below). They comprise only activities *within* a normal day at work but do not include for example, progression in a chosen career (*Chief Constable of Lothian and Borders Police* v. *Cumming* [2010] IRLR 109 (EAT) (**1.1.2**)).

Paterson v. Commissioner of Police of the Metropolis [2007] IRLR 763 (EAT)

Mr Paterson's dyslexia adversely affected his ability to sit examinations that would lead to promotion. At tribunal he was held not to be disabled on the basis that taking an exam is not a normal day-to-day activity. On appeal the EAT held that this was a normal day-to-day activity because it was relevant to his participation in professional life. Giving judgment for the claimant, Mr Justice Elias said:

> We must read s.1 [of DDA 1995] in a way which gives effect to EU law. We think it can be readily done, simply by giving a meaning to day-to-day activities which encompasses the activities which are relevant to participation in professional life. Appropriate measures must be taken to enable a worker to advance in his or her employment. Since the effect of the disability may adversely affect promotion prospects, then it must be said to hinder participation in professional life.

It might appear that *Paterson* contradicts *Cumming* (**1.1.2**). The distinction between the cases may be fine but it is suggested that there is a difference between entering a chosen profession and progressing within that profession once admitted. The latter is a normal day-to-day activity.

A decision in which no effect on normal day-to-day activities was found is as follows.

Ahmed v. Metroline Travel Ltd [2011] Eq LR 464 (EAT)

Mr Ahmed was held not to be disabled because, although he could not work in his capacity as a bus driver following a soft tissue injury to his back, he was able to play football with his children, lift weights and drive his car. These were held to be normal day-to-day activities which he seemed able to perform. His injury was assessed to be mild and gave rise to no long-term issues. His back strain was aggravated by poor posture. It did not assist Mr Ahmed that the tribunal did not believe his account of his functional deficit but he was assessed as being not disabled because he could function well other than at work.

A recent decision of the EAT in *Aderemi* v. *London and South Eastern Railway Ltd* [2012] UKEAT/0316/12 confirms that in assessing the impact of disability on normal day-to-day activities, the focus should be on what the client *cannot do*. *Aderemi* also tells us that unless an impact is minor or trivial it must be substantial (**1.1.2**).

Previously DDA 1995 contained a list of capacities which, if affected, could demonstrate that a claimant's normal day-to-day activities had been impaired. The list comprised mobility, manual dexterity, physical co-ordination, continence, ability to lift, carry or otherwise move everyday objects, speech, hearing or eyesight, memory or ability to concentrate, learn or understand, or perception of the risk of physical danger. Only if a claimant could demonstrate an impact on one of these prescribed capacities would he or she be able to show that normal day-to-day activities had been affected.

This list has been removed from the Equality Act 2010. This is significant. It widens the ambit within which claimants can seek to demonstrate an impact on normal day-to-day activities. It means they no longer have to shoehorn any impact into one of the prescribed categories. This is especially significant for those impaired by mental health conditions who previously would have been required to show an impact on memory or ability to concentrate, learn or understand. The impact of an impairment such as depression can have far-reaching effects such as reducing libido, weight loss or gain and many other features. These can now be cited to explain the impact on normal day-to-day activities where they might previously have been ignored.

The removal of the capacities list should assist claimants with mental health conditions in demonstrating that there has been an impact on normal day-to-day activities. Those representing claimants will want to explore all aspects of the impairment in order to provide a picture of the impact on the claimant.

The Guidance gives, in its Appendix, two 'illustrative and non-exhaustive' lists. The first list cites factors which it would be reasonable to regard as having a substantial adverse effect on normal day-to-day activities. The second list cites factors it would not be reasonable to regard as having that effect. These provide useful guidance to any practitioner.

1.2 SPECIFIED CONDITIONS

1.2.1 Automatic disabilities

The Equality Act 2010 prescribes conditions which automatically qualify as disabilities (Sched.1, Part 1, para.6(1)). There are currently three: HIV, cancer and multiple sclerosis. There is no requirement for these conditions to satisfy the tests of whether they are substantial, long term or have an adverse impact on normal day-to-day activities.

Under the Equality Act 2010 (Disability) Regulations 2010, SI 2010/2128 ('the Disability Regulations'), some people with severe sight impairments may also be covered automatically. A person who has been certified by a consultant ophthalmologist as being blind, severely sight impaired, sight impaired or partially sighted is deemed to be disabled.

Severe disfigurement is also an automatic disability unless it has been self-inflicted, for example by tattoos or piercings. A person who is severely disfigured does not have to demonstrate substantial adverse effect or that it is long term and affects daily activities. Under the Equality Act 2010, Sched.1, Part 1, para.3(1):

An impairment which consists of a severe disfigurement is to be treated as having a substantial adverse effect on the ability of the person concerned to carry out normal day-to-day activities.

1.2.2 Excluded conditions

The Disability Regulations, regs.3 and 4 expressly exclude a number of conditions from the definition of disability. These are:

- addictions to alcohol, nicotine or any other substance, the most common being drugs;
- exhibitionism;
- kleptomania;
- voyeurism;
- pyromania;
- a tendency to physically or sexually abuse others; and
- hayfever (seasonal allergic rhinitis).

The exclusions only apply to freestanding conditions. If there is a second impairment arising from an excluded condition, the second impairment is capable of being a disability subject to satisfying the statutory definition, i.e. that it is an impairment which is long term and which has an adverse effect on normal day-to-day activities.

An interesting example of this is *Power* v. *Panasonic UK Ltd* [2003] IRLR 151 (EAT).

Power v. Panasonic UK Ltd [2003] IRLR 151 (EAT)

Ms Power worked for Panasonic as an area sales manager. Following a reorganisation, the geographical area she was required to cover increased. She was signed off sick. She was depressed and drinking heavily. Both psychiatrists at the first tribunal hearing agreed that she suffered from both alcohol abuse and depression. Each tried to identify which came first. At first instance the tribunal held that she was not disabled. The question the tribunal considered was which of depression or alcoholism was the primary condition. If the depression was a symptom of the alcoholism, the tribunal said that Ms Power could not meet the definition of disability because addiction was an excluded condition.

On appeal the EAT held that it was irrelevant to consider which condition came first. The legislation does not require a claimant to demonstrate the cause of an impairment. What is significant is the impact of the impairment and whether the impairment meets the definition. The EAT said:

What is material is to ascertain whether the disability from which they are suffering at the material time is a disability within the meaning of the Act or whether, where it is relevant as in this case, it is an impairment which is excluded by reason of the Regulations from being treated as such a disability.

While alcoholism is an excluded condition, depression is capable of being a disability. If the depression meets the four-part test of the definition, the claimant will be disabled. It is entirely irrelevant that there is any connection between the depression and the excluded condition.

Where there are two conditions, one of which is excluded, it will be the task of the tribunal to determine whether any wrongdoing which is alleged relates to the excluded condition or the second condition. If a respondent can show that the reason for its actions was based entirely on the excluded condition, it will not be liable for disability discrimination. This was the case in *Edmund Nuttall Ltd* v. *Butterfield* [2006] ICR 77 (EAT) where Mr Nuttall suffered from both depression and exhibitionism. His employer dismissed Mr Nuttall for an offence of indecent exposure. The EAT held that the reason for the less favourable treatment, the dismissal, was the excluded condition. There was therefore no disability discrimination notwithstanding the existence of a potentially qualifying condition. The cause of the treatment in question is a matter of fact in each case.

1.3 VARIABLE CONDITIONS

1.3.1 Recurring or fluctuating conditions

The Equality Act 2010, Sched.1, Part 1, para.2(2) states that:

> If an impairment ceases to have a substantial adverse effect on a person's ability to carry out normal day-to-day activities, it is to be treated as continuing to have that effect if that effect is likely to recur.

Some medical conditions present fluctuating symptoms. For example, a person with asthma or epilepsy will have periods where they experience very few symptoms at all and little or no effect on normal day-to-day activities. The effects of such conditions, when they cease to be substantial, are treated as continuing if the effect is *likely* to recur. 'Likely' is given the same interpretation as in *SCA* v. *Boyle* (**1.1.3**).

It is accepted that the severity of the fluctuating effects will vary.

If there are recurrences within a 12-month period, the effect is treated as continuing; however, a person having two discrete episodes of a medical condition *within* a one-year period will not satisfy the long-term element of the definition.

Hayfever is an excluded condition, but if it impacts on another underlying condition which is capable of being a disability, such as asthma, it may still be treated as a condition which has a recurring or fluctuating effect.

The Guidance deals with fluctuating effect at paras.C5–C8.

The only exception to the rules about recurring or fluctuating conditions is that, where a permanent cure has been effected by medication, the condition is treated as cured and not as recurring.

1.3.2 Progressive conditions

The Equality Act 2010, Sched.1, Part 1, para.8 provides for progressive conditions as follows:

(1) This paragraph applies to a person (P) if–

    (a) P has a progressive condition,

    (b) as a result of that condition P has an impairment which has (or had) an effect on P's ability to carry out normal day-to-day activities, but

    (c) the effect is not (or was not) a substantial adverse effect.

(2) P is to be taken to have an impairment which has a substantial adverse effect if the condition is likely to result in P having such an impairment.

If the effects of a condition are not yet substantial but are *likely* to have that effect as the condition progresses, they are treated as disabilities as soon as *any* symptoms arise. At this point the requirement to show a substantial effect falls away and it is enough to show *any* effect arising from the condition.

The Guidance provides useful examples at paras.B16–B20.

Once again the test for 'likely' is 'could well happen' following *SCA* v. *Boyle*. The long-term element of the definition must also be satisfied, but with most progressive conditions this should not be an issue.

1.3.3 Cumulative conditions

Unrelated consecutive impairments cannot be assessed on a cumulative basis; however, related conditions may be aggregated in appropriate circumstances. This applies both to the question of whether or not a condition satisfies the requirement of being long term (**1.1.3**) and also to the question of whether a condition has a substantial adverse effect on an individual. One example given in the Guidance at para.B5 is of a man with depression for whom a number of tasks are difficult. Individually they are not substantial but the cumulative effect amounts to a substantial difficulty.

***Patel* v. (1) *Oldham Metropolitan Borough Council* and (2) *The Governing Body of Rushcroft Primary School* [2010] ICR 603 (EAT)**

In this case Ms Patel, a teacher at a primary school, suffered from two conditions. The first was myelitis, an inflammation of the spinal cord. She suffered from this condition from February to December 2005. Her treating clinician confirmed that this condition would not last longer than 12 months. Another condition arose from her myelitis: myofacial pain syndrome, a painful muscular disorder, and this too did not last longer than 12 months. Taken together, both conditions did span a period in excess of 12 months. Mrs Justice Slade held that, while two consecutive unrelated impairments could not satisfy the definition of long term, two related impairments could:

> in my judgment fine distinctions between one medical condition and its development into another are to be avoided…the effect of an illness or condition likely to develop or which has developed from another condition or illness forms part of the assessment of whether the effect of the original impairment is likely to last or has lasted 12 months.

1.4 PAST DISABILITIES

The Equality Act 2010 provides that people who have previously been disabled within the definition but who are now recovered or who are no longer suffering substantial effects are protected.

In deciding whether a past condition was a disability, note that it will be long term if the effects lasted 12 months or more after the first occurrence, or if there was a recurrence continuing beyond 12 months.

Some employees will therefore be protected under the Equality Act 2010 by virtue of having had a past disability, even if that was before the coming into force of the current legislation. The Equality Act 2010, Sched.1, Part 1, para.9 provides that:

(1) A question as to whether a person had a disability at a particular time ('the relevant time') is to be determined, for the purposes of section 6, as if the provisions of, or made under, this Act were in force when the act complained of was done had been in force at the relevant time.

(2) The relevant time may be a time before the coming into force of the provision of this Act to which the question relates.

1.5 THE EFFECT OF MEDICAL TREATMENT AND PROSTHESES

The Equality Act 2010, Sched.1, Part 1, para.5 states that–

(1) An impairment is to be treated as having a substantial adverse effect on the ability of the person concerned to carry out normal day-to-day activities if–

(a) measures are being taken to treat or correct it, and

(b) *but for* that, it would be likely to have that effect [our emphasis].

(2) 'Measures' includes, in particular, medical treatment and the use of a prosthesis or other aid.

(3) Sub-paragraph (1) does not apply–

(a) in relation to the impairment of a person's sight, to the extent that the impairment is, in the person's case, correctable by spectacles or contact lenses or in such other ways as may be prescribed;

(b) in relation to such other impairments as may be prescribed, in such circumstances as are prescribed.

In assessing disability, the effects of medical treatment and prostheses should be ignored. In the cases this has become known as the 'deduced effect'.

For the purposes of the Equality Act, medical treatment includes medication but it also comprises other treatments such as counselling, cognitive behavioural therapy and other similar therapies. In *Abadeh* v. *British Telecommunications plc* [2001] IRLR 23 (EAT) the tribunal acknowledged that psychotherapy falls within the definition of medical treatment. In *Kapadia* v. *London Borough of Lambeth* [2000] IRLR 699 (CA) counselling from a clinical psychologist was also held to be medical treatment.

Where a medical aid is engaged, discount should be given for the positive impact of the aid. For example:

- a person with a prosthetic limb should be assessed without the prosthesis;
- a hearing impaired person should be assessed for disability when they are not wearing any form of hearing aid;
- a person with diabetes who needs to take medication and follow a dietary regime should be assessed absent both of these elements.

The tribunal wants to know what the impact on the person's normal day-to-day activities would be in the absence of treatment or prosthesis. This is a somewhat artificial test and can give rise to some difficulties when assessing medical evidence. This is particularly the case with mental health impairments such as depression or anxiety, which are difficult to measure and where the impact of medical treatment or counselling is often difficult to quantify. Doctors and consultants should be able to give a fairly accurate prediction of how the person can function *but for* treatment, particularly if they are asked the pertinent questions (**Appendix B4**).

The exception to the *but for* rule (or 'deduced effect') is where a person wears spectacles or contact lenses to correct a sight impairment. They should be assessed while wearing spectacles or lenses. If a person with a sight impairment uses other aids, such as a magnifying glass or telescopic lens, the assessment should not take these into account.

Only once treatment has led to a permanent improvement of the condition can it be taken into account (*Abadeh* v. *British Telecommunications plc* [2001] IRLR 23 (EAT)).

1.6 THE MATERIAL TIME FOR ASSESSING DISABILITY

The material time for assessing disability is the time when the alleged discrimination occurred. It is irrelevant if at the time of the tribunal hearing a claimant can demonstrate that they have had the impairment for 12 months if the impairment was not already long term at the time of the alleged discrimination. This is unless, of course, the claimant can demonstrate that it was likely to last 12 months or the rest of their life at the time of the alleged discrimination.

Example

A woman, W, with an anxiety disorder, is dismissed as a result of sickness absence. W brings a claim for disability discrimination on the basis that her absence arises from disability and her employer has failed in its reasonable adjustments duty. At the time of her dismissal, W has only had the impairment for six weeks. The tribunal hearing is held one year after the dismissal and W seeks to demonstrate that she has met the 12-month hurdle because, as a matter of fact, she has now been impaired for 12 months. At the time of her dismissal she had been impaired for six weeks.

The relevant question for the tribunal and the medical experts is, at the time of the alleged discrimination, was the impairment long term? No, it was not. It had lasted six weeks. At the time of the alleged discrimination, was it *likely* to last 12 months? This is a question for medical opinion and for the tribunal to determine based on the evidence before it. If it was not likely to last 12 months, she was not disabled.

The issue of the time at which disability is assessed was considered in the following case:

Richmond Adult Community College v. *McDougall* [2008] EWCA Civ 4

Ms McDougall was offered a job subject to medical clearance. The job offer was rescinded when the college discovered that she was suffering from persistent delusional disorder with schizo-affective disorder. At the Court of Appeal hearing, Lord Justices Pill, Sedley and Rimer considered the approach to determining whether a condition was likely to recur, the time for making the assessment and what evidence could be used to assess this.

The material time is the time when the alleged discrimination occurred. The key question is 'what was the likelihood *then* that the condition was likely to recur?' Evidence as to facts occurring *after* the material time *cannot* be taken into consideration. The tribunal had erred in holding that they could. Pill LJ said:

> Whether a wrong has been committed must be judged on the basis of the *evidence available at the time of the act* alleged to constitute the wrongdoing. The predictive exercise may be a difficult one. Predictive exercises usually are. [our emphasis] (para.25)

Rimer LJ elaborated further. The question as to whether the condition was likely to recur:

> had to be answered *exclusively* by reference relating to the then likelihood of such recurrence. In short, the statute requires a *prophecy* to be made. It does not permit recourse to evidence as to subsequent events. [our emphasis] (para.35)

Even where the prophecy has been fulfilled, i.e. a claimant can show he or she has in fact been ill for more than 12 months from the time of the alleged discrimination, this will not assist in showing that the disability was *likely* to last. The tribunal must disregard what has happened *in fact* and cast its mind back to what the position was at the time of the alleged act. Although this test can be an exercise in mental gymnastics, it is probably the fairest way of holding the balance between an employer and employee. If an employee is found to be disabled then significant consequences follow for the employer. These obligations only arise if the employee was *at that time* disabled. The fact that the employee has later satisfied the statutory test should not retroactively impose obligations on an employer.

1.7 CONCLUSION

The definition of disability is anything but straightforward. This highly technical area of the law has given rise to a huge body of case law which assists us in determining the factors which need to be considered. From this chapter you should have a broad grasp of the concepts but of course every case is individual and fact specific. The role of medical evidence may be vital. We deal with this in more detail in **Chapter 7** and **Chapter 15**. Further assistance is also available in the Guidance. The question of whether or not a person is disabled is often determined at a pre-hearing review (**Chapter 15**). In the following chapters we look at the legal protection available for those who satisfy the statutory definition. We also examine the obligations placed on employers.

CHAPTER 2

Direct disability discrimination, associative discrimination and discrimination by perception

Direct discrimination is what most people think of when they consider discrimination. The legal definition may not reflect common understanding. In this chapter we look at the elements of a successful claim for direct discrimination (**2.1**), before considering the related concepts of associative discrimination (**2.2**), and discrimination based on perception (**2.3**). Consideration of direct discrimination also requires consideration of a number of discrete points such as positive discrimination and occupational requirements. We look at these matters at **2.4**.

2.1 DIRECT DISABILITY DISCRIMINATION

2.1.1 The s.13 definition

It is to be noted that direct discrimination was not expressly included by DDA 1995 when it came into force. It was only introduced by an amendment in 2003. In practice it has taken many years to determine how direct disability discrimination works. The cases are very instructive in this regard. The body of case law which has developed is now applied to the Equality Act 2010 provision found in s.13.

Direct discrimination is defined by the Equality Act 2010, s.13 as follows:

(1) A person (A) discriminates against another (B) if, because of a protected characteristic, A treats B *less favourably* than A treats or would treat others. [our emphasis]

If A treats B in a less favourable way *because of* their disability, this will constitute direct discrimination. In practice this involves an assessment of how a non-disabled person in broadly similar circumstances would have been treated. A claimant is required to demonstrate that the disability was the reason for the treatment and that it was not background or for another reason. We examine this at **2.1.4** when we look at the effective or substantial reason for the alleged less favourable treatment.

The case of *High Quality Lifestyles Ltd* v. *Watts* [2006] IRLR 850 (EAT) illustrates the care with which 'because of' is interpreted.

High Quality Lifestyles Ltd v. Watts [2006] IRLR 850 (EAT)

Mr Watts was HIV positive. He worked in a care centre where he had to deal with individuals with challenging behaviour on a day-to-day basis. In the course of his work he and his colleagues were regularly beaten, bitten and scratched while caring for individuals with special needs. On learning that he was HIV positive his employer dismissed him. The employer took the view that it was a risk to the patients of the care centre if Mr Watts were to transmit HIV to them. Mr Watts brought a claim for direct disability discrimination. His claim succeeded at the tribunal but the decision was overturned on appeal.

The EAT held that a fellow employee with a communicable disease in the same role would have been treated in the same way as Mr Watts. The treatment was therefore not less favourable. The findings from the tribunal on the reasons for the dismissal were inconsistent. The EAT found that he was not dismissed *because of* his disability but because of the risk of transmission to others.

The EAT did uphold findings of disability-related discrimination (the provisions for which are now repealed and replaced with provisions as to discrimination arising from disability (**Chapter 3**)) and a failure to make reasonable adjustments (**Chapter 4**).

It is not uncommon in practice for employers to take a stereotypical view, based on assumption, of the impact on an employee of a given disability. This is almost certain to land them in hot water. No decisions should be taken without first seeking up-to-date medical evidence and considering the position based on medical advice. We deal further and in more detail with this issue in **Chapter 7**. The case of *Tudor* v. *Spen Corner Veterinary Centre* (2005) ET/2404211/05 further illustrates this point.

Tudor v. Spen Corner Veterinary Centre (2005) ET/2404211/05

Ms Tudor suffered a stroke which caused blindness. The medical evidence was not conclusive on whether the blindness was temporary or permanent but the employer took the view, based on stereotype and assumption, that Ms Tudor would no longer be able to discharge her duties. Spen Corner Veterinary Centre made no further enquiries and Ms Tudor was dismissed.

Ms Tudor brought a claim of direct disability discrimination. The tribunal found in her favour. The employer had without reason taken the view that she was no longer able to provide good service. Their treatment of her was directly linked to her new status as someone with a sight impairment. The link between the treatment and the disability was evident and had motivated the employer's conduct. The employer had directly discriminated.

2.1.2 'Because of' disability

Previously the wording of the definition of direct discrimination used the words 'on grounds of' rather than 'because of'. Commentators on the Equality Act 2010 have made much of this but, in the opinion of the authors, the change of language is not intended to substantially change the meaning of the definition. It is clear that the treatment must be connected to the protected characteristic. There must be a direct link between the treatment and the disability. The only difference which is evident, however, is that the wording is wide enough to now explicitly include associative and perception discrimination (**2.2** and **2.3**) because the person alleging discrimination does not have to have a disability to present a claim for associative disability discrimination or disability discrimination by perception. These claims were previously covered under DDA 1995 to give effect to the Directive, but the wider wording in the Equality Act 2010 explicitly provides for their inclusion.

2.1.3　Comparators

In order to succeed in a claim of direct discrimination, a claimant will also have to conduct a comparison exercise. The treatment complained of must be *less favourable* than that afforded to others whose circumstances are not materially different from theirs. Historically, the case law has demonstrated that construction of the wrong comparator can be fatal to a claim of direct discrimination.

The appropriate comparator for a direct disability discrimination claim is a person, real or hypothetical, sharing the same material circumstances as the claimant *and*, in the case only of disability, sharing the claimant's abilities.

The Equality Act 2010, s.23(1) states:

> On a comparison of cases for the purposes of section 13…there must be no material difference between the circumstances relating to each case.

Section 23(2) continues:

> The circumstances relating to a case include a person's abilities if–
>
> (a)　on a comparison for the purposes of section 13, the protected characteristic is disability;

The following case illustrates the role of the comparator in determining whether direct discrimination has occurred.

Eagle Place Services Ltd v. Rudd [2010] IRLR 486 (EAT)

Mr Rudd, a solicitor, worked for just under 14 years as a specialist in personal injury litigation. He was disabled by virtue of having detached retinas in both eyes. He was summarily dismissed in May 2007 and in February 2009, at a final remedies hearing, was awarded £453,242.46 in compensation.

Mr Rudd worked exclusively for a major client of the firm, UKCoal plc. As a result of his sight impairment he was unable to drive in the dark and in rush hour traffic. Adjustments were also required, and made, to the air conditioning and lighting in his office. His hours of work were reduced from eight to seven hours a day, with a facility to take frequent breaks and leave the office to rest his eyes. He was also able to spend some time working from home. Originally he suffered only with a detached retina in his left eye. In 2006 he developed the same problem with his right eye. Following this, occupational health advised that he should work two days per week at home.

Relations between Mr Rudd and HR broke down in part over HR's insistence on inspecting his home office set-up. This eventually led to Mr Rudd's dismissal for a number of purported reasons unconnected to disability. The tribunal found that the real reason was that the respondent was concerned that it would not get an appropriate financial return in terms of the claimant's billable hours. It found that the respondent took a stereotypical view to the effect that the claimant's disability made him an inconvenient liability that would inhibit or damage the respondent's commercial objectives.

The correct comparator was a fellow lawyer of the same grade and skills as the claimant who shared a similarly good relationship with the client, who for reasons other than disability required adjustments for him to be able to work and in respect of whom reasonable adjustments had been agreed, and in respect of whom commercial performance was not an issue.

There was evidence from which an inference of discrimination might be drawn and the tribunal rejected non-discriminatory explanations by the employer. Eagle Place Services Ltd was liable for direct disability discrimination.

In *Stockton-on-Tees Borough Council* v. *Aylott* [2010] EWCA Civ 910 (**2.1.4**) the Court of Appeal held that the comparator does not have to be a 'clone' of the person alleging discrimination. Mummery LJ stated that a court need not proceed by a strict application of the comparison in every case and that, by looking at the evidence in the round, it may be possible to see from the facts that less favourable treatment has occurred. A tribunal will not be making an error of law if it fails to identify a hypothetical comparator.

2.1.4 The effective or substantial reason

Where there is more than one reason for the treatment alleged, it is for an employment tribunal to determine whether the disability was a substantial reason for the treatment. The disability need not be the main or only reason, but in order to successfully demonstrate that direct discrimination has occurred it must be an effective cause of the treatment. Sometimes this is referred to as the activating cause. The claimant must be able to demonstrate that the disability had a significant influence on the decision to treat the employee in the way he or she has been treated.

For example, where an employee alleges that he or she has been dismissed because of disability and the employer's position is that performance was the reason for the dismissal, it will be for the tribunal to decide whether it can, on the facts, find explicitly that the reason was disability or whether it can draw an inference that it was from the facts. Any subsequent failure by the respondent to provide an adequate explanation will lead to a finding against it.

The following case illustrates this point.

Stockton-on-Tees Borough Council v. Aylott [2010] EWCA Civ 910

Mr Aylott suffered from bipolar affective disorder dating back to at least 1973. There was no dispute that he was disabled for the purposes of the legislation. He began working for Stockton-on-Tees Borough Council in 2003 and in 2004 was promoted to a management position. Issues began to arise including alleged assault, bullying, harassment and a failure to have regard for his disability. It was at this time that the council became aware that he was bipolar. Mr Aylott lodged 17 grievances and underwent a long period of paid suspension while the grievances were investigated.

On return from this absence Mr Aylott was put under pressure by the council. It imposed tight deadlines on his work and subjected him to close scrutiny. The pressure culminated in Mr Aylott going off sick with stress-related chest pain in February 2006. On returning to work Mr Aylott had a confrontation with an HR representative of the council. In an email to her HR manager she referred to Mr Aylott's behaviour as being unprofessional, intimidating and wholly inappropriate and said they needed to discuss how to manage him out of work. The council began a disciplinary investigation and suspended Mr Aylott, citing erratic, unpredictable and over exuberant behaviour that made Mr Aylott uncomfortable to work with. Before a disciplinary hearing could be held Mr Aylott was admitted to hospital and the council halted the investigation. Mr Aylott never returned to work. The council dismissed him for capability on 8 November 2006. The council relied on Mr Aylott's sickness absence record. The council had not obtained any up-to-date medical evidence on Mr Aylott's bipolar disorder and in fact the evidence from Mr Aylott's treating consultant was that he may have been able to return to work 'in the not too distant future'. Mr Aylott brought claims of disability discrimination under a number of different heads.

The tribunal found in Mr Aylott's favour but the EAT reversed the decision. The unfair dismissal claim remained undisturbed. The case then went to the Court of Appeal for it to consider whether Mr Aylott's dismissal was an act of direct discrimination. The Court of Appeal found for Mr Aylott.

In giving judgment Lord Justice Mummery summed up the essence of direct discrimination:

> The essential inquiry is into why the disabled Claimant was treated less favourably than a person not having that particular disability. (para.28)

The Court of Appeal found that there were facts from which a tribunal was entitled to conclude, in the absence of adequate explanation, that Mr Aylott had suffered direct discrimination. The tribunal had found that stereotypical and prejudicial attitudes to mental health issues had coloured the council's attitude to Mr Aylott. It had been harsh to impose a disciplinary sanction when a less formal approach would have sufficed. There was also factual evidence of a change of tone in the way the council dealt with him following his return from absence. It would not have treated him in the same way if he had been suffering complications from a broken bone or surgery.

His behaviour had never in fact been threatening but the council had made assumptions because of Mr Aylott's disability:

> The Council's decision to dismiss the Claimant was based in part at least on assumptions that it made about his particular mental illness rather than on the basis of up-to-date medical evidence about the effect of his illness on his ability to continue in the employment of the Council. (para.50)

Finding the reason or substantive reason is not easy. In *O'Neill* v. *Governors of St Thomas More Roman Catholic Voluntarily Aided Upper School* [1997] ICR 33 (EAT) at 44, the EAT posed the question:

> what, out of the whole complex of facts before the tribunal is the 'effective and predominant cause' or the 'real or efficient cause' of the act complained of?

The focus, based on the facts, is on finding out *the reason why* the employer acted as it did. If it acted because of disability, a finding of direct discrimination will ensue.

2.1.5 Justification and defences

If a claimant can establish a case for direct discrimination and succeeds in persuading the tribunal that direct discrimination has occurred, it is a strict liability offence. An employer will never be able to justify direct discrimination. By contrast, other types of disability discrimination lend themselves to a justification defence as we will see in the remaining chapters in this Part of the book.

For respondents the best defence against a direct discrimination claim will be to demonstrate either that the claimant does not meet the Equality Act 2010, s.6 definition of disability or that the treatment was for another reason and not because of disability. This can be done by showing that a non-disabled employee would have been treated in the same way. Claims may also be successfully defended on the basis of a technical flaw in the construction of the comparator or on the basis of knowledge of the disability.

2.1.6 Knowledge

It is not possible to bring a direct discrimination claim if the employer does not know of the disability and knowledge cannot be reasonably imputed.

Sometimes an employer will have direct knowledge. This may be because the disability can be seen and is obvious, for example, where a mobility impaired employee makes use of a wheelchair or because the employee has declared the disability. Sometimes an employee will have declared the medical condition at the start of the employment or at some stage when it became an issue during the employment. This is explicit knowledge. Often the issue will come to the fore when an employee requires adjustments to be made to their working environment or needs time off for treatment (**Chapter 4**).

Absent an express declaration, it can be difficult for an employer to know that an invisible disability exists, such as diabetes, heart disease or mental illness. Even when explicitly asked, in the form of a medical questionnaire, employees still might not reveal a disability. Often employees prefer not to tell employers directly that they have an invisible disability. This can be problematic for employers.

If an employee has undergone medical clearance by way of an appointment with occupational health and if occupational health has direct knowledge of a disability, even if occupational health does not share this with the employer or its management, the employer is deemed to have constructive knowledge of the disability. Such an employer will not be able to escape liability for disability discrimination by relying on the defence that it did not know (*London Borough of Hammersmith & Fulham* v. *Farnsworth* [2000] IRLR 691 (EAT)).

Knowledge can also be imputed by virtue of signs of disability which have been apparent and from which, had proper enquiry and investigation been made, the employer would have gained explicit knowledge. In *HJ Heinz Co Ltd* v. *Kenrick* [2000] IRLR 144 (EAT) the EAT held that there was a dismissal for reasons relating to disability in circumstances where the employer knew of the symptoms but not the diagnosis. Lindsay J said:

> As we see it, the expression may include a reason deriving from how the disability manifests itself even where there is no knowledge of the disability as such…it does require employers to pause to consider whether the reason for some dismissal that they have in mind *might* relate to disability and, if it might, to reflect upon the Act and Code of Practice before dismissing. (para.27)

It is a question of fact whether the employer had enough information to put it on notice of disability.

If an employee has established the elements of the direct discrimination claim, it is going to be very difficult in many cases for an employer to rely on an argument that it did not know there was a disability. This is especially so if managers have been trained to spot the signs of invisible conditions like depression where usually there are signs of harm to health, for example where a previously reliable employee begins to take a lot of time off, arrives late at work or shows signs of distress at work.

2.1.7 Motive

The motive of the discriminator is irrelevant. It is not a defence to direct discrimination if an employer can show it had 'good reason' to discriminate. This was established in, among others, *Chief Constable of West Yorkshire Police* v. *Khan* [2001] UKHL 48. In *Amnesty International* v. *Ahmed* [2009] ICR 1450 (EAT), a race discrimination case, the EAT held that Amnesty's refusal to allow a UK national of Sudanese origin to work for it in Sudan was direct race discrimination. Amnesty cited two reasons: that it would adversely affect Ms Ahmed's safety and that of her colleagues if a Sudanese woman was working for Amnesty in Sudan, and that it would impinge on Amnesty's perceived impartiality. Despite Amnesty's genuine concerns about safety, its conduct was directly discriminatory and its 'good reason' was no defence. In the disability context motive will also be irrelevant. Even where an employer acts in what it believes to be the best interests of a disabled person at work, if the treatment is perceived as being less favourable the disabled employee will be able to show direct disability discrimination.

2.1.8 Proof

Direct discrimination is perhaps the most difficult discrimination claim to make out in the tribunal. There are several reasons for this. First, there is rarely overt evidence of direct discrimination and so tribunals will be required to draw inferences from facts and oral evidence. Secondly, the discriminator may not actually be aware that its treatment of an employee is based on prejudice or assumption. Thirdly, the issue of a comparator is complex and it often involves mental acrobatics to construct a comparator and then consider how an employer might have treated him or her. It is rare to have an actual comparator readily available.

It will almost always be easier for an employee to bring a claim for discrimination arising from disability than a claim for direct discrimination (**Chapter 3**).

2.2 ASSOCIATIVE DISCRIMINATION

DDA 1995 did not expressly provide for associative discrimination but following a reference to the ECJ in 2006 it is now part and parcel of disability discrimination law. The wider definition of direct discrimination under the Equality Act 2010 because of disability confirms the existence of the right to claim for associative discrimination. This means that a claimant need not be disabled to bring a disability discrimination claim. If there is an association with a disabled person, for example a spouse, child or family member, which causes less favourable treatment to occur, a non-disabled claimant may be able to bring a claim.

EBR Attridge Law LLP v. *Coleman* [2010] ICR 242 (EAT)

Miss Coleman worked for a law firm. She had a disabled son for whom she was the main carer. She alleged that she had been subjected to unfavourable comments at work, for example being called lazy when she requested time off to take care of her child. She brought claims of unfair constructive dismissal and disability discrimination pursuant to DDA 1995.

DDA 1995 did not expressly outlaw associative discrimination. In 2006 the Court of Appeal asked the ECJ whether associative discrimination fell within the provisions of the Directive. The ECJ held that it did.

In light of the ECJ ruling the tribunal held that:

> Although…the person who is subject to direct discrimination on grounds of disability is not herself disabled, the fact remains that it is the disability which, according to Ms Coleman, is the ground for the less favourable treatment…

The respondent appealed the decision of the tribunal on the basis that it had 'distorted and rewritten' DDA 1995 by reading in words so as to outlaw associative discrimination. The EAT held that:

> The proscription of associative discrimination is an extension of the scope of the legislation as enacted, but it is in no sense repugnant to it…What matters is that the putative victim has suffered adverse treatment on a proscribed 'ground', namely disability, and the fact that the disability is not his own is not of the essence.

It is to be noted that while an associate may bring a claim for discrimination, there is no obligation on employers to make reasonable adjustments for an employee who is associated with a disabled person (**Chapter 4**).

It is very likely that this area of law will see exponential growth in years to come. The increase in mental health difficulties in the elderly and the advances in medicine enabling children to live with severe disabilities are likely to lead to more employees with caring responsibilities. Employers need to be aware of their employees' personal circumstances when dealing with, for example, a flexible working request, in order to avoid potential issues with associative disability discrimination.

2.3 PERCEPTION DISCRIMINATION

Perception discrimination is, in principle, available in relation to disability discrimination claims. It is, however, a difficult concept in the field of disability.

J v. DLA Piper UK LLP [2010] ICR 1052 (EAT)

J was a barrister who had applied to work for DLA Piper as a professional support lawyer (PSL). An offer was made subject to satisfactory references and medical clearance. J disclosed a history of depressive illness which was managed with medication and would not prevent her from fulfilling the role. DLA Piper subsequently withdrew the offer on grounds that its requirements for a PSL had diminished and it did not have work for J. J presented a claim for disability discrimination.

The tribunal found that J did not meet the statutory definition of disability. J attempted to rely on the fact that even if she did not meet the definition, DLA had *perceived* her to be disabled and this had been the reason for the withdrawal of the offer. The claimant had not pleaded perception discrimination and was therefore not permitted to pursue it. The EAT noted the difficulties with this type of claim:

> What the putative discriminator perceives will not always be clearly identifiable as 'disability'. If the perceived disability is, say, blindness, there may be no problem: a blind person is necessarily disabled. But many physical or mental conditions which may attract adverse treatment do not necessarily amount to disabilities, either because they are not necessarily

25

> sufficiently serious or because they are not necessarily long-term. If a manager discriminates against an employee because he believes her to have a broken leg, or because he believes her to be 'depressed', the question whether the effects of the perceived injury, or of the perceived depression, are likely to last more or less than 12 months may never enter his thinking, consciously or unconsciously (nor indeed, in the case of perceived 'depression', may it be clear what he understands by the term). In such a case, on what basis can he be said to be discriminating 'on the ground of' the employee's – perceived – disability?

It is easy to see that in the context of other forms of discrimination perception discrimination might be possible.

Austin v. Samuel Grant (North East) Ltd (2011) ET/2503956/11

Mr Austin suffered sexual orientation discrimination based on a false perception that he was gay. In this case his fellow workers taunted him and created a hostile and intimidating environment for him to work in because they perceived him to be gay. He was subjected to less favourable treatment because of sexual orientation. It did not matter that he was in fact heterosexual: the bullying and harassment occurred because of the perception that he was gay and it was therefore discriminatory.

The central tenet of the disability discrimination legislation is that it only applies to people who meet the definition of disability in the Equality Act 2010. This is no small feat, the definition is a high test to meet (**Chapter 1**). Employees who have been seriously ill, even for long periods of time, are not certain to meet the definition. With perception discrimination, if a person who is not disabled is able to bring a claim on the basis of a perception that he or she was disabled, this would fundamentally undermine the statutory definition of disability and extend the disability protections to an undefined extent. In the view of the authors, this cannot be what was intended by Parliament and leads to unacceptable consequences. The EAT recognised the difficulties in *J* v. *DLA Piper* and was clear that, were such a claim to be brought, the first step would need to be a reference to the ECJ on the issue.

Aitken v. Commissioner of Police of the Metropolis [2011] EWCA Civ 582

The claimant failed in a claim in which he alleged that his treatment by the respondent was founded on a perception that he had a dangerous mental illness. Mr Aitken suffered from depression and obsessive compulsive disorder. He demonstrated behaviours at work that his colleagues found frightening. He alleged, but failed to provide evidence to confirm, that his condition caused the behaviour in question.

The lack of medical evidence adduced to prove the link between his behaviour and his disability meant that the behaviours were not because of disability. A colleague who was not disabled who demonstrated these behaviours would have been treated in the same way.

> In this case it was held that this was not about assumptions about mental health but about observed conduct which was not, on the evidence, shown to be linked to disability. Mr Aitken's claim for direct discrimination, based on perception, failed. The case is a useful reminder of the importance of obtaining the right medical evidence (**7.2** and **Chapter 15**). Were he to present his claim under the Equality Act 2010 with appropriate medical evidence, he would now be more likely to succeed under s.15 discrimination arising from a disability (**Chapter 3**).

What we see from both *J* v. *DLA Piper* and *Aitken* v. *Commissioner of Police of the Metropolis* is reluctance on the part of the tribunals to extend perception discrimination to disability. It is the opinion of the authors that this will continue to be the case. At the time of writing there has not been a successful claim brought on grounds of disability discrimination by perception.

2.4   OTHER ASPECTS OF DIRECT DISCRIMINATION

2.4.1   Positive discrimination: s.13(3)

In relation to disability as a protected characteristic, the Equality Act 2010 states at s.13(3):

> If the protected characteristic is disability, and B is not a disabled person, A does not discriminate against B only because A treats or would treat disabled persons more favourably than A treats B.

This is the only example in English discrimination law of permissible positive discrimination. Disabled employees may justifiably be treated *more favourably* than their non-disabled counterparts. The aim of the disability discrimination legislation is to create a level playing field for people with disabilities. To meet the definition a person must show a substantial disadvantage so creating a level playing field will necessarily involve going the extra mile to provide the person with resources and adjustments which will enable them to obtain work and remain in employment without their disabilities causing unnecessary obstacles. It is fundamental to disability discrimination that this element of positive discrimination is permitted. As a result, employees who are not disabled are not permitted by law to complain that they have been treated less favourably than colleagues with disabilities.

2.4.2   Occupational requirements: Sched.9, Part 1

The Equality Act 2010, Sched.9, Part 1, para.1(1) states:

> A person (A) does not contravene a provision mentioned in sub-paragraph (2) by applying in relation to work a requirement to have a particular protected characteristic, if A shows that, having regard to the nature or context of the work—

(a)   it is an occupational requirement,

(b)   the application of the requirement is a proportionate means of achieving a legiti-
        mate aim, and

(c)   the person to whom A applies the requirement does not meet it (or A has reasonable
        grounds for not being satisfied that the person meets it).

The provisions in para.1(2) include arrangements for offering employment and opportunities for promotion for the range of types of employees and applicants listed.

It will not be discriminatory for an employer to offer work to a person who is disabled on the basis of their disability.

Example

A charity working to promote awareness of mental health issues in the workplace may favour a candidate with bipolar affective disorder over one who does not have that (or any other) disability. Provided the appointment is a proportionate means of achieving a legitimate aim, no discrimination will have occurred.

It may be an occupational requirement that a disabled person is needed to fill a role. In any event, and only in the case of disability, positive discrimination is acceptable.

2.4.3   The alleged discriminator's characteristics: s.24

The Equality Act 2010, s.24 states:

Irrelevance of alleged discriminator's characteristics

(1)   For the purpose of establishing a contravention of this Act by virtue of section 13(1), it does not matter whether A has the protected characteristic.

If the alleged discriminator shares the protected characteristic of the person alleging disability discrimination, i.e. the discriminator is also disabled, this cannot be a defence to the treatment. Section 24 states that it is irrelevant for the purposes of a direct discrimination claim if the discriminator shares the protected characteristic. As a matter of evidence, a claimant may find it more difficult to persuade a tribunal to draw an inference of discrimination where the alleged perpetrator shares the protected characteristic but a disabled employee who discriminates against another disabled employee still discriminates.

2.4.4   Dual discrimination: s.14 (not in force)

At the time of writing, s.14 relating to combined or dual discrimination has not been brought into force. Many consider it unlikely to be brought in. We mention it for completeness only.

The Equality Act 2010 states at s.14(1) that:

A person (A) discriminates against another (B) if, because of a combination of two relevant protected characteristics, A treats B less favourably than A treats or would treat a person who does not share either of those characteristics.

It goes on to say at s.14(3) that:

For the purposes of establishing a contravention of this Act by virtue of subsection (1), B need not show that A's treatment of B is direct discrimination because of each of the characteristics in the combination (taken separately).

Example

A woman of 55 is a news presenter on television. She is dismissed. She cannot demonstrate that it is because she is a woman that she has been dismissed. The channel has many women newsreaders. She cannot demonstrate that it is because of age, because the channel has many older (male) newsreaders. What she can demonstrate, however, is that the channel has no older female newsreaders because once they reach a certain age they are taken off air to make way for younger models. This is dual discrimination in action.

As with all direct discrimination, dual discrimination requires a comparator.

2.5 CONCLUSION

The ambit of direct disability discrimination has been widened significantly with the specific inclusion of associative discrimination and discrimination by perception. Proving that direct disability discrimination has occurred is quite a high hurdle. It is a rare case where there has been blatant direct discrimination and an even rarer one where there is some objective evidence beyond the oral testimony of the parties to demonstrate the claim to the tribunal. It is the job of the tribunal to draw inferences from the facts before applying law. As we will see in the following chapters, some of the other forms of disability discrimination present lower hurdles to a claimant. It is perhaps for this reason that direct disability claims are less prevalent in practice.

CHAPTER 3

Section 15 discrimination arising from disability

This chapter examines the new concept of discrimination arising from disability in the Equality Act 2010, s.15. We take a brief look at the background to this provision (**3.1**) before explaining the elements of s.15 discrimination (**3.2**) and considering the key differences between s.15 and other forms of disability discrimination. We will then review some early first instance cases (**3.3**), which help to illustrate how the provision may be interpreted by tribunals. Finally we consider the overlap between s.15 and indirect discrimination (**3.4**) and its relationship with the reasonable adjustments duty (**3.5**). Section 15, discrimination arising from a disability, is a new form of discrimination. There is very little case law and no historical precedent to follow. In this chapter therefore we explore the Explanatory Notes to the Equality Act 2010 and the Code, for instructive guidance.

3.1 BRIEF BACKGROUND

3.1.1 Disability-related discrimination under DDA 1995 and *Novacold*

Discrimination arising from disability, as compared to disability-related discrimination, is a new concept. The old cases under DDA 1995, s.3A on disability-related discrimination have no application to the Equality Act 2010, s.15. There are key differences between the two regimes. There was no intention, when the Equality Act 2010 was at the bill stage, to change the concept. The change came about because of the House of Lords decision in *London Borough of Lewisham* v. *Malcolm* [2008] UKHL 43.

Pre-*Malcolm* the key case on disability-related discrimination was *Clark* v. *TDG Ltd t/a Novacold* [1999] ICR 951 (CA). In *Novacold* Mr Clark was dismissed following sickness absence. The Court of Appeal held that the correct comparator was a person who had not been absent from work and was able to carry out their job. This was the standard test until *Malcolm* and was relatively easy for an employee to meet.

3.1.2 *Malcolm*

The House of Lords decision in *Malcolm* radically undermined the protections for those with disabilities. This was a housing case which related to a man who was a schizophrenic who had, in contravention of council rules, sublet his flat. The House of Lords decided that the correct comparator was someone who shared all the characteristics and behaviour of the claimant except the mental health disability. Therefore the comparator would be someone who had sublet the flat but did not have schizophrenia. Such a person would have been treated in the same way as the claimant and there was therefore no discrimination. The decision had a devastating impact on DDA 1995, completely undermining the disability-related provisions. The Explanatory Notes to the Equality Act 2010 state in relation to s.15:

> those provisions [disability-related discrimination] no longer provided the degree of protection from disability-related discrimination that is intended for disabled people.

It effectively made it almost impossible for a disabled claimant to show that they had been treated less favourably for a disability-related reason. As compared to *Novacold*, a *Malcolm* comparator would be a non-disabled person who had been absent from work on leave for a reason other than disability. In most cases the comparator would be treated in the same way as the disabled employee so there would be little prospect of the disabled employee being able to show that discrimination had occurred.

3.1.3 Parliament addresses disability post-*Malcolm*

The *Malcolm* decision was issued by the House of Lords while the Equality Bill was going through Parliament. The aim of the Equality Bill was to harmonise all the strands of discrimination law and bring all the protected characteristics (sex, age, race, etc.) together into one piece of legislation. Indirect discrimination which had hitherto not applied in the field of disability discrimination was already proposed but a further amendment was required as a result of the *Malcolm* decision if the legal protections introduced by DDA 1995 and which had previously been enjoyed were to remain in place. That amendment was the introduction of a new form of discrimination, s.15, discrimination *arising from* disability. This is also referred to as detriment arising from disability.

3.1.4 Comparing the old and new regimes

We have no desire to dwell on DDA 1995, s.3A which is now repealed; however, it is perhaps instructive to briefly compare the old and new regimes. This may be

31

particularly useful for practitioners who have practised under the old regime and who have previously relied on the older case law. Section 15 is new territory.

	DDA 1995, s.3A	**Equality Act 2010, s.15**
Type of treatment	Less favourable treatment (a comparison).	Unfavourable (showing only that the treatment adversely affects the person).
Comparator	Required (different comparators were required under *Novacold* and *Malcolm* – this is now history).	No comparator required.
Group disadvantage	Must be able to show the provision, criterion or practice affects or would affect others more widely.	No requirement to demonstrate group disadvantage.
Reason for treatment	The reason had to be related to the disability itself.	The reason does not have to relate directly to the disability. It can be from something arising in consequence of disability.
Defences	If the reason for the treatment was substantial and material in the circumstances there could be no discrimination.	The treatment may be justifiable if it can be shown to be a proportionate means of achieving a legitimate aim.
Knowledge	Pre-*Malcolm* the employer was not required to know there was a disability. Post-*Malcolm* knowledge was required.	If the employer did not know and could not reasonably be expected to know then there can be no discrimination.

3.2 SECTION 15

3.2.1 The definition

The Equality Act 2010, s.15 states:

Discrimination arising from disability

(1)   A person (A) discriminates against a disabled person (B) if–

    (a)   A treats B unfavourably because of something arising in consequence of B's disability, and

    (b)   A cannot show that the treatment is a proportionate means of achieving a legitimate aim.

(2)   Subsection (1) does not apply if A shows that A did not know, and could not reasonably have been expected to know, that B had the disability.

The definition comprises four elements which must be satisfied for a claim of discrimination to be made out. These are:

(a)   the treatment must be unfavourable;
(b)   the treatment must arise from, i.e. be connected with or linked to, the claimant's disability;
(c)   the treatment is not capable of being a proportionate means of achieving a legitimate aim; and
(d)   the employer must know or ought reasonably to know of the disability.

Paragraph 70 of the Explanatory Notes states in relation to s.15:

> This section is aimed at re-establishing an appropriate balance between enabling a disabled person to make out a case of experiencing a detriment which arises because of his or her disability, and providing an opportunity for the employer or other person to defend the treatment.

Someone in the same circumstances as Mr Rudd in *Eagle Place Services* v. *Rudd* (**2.1.3**) would now be able to present a s.15 claim and the employer would have to provide a justification.

In the absence of many precedents from case law, the Code will, for now, to a very great extent, guide tribunals and courts on the interpretation of s.15. At the time of writing there have been only non-binding first instance decisions and none from the higher appellate courts.

3.2.2   No comparator

Section 15 requires a claimant to demonstrate that they have suffered *unfavourable* treatment. Less favourable treatment, for direct and indirect disability discrimination, requires a comparison to be undertaken between the person alleging disability and others. Under s.15 there is no requirement to compare that treatment to the way another employee has been or may be treated. There is therefore, in contrast to direct and indirect disability discrimination, no requirement to identify a comparator. This removes a significant burden from the claimant – note the difficulties a comparator can give rise to (**2.1.3**) – and obviates any difficulties that could arise in litigation if an incorrect comparator has been applied. This is a welcome development in disability discrimination law for claimants.

3.2.3   Unfavourable treatment

Unfavourable treatment is not defined in the Equality Act 2010. The Code uses the words 'being put at a disadvantage'. Some commentators use the term 'subjecting to a detriment'. Disadvantage is not defined in the Equality Act 2010. It is given its common-sense meaning.

What is clear is that the impact on the individual alleging discrimination must demonstrate some form of negative treatment. Only the courts and tribunals will determine how wide this provision will be.

Examples of unfavourable treatment include:

- being denied a promotion;
- being disciplined;
- being put under undue pressure in a performance management exercise; and
- being dismissed.

In practice a common scenario might be that of disabled employees who return to work after a period of sickness absence related to anxiety. They are put under pressure to catch up with the work they have missed during their absence. Unreasonable deadlines are set and the employees are put on a performance improvement plan (PIP). This unfavourable treatment causes the employees to have a relapse of their symptoms. It would have been a reasonable adjustment to delay the PIP pending their full immersion back into work and after establishing that they were in fact fit for work at full speed. The employee has suffered a detriment, being put on a PIP and under pressure, for a reason arising in consequence of his or her disability, the sick leave.

A disciplinary procedure is capable of being discriminatory if actions or failures giving rise to the procedure are related to disability. This provision does not mean that it will be an act of discrimination, in every case, to dismiss or discipline a disabled employee. An employer has an opportunity to justify any of its decisions. What it does mean is that careful thought and clear reasoning need to be applied to any sanctions imposed on a disabled employee in the light of this new provision.

An employer may still be capable of discrimination where it believes it is acting in the best interests of the employee. For example, a person with clinical depression is denied a promotion on the basis that the employer believes the worker will be unable to cope with the new role without getting excessively fatigued. The employer's motives are honourable but it is treating the worker unfavourably for a reason related to disability. If the employer was given a medical opinion which suggested that the promotion may cause a relapse in the employee's symptoms then refusing the promotion may be justifiable. The legitimate aim might be the protection of the employee's welfare. Whether this is proportionate will depend on the facts of the case. If the job could have been performed as a job share, this might suggest that denial of the promotion was not proportionate. By exploring this example a little we wish to demonstrate that employers with disabled employees are not prevented from taking action, they are simply required to act proportionately and in line with medical advice rather than on the basis of suspicion or speculation.

3.2.4 Arising in consequence of disability

The Explanatory Notes describe the effect of s.15 as follows:

it is discrimination to treat a disabled person unfavourably not because of the person's disability itself but because of something arising from, or in consequence of, his or her disability, such as the need to take a period of disability-related absence.

If the treatment was because of disability itself, it would be direct discrimination.

It is for the person alleging discrimination to demonstrate that there is a *connection* between the disadvantage or detriment and the disability. The Code tells us that the consequences of disability are anything which is the:

- result;
- effect; or
- outcome

of a disability.

The consequences of disability vary considerably and depend on the individual and the disability. Some consequences may be obvious, for example being unable to walk unaided or needing to use specialist equipment to alleviate the effects of disability. Other consequences might relate to mood, for example if a person has diabetes or a mental health condition which has an effect on mood. It may be appropriate to discuss with the employee a report from his or her treating physician in order for both parties to have a clear understanding of the consequences of the disability on the individual (see **7.2**). The advantage of a medical report is that problems can be addressed before they arise, adjustments may be made, misunderstandings can be avoided and, should the matter proceed to a tribunal, there is a clear record of the impact on the claimant *at the time* and of the knowledge of the respondent.

The draft version of the Code included some examples of consequences of disability. These are absent in the final version. The list below is taken from some of the examples in the draft version and some of the case study examples in the final version:

- a need for regular breaks;
- slower typing or output speeds;
- regular hospital appointments;
- a need for a private or quiet working environment;
- a need for specialist computer equipment;
- a period of absence related to disability;
- a need to work reduced hours.

The Code devotes an entire chapter to s.15 at pp.71–77. Chapter 5 of the Code explains the duty on employers not to treat disabled people unfavourably because of something arising in consequence of disability.

Example from the Code, para.5.3

A worker is dismissed for having taken three months' sick leave. The employer is aware that the worker has multiple sclerosis and most of the sick leave is disability-related. The employer's decision to dismiss is not because of the disability itself. However the worker has been treated unfavourably because of something arising in consequence of disability, the sick leave.

Example from the Code, para.5.9

The Code gives another example of a woman who is disciplined for losing her temper at work. Her behaviour was out of character and was a result of severe pain caused by cancer. The disciplinary action is unfavourable treatment. The loss of temper is the reason for the treatment and this arises in consequence of her disability. There is a direct connection between the reason she is being subjected to unfavourable treatment and her disability. She is not being disciplined because she is disabled. The employer will need to justify its decision to discipline this employee if it is to avoid liability for discrimination.

In order to succeed with a claim under s.15, a claimant must be able to persuade the tribunal that there is a link between the unfavourable treatment and the claimant's disability. Absent this link the claim will fail. The two cases below at **3.3** illustrate this very neatly.

3.2.5 A proportionate means of achieving a legitimate aim

Employers may be able to justify discrimination if they can show that there is a business need which needs to be achieved and the unfortunate side effect of this need is that some employees suffer discrimination as a result. The test is one of standard objective justification. The aim pursued must be appropriate and proportionate. The need to achieve this aim must be reasonably necessary. The aim must not be discriminatory itself. The employer does not have to be able to show that there was no alternative course of action. It is enough to show that there is no less discriminatory means of achieving the same aim. If there is a less discriminatory means of achieving the same aim then it can never be proportionate.

It is a balancing exercise to achieve the needs of a business and not produce an adverse impact on protected groups. As the law currently stands, substantially cost-driven aims are capable of justification but at present it is still necessary to show something more than cost alone as the aim (*Woodcock* v. *Cumbria Primary Care Trust* [2012] EWCA Civ 330).

The Code tells us that an employer will not be able to rely on 'mere generalisations' about why it took the actions it did. The employer will be expected to adduce concrete evidence.

3.2.6 The knowledge defence

In contrast to indirect discrimination, which does *not* require knowledge of the discriminatory impact of a provision, criterion or practice (PCP) (**4.3.1**), s.15 requires that an employer knows about the employee's disability. Parliament considered it unfair for employers to have liability for discrimination without knowing about disability because in many cases employees choose not to reveal hidden disabilities. This is particularly so in the case of mental health conditions. If an employer does not know, cannot reasonably be expected to know, cannot be imputed to know or cannot be fixed with constructive knowledge (**2.1.6**) then it cannot be liable under s.15.

This does not mean that an employer can simply ignore the issue of disability until an express disclosure is made. The Code requires an employer to take all such steps as are reasonable in the circumstances to find out whether there is a disability (Code, para.5.15). What is reasonable will depend on the facts but to illustrate the obligation it is suggested that, for an applicant with no visible impairment, it may be reasonable to rely on a declaration that there is no disability. For a long-standing employee who has recently demonstrated an inexplicable change in attitude, greater enquiries may be required. For an employee who has had, or is on, an extended period of sickness absence, it may be appropriate to make substantial enquiries or seek a medical opinion (**7.2**).

For many employers this is an important line of defence to a disability discrimination claim, possibly combined with an argument that the condition does not meet the statutory definition. Both of these defences go to the heart of a discrimination claim without the need to explore the conduct of the employer.

3.3 SOME EARLY CASES

Two relatively recent tribunal decisions, from 2011, give us an early indication of how employment tribunals are approaching s.15 and discrimination arising from a disability. They are both first instance decisions. At the time of writing the higher courts, the EAT, the Court of Appeal and the Supreme Court, are yet to consider any cases dealing with s.15.

Below is a first example of a successful claim under s.15. To succeed it was vital that a link was established between the unfavourable treatment and the disability.

Williams v. *Ystrad Mynach College* (2011) ET/1600019/11

Mr Williams was a lecturer who, due to a number of serious illnesses, had a high sickness absence rate. In 2007 he was diagnosed with hydrocephalus, fluid retention on the skull. This caused headaches and in 2010 led to a diagnosis of haematoma on the brain. This meant that Mr Williams was no longer suitable for full-time work as a lecturer. There was an occupational health report at the time of the haematoma diagnosis

---

suggesting that he was 'certainly not fit to work in any capacity at present'. Subsequently Mr Williams's GP wrote to the college saying that Mr Williams would possibly be fit to resume work on a part-time basis or 'possibly half his original workload'. Shortly after this the college commenced a capability procedure and invited Mr Williams to a capability hearing.

At the capability meeting Mr Williams made it clear he was willing to work reduced hours, with reduced pay and that his health was improving. Mr Davies, the college principal who chaired the meeting, suggested that ill health retirement might be a better option and that if Mr Williams did not retire he should be moved from a permanent contract to an F4 contract. The F4 contract was unfavourable. Mr Williams did not want to move to an F4 contract.

The outcome of the capability meeting was that Mr Williams was moved to an F4 contract. Mr Williams treated this move as a dismissal from his permanent contract and appealed. Despite inconsistent medical evidence about Mr Williams's capability, the college failed to seek any further medical evidence. It seemed to have decided that Mr Williams was no longer able to function at his previous high level. The College reached its own medical conclusions based on the fact that it believed Mr Williams would fall ill again. Mr Williams claimed unfair dismissal and two counts of disability discrimination, for failure to make reasonable adjustments and for discrimination arising from disability under s.15.

The tribunal was in no doubt that replacing a permanent contract with an F4 contract was unfavourable treatment. The college acknowledged that its actions arose in consequence of Mr Williams's disability, therefore the requisite link was established. The sole remaining issue for the tribunal to consider was whether the college's actions could be objectively justified. The tribunal accepted that it could be a legitimate aim for the college to need to provide teaching services to its students. However the tribunal believed that although the college had formed the view that Mr Williams was incapable of providing service and was no longer capable of doing his job, this view was not supported by up-to-date medical evidence. The tribunal believed that the new contract arrangement was designed to minimise any disruption which could arise from Mr Williams's future absences and the college should not be entitled to retrospectively rely on an objective justification that had not been considered at the time the decision to change the contracts had taken place. The tribunal also concluded that even if this aim had been in the minds of the decision makers at the time of their decision, they had gone about implementing their aim in a disproportionate manner. The justification defence was therefore not made out. Mr Williams had sought, as a reasonable adjustment, to be retained on a permanent contract on reduced hours. The college could have and should have provided this adjustment. Mr Williams succeeded on all three heads of claim.

Below is an example of a s.15 claim which failed because the claimant could not satisfy the tribunal that there was a link between the unfavourable treatment and the disability.

McGraw v. London Ambulance Service NHS Trust (2011) ET/3301865/11

Mr McGraw, a paramedic, was dismissed for gross misconduct on grounds that while off sick with depression he went to the ambulance station with the intention of misappropriating Entonox, an anaesthetic which he had been abusing for a number of years. This contravened the service's policy on alcohol, drugs and solvent misuse. The

Ambulance Service took the decision on the basis that it would not tolerate substance abuse, Entonox was reserved for patient use, Mr McGraw had easy access to drugs in his role as a paramedic and he could not be relied on to provide services to the public. Mr McGraw brought claims of unfair dismissal, direct disability discrimination and discrimination arising from disability under s.15.

The tribunal gave considerable thought as to whether London Ambulance's treatment was because of something arising in consequence of disability. Following the wording of the Code, the tribunal asked itself whether the attempted theft was a *result, effect or outcome* of Mr McGraw's disability. The tribunal could find no evidence of a link between the depression, any medication Mr McGraw was taking for depression and the theft. The evidence before the tribunal suggested that the depression medication was likely to make Mr McGraw drowsy but not that it would incline him to theft.

The tribunal concluded that even if its analysis on disability was wrong, the actions of the Ambulance Service were a proportionate means of achieving a legitimate aim, namely providing service to the public by paramedics who were not under the influence of drugs. As a matter of fact the tribunal found that Mr McGraw's conduct arose from his addiction and not from his disability. The actions of the Ambulance Service could not therefore amount to discrimination arising from a disability.

3.4 RELATIONSHIP WITH INDIRECT DISCRIMINATION

Many circumstances giving rise to a *prima facie* claim of discrimination under s.15 will also give rise to a claim for indirect disability discrimination under the Equality Act 2010, s.19 (**Chapter 5**). However the differences between s.15 and s.19, in a disability discrimination context, make s.15 a more attractive claim for most claimants. The differences include:

- s.15 does not require a comparator;
- there is no need to show a provision, criterion or practice for s.15;
- group disadvantage need not be shown under s.15; and
- the knowledge requirement is different (**2.1.6** and **5.2.7**).

Discrimination under s.15 requires that the employer knows of the disability. Indirect discrimination does not. There may be occasions where, because the employee has not revealed his or her disability and there is no way the employer could have known or can be fixed with knowledge, a s.15 claim is ruled out and s.19 is relied upon. In almost all other cases, where there is knowledge, a s.15 claim will be preferable.

3.5 OVERLAP WITH THE REASONABLE ADJUSTMENTS DUTY

Employers will in many cases be able to avoid unfavourable treatment by making reasonable adjustments for disability (**Chapter 4**). It will be very difficult for an employer who has failed to consider or make reasonable adjustments to show that its actions can be objectively justified. Making reasonable adjustments is not a complete answer to a claim of discrimination under s.15 but it will certainly be relevant.

Example from the Code, para.5.22

A company alters the hours of work for a female employee who is disabled by virtue of multiple sclerosis. The employee is dismissed for having taken three months' sick leave. In spite of the fact that the employer has previously made reasonable adjustments, it may still be liable under s.15 for discrimination arising from a disability unless it can show a justification.

3.6 CONCLUSION

There is no question that s.15 will achieve what it sets out to do: redress the balance in a post-*Malcolm* world so that it is easier for claimants to demonstrate that they have suffered detriment for a reason connected with their disability. There is also no question, as stated in **Chapter 5**, that indirect discrimination will have very limited application in the field of disability discrimination because s.15 removes so many barriers for claimants, in terms of technicalities and hurdles to be crossed. Section 15 imposes additional responsibilities on employers who will need to consider whether an employee has a disability before taking steps which could be perceived as unfavourable: disciplinaries, performance management, dismissal and so on. In addition to the reasonable adjustments duty, employers now need to be mindful of falling foul of s.15.

CHAPTER 4

Reasonable adjustments

This chapter looks at the law around the duty to make reasonable adjustments. We start with a brief look at the background to this important provision (**4.1**). When the duty arises it is very broad and can be quite onerous on employers (**4.2**). The duty is widely invoked in practice but it is still misunderstood. We set out the three requirements which may lead to the imposition of the duty (**4.3**). We also set out the steps the tribunal is required to follow in assessing whether the duty has arisen (**4.4**). The duty arises when substantial disadvantage is caused to a disabled employee (**4.5**) in comparison with a non-disabled employee (**4.6**). We then consider the requirement of reasonableness (**4.7**). The duty on employers is neither a general nor a blanket duty. The duty does depend on actual or imputed knowledge (**4.8**) often connected to consultation with the employee (**4.9**). We consider the duty in a number of situations including in relation to sick pay (**4.10**), disability leave (**4.11**) and dismissals (**4.12**). Finally it is to be noted that once the reasonable adjustments duty is triggered, employers are compelled to make adjustments. A failure to do so can never be justified if the adjustment is reasonable and the employee is disabled (**4.13**).

4.1 BACKGROUND

The employer's duty to make reasonable adjustments is a core tenet of the Equality Act 2010 as it was with DDA 1995. It is central to the disability discrimination legislation. The intention behind the duty is neatly summarised by Baroness Hale in her judgment in *Archibald* v. *Fife Council* [2004] UKHL 32:

> The making of adjustments is not an end in itself. The end is reached when the disabled person is no longer at a substantial disadvantage.

The aim is to alleviate the substantial disadvantage suffered by disabled employees. It is about creating a level playing field, giving disabled employees a leg up so that they can work alongside non-disabled colleagues without suffering detriment. Clearly there is a balance to be struck between removing all disadvantage and what the law requires an employer to do. What is clear is that once the duty arises it cannot be avoided.

The duty to make reasonable adjustments:

- requires employers to take proactive steps;
- applies to all stages of the employment process (including dismissal and post-termination);
- applies to employers of all sizes;
- applies only where the employee meets the statutory definition of disability, it does not cover all sick employees; and
- in some cases involves treating disabled employees *more favourably* than those employees who are not disabled – permissible positive discrimination.

However, the duty to make reasonable adjustments is *not* a general, blanket duty to assist a disabled employee.

4.2 THE BREADTH OF THE DUTY

The seminal case on reasonable adjustments has for many years been *Archibald* v. *Fife Council* [2004] UKHL 32, a DDA 1995 case which is a decision of the House of Lords. The judgment of Baroness Hale set the mark for the extent of the reasonable adjustments duty and has been relied on and reiterated ever since.

Archibald v. *Fife Council* [2004] UKHL 32

Mrs Archibald worked for the council as a road sweeper. Following minor surgery she became mobility impaired. She could no longer fulfil her role and wanted to be moved to a clerical post. Mrs Archibald was subjected to competitive interviews. She failed to get another post within the organisation and was dismissed. She brought a claim alleging that the council had failed in its duty to make reasonable adjustments.

The House of Lords, Baroness Hale giving judgment, said the council *had* failed in its duty. Mrs Archibald should have been transferred to another post and been given training without the need to undergo interviews. Baroness Hale said the duty to transfer can involve a move up, down or sideways. She also said the making of the adjustment was not an end in itself. The aim is to end the substantial disadvantage. The law not only requires employers to treat those with disabilities *more* favourably, it *requires* them to take reasonable steps to alleviate the disadvantage. She went on to say that training should be provided to enable the person to fulfil the new role.

This decision requires employers only to move disabled employees to fill *vacant* posts. There is nothing to suggest the creation of a new post. Larger companies which have a broad base of roles will have to justify a decision not to transfer to any other available roles within the organisation.

More recently the case of *Chief Constable of South Yorkshire* v. *Jelic* [2010] IRLR 744 (EAT) appears to widen the duty further, although it is questionable whether it would be reasonable, in a general commercial context, to bump a non-disabled employee from their position to make room for a disabled person. The case concerned a policeman. In the police force the power structure and chain of command enable an order to be made which might not be possible in a wider commercial context but the case does demonstrate the length to which employers are expected to go to comply with the reasonable adjustments duty.

Chief Constable of South Yorkshire v. *Jelic* [2010] IRLR 744 (EAT)

PC Jelic suffered from chronic anxiety syndrome. His disability made it very difficult for him to work in a confrontational environment where he had contact with the public. He needed to be moved into a role which was not public facing in order to alleviate the substantial disadvantage that he has suffered in his existing role. The PCP which disadvantaged him was the requirement to do face-to-face duties. The reasonable adjustment he sought was to move to a desk-based role. His colleague PC Franklin's role was better suited to him. PC Franklin was bumped from his role to make room for PC Jelic.

4.3   THE THREE REQUIREMENTS

The reasonable adjustments duty comprises three requirements which are set out in the Equality Act 2010, s.20:

...
(2)   The duty comprises the following three requirements.
(3)   The first requirement is a requirement, where a provision, criterion or practice of A's puts a disabled person at a substantial disadvantage in relation to a relevant matter in comparison with persons who are not disabled, to take such steps as it is reasonable to have to take to avoid the disadvantage.
(4)   The second requirement is a requirement, where a physical feature puts a disabled person at a substantial disadvantage in relation to a relevant matter in comparison with persons who are not disabled, to take such steps as it is reasonable to have to take to avoid the disadvantage.
(5)   The third requirement is a requirement, where a disabled person would, but for the provision of an auxiliary aid, be put at a substantial disadvantage in relation to a relevant matter in comparison with persons who are not disabled, to take such steps as it is reasonable to have to take to provide the auxiliary aid.

Section 20(6) goes on to say that where the first or third requirement relates to the provision of information, the steps which it is reasonable for an employer to have to take include steps for ensuring that the information is provided in an accessible format. An employee will never be required to meet the employer's costs of complying with the duty (s.20(7)).

The elements of each of the requirements are that:

(a)   there is a PCP, physical feature or lack of an auxiliary aid;
(b)   which *substantially* disadvantages a disabled employee;
(c)   which would not produce the same effect on a non-disabled employee;
(d)   the employer is *required* to take such steps as it is reasonable to take; and
(e)   the steps should alleviate the disadvantage.

In this chapter we will examine each of the elements of the definition.

4.3.1   Provisions, criteria or practices

The concept of PCP is widely construed. A PCP is capable of being any policy, procedure, practice, requirement, management decision, provision, criterion, workplace rule or similar which applies at work. It need not be a formal policy or one that is expressed in writing. It can be a way of doing things, a common practice which is expected of staff. It can be applied to everyone, some people, or even to only one person.

Examples of PCPs include:

- a grievance and disciplinary policy;
- the requirement to work fixed hours;
- a staff uniform requirement or dress code restriction;
- a formal candidate selection process for internal job vacancies;
- open-plan office working;
- hot-desking;
- rules contained in a staff handbook;
- appraisal processes and PIPs;
- a requirement to undertake exams/qualifications in order to obtain promotion;
- redundancy criteria; and
- attendance records.

The PCP must apply or be capable of applying to the employee alleging discrimination *and* to other non-disabled colleagues.

The following case demonstrates that even if a PCP does not apply directly to an employee, it is still capable of being a PCP on which that employee can rely.

Roberts v. North-West Ambulance Service **[2012] Eq LR 196 (EAT)**

Mr Roberts suffered from a social anxiety disorder which amounted to a disability. He found his working environment challenging for two reasons. First, the room he worked in was open plan and very busy, which caused anxiety. Secondly, employees hot-desked and Mr Roberts found it very difficult not having a fixed desk to call his own. He tried on occasion to reserve a desk, the same desk each time, for his use, but if he did not start work on an early shift it was not always available.

Although on the facts Mr Roberts was not strictly hot-desking himself, the practice of others hot-desking was found, by the EAT, to be a PCP which applied to him. The case was remitted to the tribunal to consider whether the PCP placed Mr Roberts at a substantial disadvantage.

In the course of tribunal proceedings the first hurdle which the claimant must pass is the correct analysis and identification of the PCP. It is open to employers to raise evidence to counter the claim that a PCP exists and has been applied. Given the broad interpretation, this may not be a particularly fruitful point of challenge.

Example from the Code, para.6.10

An employer has a policy that designated car parking spaces are only available for senior managers. A worker who is not a manager but who is mobility impaired needs a parking space near the office. The employer gives this employee a designated space. The employer has made a reasonable adjustment to its policy of only giving spaces to senior managers.

A PCP can be as simple as a requirement to fulfil a job specification (*Archibald* v. *Fife Council* [2004] UKHL 32). A PCP can also arise from a one-off decision, as found in *British Airways plc* v. *Starmer* [2005] IRLR 863 (EAT) and, more recently *Roberts* v. *North-West Ambulance Service* [2012] Eq LR 196 (EAT). Although the definition is given a broad interpretation there are limits. In *Newcastle Upon Tyne Hospitals NHS Foundation Trust* v. *Bagley* [2012] Eq LR 634 (EAT) ineptitude by HR was held not to be a PCP.

British Airways plc v. *Starmer* [2005] IRLR 862 (EAT)

This was a case under the Sex Discrimination Act 1975. Ms Starmer was a pilot for BA. Following her return from maternity leave she applied to work 50 per cent of her full-time hours. BA refused her request but was able to offer her 75 per cent of her hours. Ms Starmer alleged that BA's requirement for her to work 75 per cent of full hours was a PCP. BA resisted this on the basis that the decision applied only to Ms Starmer and therefore could not be a PCP. The EAT held that the decision was a PCP and that there is nothing in the wording of the statute which precluded a one-off decision applied to one person from being a PCP.

The scope of a PCP is not, however, without limit. In contrast to *Starmer*, the EAT recently held that where the practice relied upon was a one-off flawed disciplinary process this could not amount to a PCP (*Nottingham City Transport Ltd* v. *Harvey* [2013] Eq LR 4 (EAT)).

Yorkshire Housing Ltd v. *Cuerden* [2010] UKEAT/0397/09

The requirement to attend a return to work meeting was held to amount to a PCP. By way of reasonable adjustment Ms Cuerden requested that her solicitor be allowed to attend the meeting with her. She suffered from a major depressive disorder. She alleged that a substantial disadvantage (extreme anxiety) arose from the requirement to meet with the company. Her employer declined. Ms Cuerden resigned claiming constructive dismissal and a breach of the duty to make reasonable adjustments. The EAT held that it was a reasonable adjustment and one which the company should have made. She was awarded £174,000 in damages.

Care should be taken to define and clarify the PCP relied upon if a claim is brought. Alternatively if the matter is a one-off failure by the employer the appropriate claim may be one under s.15 as that does not require the identification of a PCP (**Chapter 3**).

4.3.2 Physical features

The Equality Act 2010, s.20(9) records that avoiding a substantial disadvantage caused by a physical feature includes:

- removal of the physical feature in question;
- altering it; or
- providing a reasonable means of avoiding it.

'Physical feature' is also very widely defined. The following are to be treated as physical features (s.20(9) and (12)):

- any feature of the design or construction of a building;
- any feature of an approach to or exit from or entrance to a building;
- a fixture, fitting, furniture, furnishings, materials, equipment or other moveable property in or on the premises; and
- any other physical element or quality of the premises.

This definition applies equally to permanent and temporary features of premises.

The Code gives a non-exhaustive list of physical features including steps, stairways, kerbs, paving, internal and external doors, gates, toilets, lighting and ventilation, signs, furniture, and so on, at para.6.12.

The Explanatory Notes to the Equality Act 2010 give an example of reasonable adjustments to the physical features of a workplace.

Example from the Explanatory Notes to the Equality Act 2010, para.86

A bank is obliged to consider reasonable adjustments for a newly recruited financial adviser who is a wheelchair user and who would have difficulty negotiating her way around the customer area. In consultation with the new adviser, the bank rearranges the layout of furniture in the customer area and installs a new desk. These changes result in the new adviser being able to work alongside her colleagues.

The Code gives a further example of a reasonable adjustment to a physical feature at para.6.12.

4.3.3 Auxiliary aids

The Code describes an auxiliary aid at para.6.13 as:

> something which provides support or assistance to a disabled person.

Examples cited include an adapted keyboard or text-to-speech software. Auxiliary aids also include auxiliary services (Equality Act 2010, s.20(11)), for example, providing a sign language interpreter or a support worker for a disabled employee. 'Something' also means 'someone'.

4.4 THE REQUIRED STEPS

The reasonable adjustments duty is not a general duty to support disabled workers (*Royal Bank of Scotland* v. *Ashton* [2011] ICR 632 (EAT)). Employers and tribunals must go through the formula of analysing whether the duty arises by going through the steps set out below.

For the duty to arise on an employer, an employee needs to be able to demonstrate that:

(a)   they are suffering a disadvantage because of a PCP, physical feature or the absence of an auxiliary aid or support;

(b)   the disadvantage is substantial;

(c)   non-disabled colleagues are not affected in the same way; and,

(d)   the proposed adjustment will alleviate the disadvantage.

The diagram at **Figure 4.1** demonstrates how to assess whether an adjustment is needed and whether it is reasonable.

Only once these four matters are established does the obligation arise on the employer to make the adjustments. The case of *Environment Agency* v. *Rowan* [2008] ICR 218 (EAT) illustrates this very neatly.

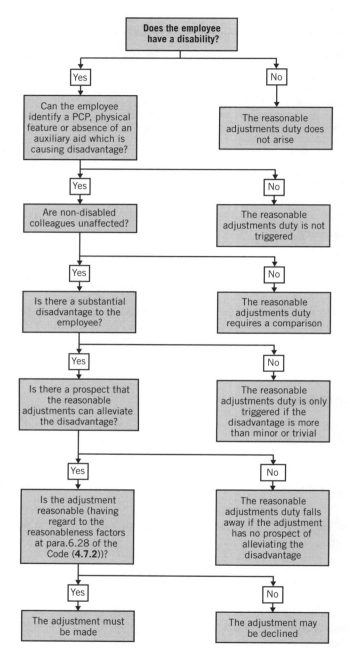

Figure 4.1 Assessing the reasonable adjustments duty

Environment Agency v. Rowan [2008] ICR 218 (EAT)

Ms Rowan worked for the Environment Agency as a clerk. Following a back injury Ms Rowan could not sit for long periods and needed bed rest. She was off sick for five months during which time she moved home. She now lived 50 miles further away from her place of work and by way of reasonable adjustment requested to be able to work from home. The tribunal at first instance found in favour of Ms Rowan. This was in part due to the 'absolutely shocking' exchanges which took place between HR and occupational health and which demonstrated a poor attitude towards the claimant. On appeal the EAT held that a trial period of home working was *not* a reasonable adjustment because it did not address the issues of working in the office. Working from home would not alleviate the difficulties of office working arising from her disability, therefore it could not be a reasonable adjustment.

In *Rowan* His Honour Judge Serota QC recommended the correct process for an employment tribunal to consider when determining whether there has been a failure in the reasonable adjustments duty. The steps are:

(a)   for the employee to identify the provision, criterion or practice applied by or on behalf of the employer; or

(b)   for the employee to identify the physical feature of premises occupied by the employer; and

(c)   for the employee to identify non-disabled comparators, where appropriate; and

(d)   to assess the nature and extent of the substantial disadvantage suffered looking at the overall picture.

His Honour Judge Serota QC helpfully stated:

> In our opinion an Employment Tribunal cannot properly make findings of a failure to make reasonable adjustments…without going through that process. Unless the Employment Tribunal has identified the four matters…it cannot go on to judge if any proposed adjustment is reasonable. It is simply unable to say what adjustments were reasonable to prevent the provision, criterion or practice, or feature, placing the disabled person concerned at a substantial disadvantage. (para.27)

Looking at *Rowan* in more detail, the PCP is the requirement to work in the office. The substantial disadvantage alleged is that she cannot do her job because she needs to be able to take bed rest during the day to manage her back condition. It is a matter of common sense that a non-disabled colleague would not require bed rest during the day therefore there is no disadvantage to a non-disabled colleague when there clearly is to Ms Rowan. Ms Rowan's claim failed on the last head: the proposed adjustment would not alleviate the disadvantage. Working from home would not enable Ms Rowan to be able to work in the office. Working from home, based on the facts of this case, was not capable of amounting to a reasonable adjustment.

4.5 SUBSTANTIAL DISADVANTAGE

The focus of reasonable adjustments should be to remove an impediment. For an adjustment to be *required* by law it must be capable of alleviating the substantial disadvantage suffered by the disabled employee. If the adjustment cannot alleviate the disadvantage, the employer is not required to comply with it. It is therefore necessary to identify the substantial disadvantage caused by the PCP, physical feature or lack of auxiliary aid.

In DDA 1995 'substantial' was not defined. The Equality Act 2010 does define substantial at s.212(1) as meaning 'more than minor or trivial'. This is discussed in more detail at **1.1.2**.

The substantial disadvantage must be identified so that any proposed adjustment can be tested to see whether it could alleviate the disadvantage.

4.6 THE COMPARISON WITH NON-DISABLED PEOPLE

An employee alleging a reasonable adjustments failure must be able to demonstrate that they are suffering a disadvantage as compared to their non-disabled colleagues. The disadvantage suffered by a disabled employee must be one which disadvantages the disabled person in a way that would not disadvantage a non-disabled person.

Unlike direct and indirect discrimination, there is no requirement to identify a comparator. If there is an obvious comparator, this may be relied on. With reasonable adjustments the comparison is, however, a more general comparative exercise. It will not always be necessary to identify a non-disabled comparator. On many occasions the facts will speak for themselves. The purpose of the comparison is to establish whether the disadvantage suffered by the disabled employee is substantial. This may be a matter of common sense. In many cases the comparison may be obvious.

Fareham College Corporation v. *Walters* [2009] IRLR 991 (EAT)

Ms Walters alleged that the college had breached its duty to make reasonable adjustments following her dismissal. She won her case in the tribunal but the college appealed the decision, partly on the basis that the tribunal had failed to carry out the appropriate comparative exercise to determine whether there had been a substantial disadvantage and that this was an error of law.

The EAT found that, for reasonable adjustments only, a general comparison is required. It is not the like-for-like test that applies in direct and indirect disability discrimination. The EAT stated that in many cases the general class of people who would be disadvantaged would often be clearly discernible from the PCP being applied. It was not necessary for Ms Walters to identify someone who did not have a disability

---

but whose circumstances were not materially different from hers. The EAT said that if this was required it would 'defeat the purpose of the disability discrimination legislation'.

The Code mirrors this position at para.6.16. The purpose of the comparison is different from that of the test in direct and indirect discrimination. The aim of the comparison exercise with reasonable adjustments is simply to establish whether because of disability there is a PCP, physical feature or absence of an auxiliary aid which disadvantages the disabled person.

4.7 REASONABLENESS

4.7.1 The burden on a claimant

Unless there is evidence before the tribunal of an adjustment which at least on its face appears reasonable and which would mitigate or eliminate the substantial disadvantage to which the employee was subjected, the burden does not shift to the employer (*Project Management Institute* v. *Latif* [2007] IRLR 579 (EAT)).

Although the claimant must be able to identify a reasonable adjustment to commence the claim, the tribunal is not limited to consideration of reasonable adjustments identified by the claimant. Consideration may be given to any reasonable adjustment raised, even by the tribunal itself.

There must be *some* prospect that the adjustment will alleviate the disadvantage alleged in order for the duty to arise on the employer. However the employee does not have to be able to show that it will work with total certainty. As long as there is a *chance* it will work the duty will arise.

Foster v. *Leeds Teaching Hospital NHS Trust* [2011] Eq LR 1075 (EAT)

Mr Foster was placed at a substantial disadvantage by the requirement for him to work in the security department because his disability, a stress-related disorder, was caused by that department. There was evidence of bullying and harassment. It would have been a reasonable adjustment to put him on the redeployment register.

The EAT held that it was not necessary to find that there would have been a good prospect of redeployment or of Mr Foster being well enough to be able to work. The key factor was that there was *a prospect* of that adjustment alleviating the effects of the disability at the date of the decision. The trust's failure to place him on the redeployment register was a failure of the reasonable adjustments duty.

4.7.2 The question of reasonableness

The law only requires adjustments to be made for disability if they are reasonable, hence the name *reasonable* adjustments. Reasonableness depends on all the circumstances of the case, including the size and resources of the employer.

The Code at para.6.28 lists some of the factors which an employer might take into account in order to determine whether an adjustment is reasonable. They are:

- Whether taking any particular steps would be effective in preventing the substantial disadvantage.
- The practicability of the step. Can it be taken? Is it possible?
- The financial and other costs of making the adjustment and the extent of any disruption caused.
- The extent of the employer's financial or other resources.
- The availability to the employer of financial or other assistance to help make an adjustment, such as advice from Access to Work.
- The type and size of the employer.

The test of reasonableness is an objective one and will depend on the circumstances.

Example

A large multinational company is asked to provide specialist computer software, specialist computer hardware, specialist furniture and various other items which will alleviate the disadvantages suffered by a paraplegic employee. The cost of these adjustments is significant. It is likely that these adjustments will be viewed as reasonable as long as there is a chance they can alleviate the disadvantage. By contrast a small firm which employs five people simply does not have the financial resources to make the changes and no financial assistance is available. This adjustment is likely to be unreasonable in terms of costs for the smaller firm.

Below are some examples of adjustments which may be reasonable and some which may not be reasonable. Each case will turn on its own facts.

4.7.2.1 Adjustments which may be reasonable

In the following cases the courts have found that the proposed adjustments would have been reasonable:

- *Archibald* v. *Fife Council* [2004] UKHL 32 (**4.2**): it would have been a reasonable adjustment to move the employee to a new post without competitive interview, placing her in a new role and providing training.
- *Yorkshire Housing Ltd* v. *Cuerden* [2010] UKEAT/0397/09 (**4.3.1**): it was reasonable to allow an employee to be accompanied by her solicitor at an internal company meeting.

- *Hinsley* v. *Chief Constable of West Mercia Constabulary* [2010] UKEAT/0200/10: it would have been a reasonable adjustment to reinstate a police officer who resigned from the force while depressed.

The Code, para. 6.33 lists a number of examples of reasonable adjustments which employers might reasonably be required to take. They include:

- making adjustments to premises;
- providing information in accessible formats;
- allocating some of the disabled person's duties to another worker;
- transferring a disabled worker to fill an existing vacancy;
- altering the disabled worker's hours of work or training;
- assigning the disabled worker to a different place of work or training or arranging home working;
- allowing the disabled worker to be absent during working or training hours for rehabilitation, assessment or treatment;
- giving or arranging for training or mentoring;
- acquiring or modifying equipment;
- modifying procedures for testing or assessment;
- providing a reader or interpreter;
- providing supervision or other support;
- allowing a disabled worker to take a period of disability leave;
- participating in supported employment schemes such as Workstep;
- employing a support worker to assist a disabled worker;
- modifying grievance or disciplinary procedures;
- adjusting redundancy selection criteria; and
- modifying performance-related pay arrangements.

A common example in practice of a reasonable adjustment is the arrangement of a phased return to work for a disabled employee following long-term sickness absence. This has become common currency in workplaces across the UK.

The Equality Act 2010, s.20(9) explains the steps which it may be reasonable to take to remove a substantial disadvantage arising from a physical feature (**4.3.2**).

A substantial disadvantage can be alleviated in the case of an auxiliary aid or support worker by providing the equipment or support requested if such provision is reasonable.

Example

A severely dyslexic man commences work for a commercial organisation in the City. He requires specialist computer software to assist him in his job and a laptop computer which will allow him to catch up with work at home because he is slower than his colleagues in processing information. The substantial disadvantage he is suffering is that he cannot work effectively without the equipment and needs to be able to keep pace with his non-disabled colleagues. The right equipment will entirely alleviate these disadvantages which would not be suffered by a person without severe dyslexia. His employer is required to provide the necessary equipment.

4.7.2.2 Adjustments which might not be reasonable

It is clear that the duty is wide and far reaching. There will still be circumstances, however, when it may not be necessary for an employer to make adjustments. The question can only be determined by a tribunal so employers who decide not to make an adjustment must be prepared to defend that decision through the tribunal process.

Adjustments might not be reasonable in a case such as that set out in the example above of a small company which lacks financial assistance. The case of *Cordell* v. *Foreign and Commonwealth Office* [2012] ICR 280 (EAT) provides a good example of when the costs of implementing adjustments might not be reasonable if they are significant. In this case there was no failure in the duty to make adjustments by not implementing them, even though the organisation in question cannot sensibly be described as small.

Cordell v. Foreign and Commonwealth Office [2012] ICR 280 (EAT)

Ms Cordell was a high-flying diplomat in the Foreign and Commonwealth Office (FCO). She was disabled by profound deafness and needed the assistance of lip speakers to be able to perform her duties. Ms Cordell was offered a promotion working in Kazakhstan. The cost of providing a team of lip speakers for the three-year assignment was in excess of £250,000 per year. Including one-off costs the posting would cost the FCO around £1 million. This cost accounted for more than one half of the FCO's reasonable adjustments budget. The EAT held that the cost was not reasonable and the FCO had therefore not failed in its duty to make reasonable adjustments.

Judge Underhill, then President of the EAT, presiding, said:

It is a great misfortune for her that her disability may limit her opportunities. But the law does not require it to compensate for that misfortune *at whatever cost*. [our emphasis] (para.36)

Adjustments must have a chance of alleviating the disadvantage suffered (**4.7.1**). This means that an adjustment which has no prospect of alleviating the disadvantage will not be a reasonable adjustment.

Salford NHS Primary Care Trust v. Smith [2011] Eq LR 1119 (EAT)

Ms Smith worked as an occupational therapist. She went off sick long term due to her disability of chronic fatigue syndrome. During her sickness absence her role disappeared. She was offered other posts and training but she wanted a career break which was denied. She ultimately resigned claiming unfair dismissal and a failure of the reasonable adjustments duty.

The EAT held that a career break did not constitute a reasonable adjustment. It was not aimed at getting her back to work which is the raison d'être of the duty. The EAT also commented that in this particular case the employer could not have done more by way of suggestions to get her back to work. It had complied with its duty.

Further examples from the cases where adjustments were held not to be reasonable include:

- *Environment Agency* v. *Rowan* [2008] ICR 218 (EAT) (**4.4**): offering home working on a permanent basis was not a reasonable adjustment because it did not help address the issue of returning Ms Rowan to work.
- *O'Hanlon* v. *Commissioners of the Inland Revenue* [2007] EWCA Civ 283 (**4.10**): a requirement to pay full pay to a disabled person who is off work on sick leave was held not to be a reasonable adjustment.

4.8 KNOWLEDGE

No duty to make adjustments arises unless the employer knows, actually or constructively, *both* that the employee is disabled and that the employer's PCPs, or a physical feature of the workplace or the lack of an aid, place the employee at a disadvantage compared with people who are not disabled (*Wilcox* v. *Birmingham CAB Services Ltd* [2011] Eq LR 810 (EAT)).

The Equality Act 2010, Sched.8, Part 3, para.20 sets out the test for knowledge as follows:

Lack of knowledge of disability, etc.

(1) A is not subject to a duty to make reasonable adjustments if A does not know, and could not reasonably be expected to know–

    (a) in the case of an applicant or potential applicant, that an interested disabled person is or may be an applicant for the work in question;

    (b) in any other case referred to in Part 2 of this Schedule, that an interested disabled person has a disability and is likely to be placed at the disadvantage referred to in the first, second or third requirement.

The Code, para.6.21 says that where an employer does not have explicit knowledge of a person's disability it will be assumed to know if the knowledge is within the organisation, for example if the occupational health or HR department knows but has not shared this information with the employee's managers. This presents some difficulties for employers and conflicts with the case of *Hartman* v. *South Essex Mental Health and Community Care NHS Trust* [2005] EWCA Civ 6. The Court of Appeal held that an employer could *not* be fixed with knowledge if occupational health knew but did not share the information. The position is therefore unclear. On a practical level it must be good advice to say that where an employer is considering making reasonable adjustments and it has the resources of an occupational health department, relevant enquiries must be made. Where employee services are provided by an external provider, independently of the organisation, the employer will not be imputed to know (Code, para.6.22).

Given the risk for employers of having knowledge imputed to them after the event, it is wise to put in place systems to ensure that those with disabilities are provided with reasonable adjustments whenever the need arises. For example, one possibility is to operate an alert system such that the employee's file is coded for HR to mean that no disciplinary step can be taken and no changes to contract terms can be made without approval from occupational health. This would enable confidentiality to be maintained *and* the duty to make reasonable adjustments to be met.

4.9   EMPLOYER DUTY TO CONSULT

There is no specific duty to consult an employee around reasonable adjustments in the Equality Act 2010 and there was no such duty under DDA 1995 either. In *Tarbuck* v. *Sainsbury Supermarkets Ltd* [2006] IRLR 664 (EAT) the EAT held that there was no breach of DDA 1995 arising from a failure to consult around reasonable adjustments. However, Mr Justice Elias said:

> any employer would be wise to consult with a disabled employee in order to be better informed and fully acquainted of all of the factors which may be relevant to a determination of what adjustment should reasonably be made in the circumstances. If the employer fails to do that, then he is placing himself seriously at risk of not taking appropriate steps because of his own ignorance. He cannot then pray that ignorance in aid if it is alleged that he ought to have taken certain steps and he has failed to do so. (para.69)

This has to be correct. The disabled person who is suffering substantial disadvantage is likely to be the best person to offer suggestions for alleviating that disadvantage.

Cosgrove v. *Caesar and Howie* [2001] IRLR 653 (EAT)

The EAT held that where a disabled employee is unable to suggest any amendments this does not absolve the employer of the responsibility to make further enquiries. In this case Ms Cosgrove was a legal secretary who had been off sick for a year by reason of depression. Neither she nor her GP could come up with any ideas of how to get Ms Cosgrove back to work. Her employer took the view that it had discharged its responsibility and that nothing further could be done.

The EAT held that this was incorrect and that the employer should at the very least have *turned its mind* to possible adjustments, such as transferring her to another office or changing her working hours. The EAT took the view that no stone should be left unturned once the duty had arisen. Note that by the time a claim is brought, the claimant must be able to identify a reasonable adjustment in order to make out the claim (**4.7.1**).

There is no freestanding duty on the employer to make a proper assessment of what is required to eliminate a person's disadvantage (*Tarbuck*). However an employer who fails to apply its mind to an issue cannot rely on that failure as a defence to a reasonable adjustments claim. If the adjustment is reasonable then whether or not the employer considered it at the time or whether it was raised by the employee at the time, the employer is liable for failing to provide the adjustment.

In many cases it will be appropriate for a workplace assessment to be conducted. This is an assessment by an internal representative or an external consultant. The assessment considers the employee's working environment and general duties to see what adjustments can or might be made.

4.10 REASONABLE ADJUSTMENTS AROUND SICK PAY

The leading case on reasonable adjustments and sick pay is *O'Hanlon v. Commissioners of the Inland Revenue* [2007] EWCA Civ 283. The approach adopted in this case means that disabled employees who have exhausted their right to pay during sick leave will find it very difficult to claim any further pay during sick leave by way of a reasonable adjustment. This decision came as a relief for employers.

O'Hanlon v. *Commissioners of the Inland Revenue* [2007] EWCA Civ 283

Mrs O'Hanlon exhausted her right to sick pay due to the duration of her sickness absence. She brought a claim alleging that the failure by the Inland Revenue to continue to pay her constituted a failure to make reasonable adjustments. There was also a claim for disability-related discrimination under DDA 1995, s.3A (now repealed).

The Court of Appeal held that it will rarely, if ever, other than in the most exceptional circumstances, constitute a reasonable adjustment to pay a disabled employee who is absent from work. The tribunal said, and the EAT accepted, that payment for absences related to disability would provide a disincentive to return to work.

By contrast, however, where the actions of an employer are actively preventing an employee from returning to work, a different rule applies.

Meikle v. *Nottinghamshire County Council* [2004] EWCA Civ 859

In *Meikle* the Court of Appeal held that where an employee was unable to return to work because of an employer's failure to implement reasonable adjustments, the employee was entitled to be paid while the employer addressed the adjustments.

More recently the approach in *O'Hanlon* has been reiterated.

Newcastle Upon Tyne Hospitals NHS Foundation Trust v. Bagley [2012] Eq LR 634 (EAT)

The EAT overturned a tribunal's finding that the hospital had failed to make reasonable adjustments for Mrs Bagley. The facts of the case were that Mrs Bagley was a radiographer who was injured at work in late 2009 and became disabled within the meaning of DDA 1995. Mrs Bagley exhausted her entitlement to sick pay and subsequently became entitled to receive temporary disablement allowance. She also claimed state benefits to top up her pay.

In spring 2009 a phased return to work was recommended by occupational health. Mrs Bagley was entitled to be paid only for the hours worked under the graded return (this was the trust's policy) and she was no longer eligible to receive the disablement allowance which was only payable to staff who were completely off work. Mrs Bagley commenced the phased return but became concerned that she could not afford to be on part-time wages but could not work full-time for reasons of her disability. Mrs Bagley used up her accrued holiday to boost her pay and in May 2009 asked if she could apply for permanent injury benefit (PIB) which would top up her salary to 85 per cent of earnings. She then went off sick again and once more was in receipt of the disablement allowance.

Over a year later the trust wrote to Mrs Bagley stating that if she was not fit for work, termination of her employment might have to be considered. On termination her disablement allowance ceased and she started to receive PIB. She brought a tribunal claim for failure to make reasonable adjustments. At first instance the tribunal found that a reasonable adjustments failure had taken place on several counts including:

- for failing to pay the disablement allowance or PIB so as to facilitate a phased return;
- for requiring her to agree to a permanent reduction in hours before considering her application for PIB; and
- for failing to support her through a 'maze' of policies and 'washing its hands' of matters concerning Mrs Bagley's financial problems.

The EAT found that the tribunal had erred in finding failures in the reasonable adjustments duty. The EAT focused on the fact that the duty to make reasonable adjustments is not a general duty. It is a duty, where there is a PCP which can be identified and which places disabled people at a disadvantage compared to non-disabled people, to take such steps as are reasonable to stop the PCP placing them at that disadvantage. In this case a non-disabled person would have been affected in the same way by the confines of the pay policies and therefore there is no comparative disadvantage. Paying only for work done in a phased return is not a disadvantage. Mrs Bagley was in the same position as anyone else returning to work part-time, for example a new mother wanting family-friendly hours. Also, paying 85 per cent of salary for 60 per cent of work would not have been a reasonable adjustment, in line with the decision in *O'Hanlon*.

Under the Equality Act 2010 the same rules continue to apply to sick pay. It will rarely, if ever, be a reasonable adjustment save in the most exceptional circumstances and only where the employer's actions or inaction are causing the loss to accrue, most often by preventing a return to work. As with any work, payment need only be made where work is actually being done, other than in accordance with the sick pay policies applicable in the relevant organisation.

4.11 DISABILITY LEAVE

The thrust of the disability discrimination laws is to get the disabled person back to work and to keep them in work. The policy of offering a career break would not, in the opinion of the tribunals, further this objective (*Salford* (**4.7.2.2**)). However, in contrast, the Code, para.6.33 says that allowing a disabled person to take a period of disability leave to undergo treatment and rehabilitation might be a reasonable adjustment.

The EAT in *Salford* makes the point that the employee may be barred from being paid under a permanent health insurance scheme or from the possibility of ill health retirement because they would be having a career break rather than being off sick long term. In these situations it is difficult to see how a career break would be favourable to the employee.

There may be a distinction to be drawn between a break which would allow an employee to recover and undergo rehabilitation and a break which is not likely, on medical evidence, to make any difference to the employee's health or ability to return to work. There are clearly occasions when, although it might not be a reasonable adjustment, it might be reasonable for an employer to offer a period of disability leave. Consider, for example, employees with post-traumatic stress disorder: if they are able to take six months off work to recover they may then return to their job as before, whereas if such employees attempt to soldier on they may find themselves permanently unable to work. Allowing a period of disability leave must be good employment relations practice provided the employer has the resources to accommodate it. It would also probably be less disruptive than an employee having to take intermittent short-term absences during recovery. Remember, however, that the longer absence goes on the harder a return to work becomes.

4.12 REASONABLE ADJUSTMENTS AND DISMISSALS

There is a commonly held misconception that it is impossible to dismiss a disabled worker. This is incorrect. What is true, however, is that it will never be lawful to dismiss a disabled worker unless the reasonable adjustments duty has been fully explored and the process exhausted. Any steps taken to dismiss a disabled worker which do not include a proper assessment of the duty will amount to unlawful disability discrimination.

Under the old law, DDA 1995, and following the case of *Novacold* (**3.1.1**), the reasonable adjustments duty did not apply to dismissals. This is no longer good law. *Stockton-on-Tees Borough Council* v. *Aylott* [2010] EWCA Civ 910 reiterated in 2010 that the duty does indeed apply to dismissals.

Again the case of *Salford* is interesting because it highlights that the reasonable adjustments duty on the employer is designed to enable keeping a long-term sick employee on the payroll *and in work*. It is not intended to make the employee better and if the employee cannot do any work the employer is entitled at a certain point to determine the relationship by means of a capability dismissal. It is important for employers to follow a stringent and thorough procedure, including medical examination and evidence, before dismissing for capability (**8.4**).

4.13   NO JUSTIFICATION

Where the duty has arisen, an employer will *never* be able to justify a failure in the duty to make reasonable adjustments.

4.14   CONCLUSION

The reasonable adjustments duty is wide and far reaching but it is *not* a general duty to assist disabled employees. The duty only arises in specific circumstances which should be assessed by reference to the four-stage test (**Figure 4.1**). The duty only arises where the statutory test for disability is met. There must be a substantial disadvantage which can be alleviated and the adjustments proposed must have some prospects of succeeding in alleviating the disadvantage. The law does not require employers to make adjustments at whatever cost. Ultimately it may be for the tribunal to assess what is reasonable and whether an employer has done all that it should. Having considered a key tenet of disability protection in this chapter, in the next chapter we look at the largely irrelevant concept of indirect disability discrimination.

CHAPTER 5

Indirect disability discrimination

This chapter examines indirect disability discrimination which is another new concept in the Equality Act 2010 (**5.1**). As we will see, indirect disability discrimination requires claimants to jump a number of significant hurdles. The relative accessibility of s.15 makes it likely that indirect discrimination will have extremely limited application in practice. We explore the elements of the definition (**5.2**) and consider the issue of knowledge (**5.2.7**). The rare cases where indirect disability discrimination may be relevant are those where the employer cannot be shown to have knowledge of the disability. Other than in such an instance, it is hard to see how indirect disability discrimination will be used in practice.

5.1 INDIRECT DISABILITY DISCRIMINATION

5.1.1 Background to this new provision for disability

Indirect disability discrimination is new to the Equality Act 2010. It did not exist under DDA 1995. Indirect discrimination was introduced for disability as part of the process of harmonising all the strands of discrimination legislation when the Equality Bill went through Parliament.

It is easy to see why, where an employer has knowledge of the employee's disability, a claim under s.15 will almost always be preferable to a claim under s.19 (**3.4**). For this reason the authors and many commentators believe that indirect discrimination will, in practice, have a very limited application in the field of disability.

Since this is a new provision there is no reported or appellate case law on it in relation to disability as yet. There are many cases dealing with the elements of the definition in the context of other strands of discrimination such as race, sex or religion. We will touch on these authorities as we consider the definition; however, the authors are doubtful that there will be many new cases in this area.

5.2 THE S.19 DEFINITION

Indirect disability discrimination is defined by the Equality Act 2010, s.19 as follows:

(1)   A person (A) discriminates against another (B) if A applies to B a provision, criterion or practice which is discriminatory in relation to a relevant protected characteristic of B's.

(2)   For the purposes of subsection (1), a provision, criterion or practice is discriminatory in relation to a relevant protected characteristic of B's if–

(a)   A applies, or would apply, it to persons with whom B does not share the characteristic,

(b)   it puts, or would put, persons with whom B shares the characteristic at a particular disadvantage when compared with persons with whom B does not share it,

(c)   it puts, or would put, B at that disadvantage, and

(d)   A cannot show it to be a proportionate means of achieving a legitimate aim.

It is clear to see from the definition that indirect discrimination comprises many elements. The elements of the definition are:

(a)   the application of a PCP;

(b)   the PCP applies or would apply to everyone in a group including the disabled employee (group disadvantage);

(c)   the PCP puts or would put other disabled employees at a disadvantage as compared to non-disabled employees (shared disability);

(d)   the PCP puts or would put the disabled employee at that disadvantage (particular disadvantage); and

(e)   the employer cannot objectively justify the application of the PCP.

The test is a stringent and highly technical one, placing a considerable burden on a claimant alleging indirect disability discrimination. It is for a claimant to establish a *prima facie* case of indirect disability discrimination and then the burden of proof shifts to the employer to show that either there is no discrimination or, if discrimination is established, that it can be objectively justified. Note that of the five elements of the definition above, the first four are to be satisfied by the claimant before an indirect disability discrimination claim can get off the ground.

5.2.1 Provision, criterion, practice

Indirect discrimination can only be established where a PCP which is apparently neutral adversely affects a particular group, in our case, people with disabilities. The starting point for a claim of indirect disability discrimination is therefore for the aggrieved claimant to point to a PCP which is being applied by an employer and which is causing disadvantage.

Example

A person with a depressive condition which makes mornings particularly challenging might say that a requirement that they have to start work at 9 am is a PCP which puts them at a disadvantage. Their work is a set amount of work which needs to be completed during the day. They are not client facing so it makes no difference really whether they work from 9 am to 5 pm or from 11 am to 7 pm. This person might allege that the 9 am start is a PCP which adversely prejudices them and others with their condition.

For further details on PCPs, see **4.3.1**.

5.2.2   Disadvantage

Disadvantage must be found in relation both to a group of employees and to the claimant in question. Disadvantage is not defined in the Equality Act 2010. The Code describes it as:

- denial of an opportunity or choice;
- a deterrence;
- a rejection;
- an exclusion; and
- detriment.

5.2.3   Group disadvantage

Indirect discrimination is based on group disadvantage. A claimant must be able to demonstrate that:

(a)   the PCP does or would put other disabled employees at a disadvantage, by comparison to non-disabled employees; *and*

(b)   that it puts, or would put the claimant at that disadvantage.

The claimant needs to identify a pool for comparison which will contain people who are disadvantaged by the PCP and people who are not. The claimant will then have to demonstrate that the same disadvantage that the affected members of the group suffer is the one that applies to the claimant. This involves several steps which are summarised in the Code.

The Code, para.4.21 sets out the questions a tribunal will generally have to consider when assessing group disadvantage in the context of an indirect discrimination claim:

1.   What proportion of the pool has the protected characteristic, for our purposes disability?

2.   Within the pool does the PCP affect those without the protected characteristic? How many of those affected are put at a disadvantage? How is this expressed as a proportion ('X')?

3.   Within the pool does the PCP affect those with the protected characteristic? How many of those affected are put at a disadvantage? How is this expressed as a proportion ('Y')?

It is then possible to compare the proportion of disadvantaged people without the protected characteristic X with the proportion of disadvantaged people with the protected characteristic Y. This should show whether there is a particular disadvantage. The final question is whether any difference is significant. This will depend on the context but it is clear that it is not necessary to show a majority of people with the affected characteristic are affected in order to demonstrate significance.

As mentioned, there is at the time of writing no case law on indirect disability discrimination because it is a new provision. The case of *Eweida* v. *British Airways plc* [2010] EWCA Civ 80, considered below, was brought on grounds of religion and belief but is instructive when considering group disadvantage.

Eweida v. British Airways plc [2010] EWCA Civ 80

Ms Eweida was required, under the terms of BA's dress code, to hide the crucifix that she wore around her neck. She alleged discrimination on grounds of religion and belief. She wanted to manifest her religion and was not happy that BA asked her to cover her cross.

The case went to the Court of Appeal. Lord Justice Sedley noted that indirect discrimination can only be invoked where an apparently neutral PCP (in this case, the dress code) caused an adverse effect on a group of employees. Ms Eweida's claim failed at the Court of Appeal because she could not demonstrate group disadvantage. She was unable to identify a group of other people at work who shared her disadvantage. Ms Eweida subsequently took her case to the European Court of Human Rights which considered it under Article 1.

Establishing a pool for comparison can be a difficult exercise in itself. For other forms of indirect discrimination, statistical evidence has proved a useful tool. It is for the claimant to demonstrate a pool from within which they can show disadvantage. There are various tactical approaches to identifying the pool for comparison and legal advice should be sought if the issue arises. It is not anticipated that this is an area which is likely to prove popular with disabled claimants and therefore it is unlikely to trouble the tribunals.

5.2.4   Shared disability

The Equality Act 2010, s.6(3) states:

In relation to the protected characteristic of disability–

(a)   a reference to a person who has a particular protected characteristic is a reference to a person who has a particular disability;

(b)   a reference to persons who share a protected characteristic is a reference to persons who have the same disability.

It remains to be seen, as the case law develops, how close the disability of another person with the 'same' disability will have to be to be able to demonstrate disadvantage. For example does a person with one mental health disability share the same disability with someone with another mental health disability which is not exactly the same? Is a person with bipolar to be compared with a person with obsessive compulsive disorder? What about disabilities which are part of a spectrum such as autism or dyslexia? Does the legislation demand that the shared disability is exactly the same? If it is to be exactly the same, many employees may struggle to even identify a person with the same disability, especially in smaller organisations. Unless and until the law is developed through the courts, this is an area that is very uncertain.

5.2.5   Particular disadvantage

It is not enough for the claimant to establish that there is a group of employees suffering a group disadvantage. A claimant will then have to demonstrate that the PCP causes particular, personal disadvantage to them. 'Disadvantage' means that the employee alleging discrimination would have preferred to have been treated differently.

Example of indirect discrimination (not disability) from the Code, para.4.18

A marketing company employs 45 women, 10 of whom are part-timers, and 55 men who all work full-time. One female receptionist works Mondays, Wednesdays and Thursdays. The annual leave policy requires that all workers take time off on public holidays, at least half of which fall on a Monday every year. The receptionist argues that the policy is indirectly discriminatory against women and that it puts her at a personal disadvantage because she has proportionately less control over when she can take her annual leave. The appropriate pool for comparison is all the workers affected by the annual leave policy. The pool is not all receptionists or all part-time workers, because the policy does not only affect these groups.

It is difficult to envisage a situation where a claimant would choose to bring an indirect disability discrimination claim in preference to a s.15 claim, but the following example has been created to demonstrate the concept.

Example of indirect disability discrimination

As part of an annual team-building exercise which is scored and counts towards performance appraisal, employees are required to complete an outdoor army assault course. The PCP applies to all employees from senior management down. Mobility impaired employees and any suffering with cardiac disabilities or similar will not be able to complete the course and will not earn points towards their appraisal (which leads to their bonus being determined). The pool is all employees. The group disadvantage is shared by all employees whose disability precludes participation in the training event. A claimant would then have to show that because of this requirement he or she has personally suffered a disadvantage, be that financial loss for a reduced bonus, lack of promotion opportunities or similar.

It will be an unusual case where indirect discrimination will be preferable to a s.15 claim. A s.15 claim would avoid the need to demonstrate a pool with other employees who are disadvantaged by the PCP, any statistical analysis and so on.

5.2.6   Justification

Indirect disability discrimination is capable of justification. It is the same test as in **3.2.5**.

5.2.7   Knowledge

Indirect disability discrimination does not require that an employer is on notice of disability. This is unusual among other forms of disability discrimination which require some form of notice. The authors anticipate that because of the substantial burden of proof on the claimant, bringing an indirect disability discrimination claim will only really be viable in cases where knowledge cannot be attributed to the employer. Even then it is a complex claim which is likely to be expensive.

5.3   CONCLUSION

It is notable that the Code does not contain any examples of indirect disability discrimination. With the introduction of s.15, it is highly questionable how much of a role indirect discrimination will play in disability claims. Indirect disability discrimination is included in this book for the sake of completeness but in practical terms it is likely to be largely ignored. We turn next to some very important provisions in terms of disability discrimination protection: the prohibition of harassment and victimisation.

CHAPTER 6

Other prohibited conduct: harassment, victimisation and other unlawful acts

> Harassment, victimisation and other unlawful acts are key to disability discrimination protection. In practice harassment and victimisation occur frequently and often lead to claims. Frequently what gives rise to issues in the workplace is not the fact of disability but the manner in which it is managed. We take a detailed look at what constitutes harassment (**6.1**) and victimisation (**6.2**). The distinction between the concepts is widely misunderstood. We also look at liability for discriminatory acts (**6.3**). All employers are vicariously liable for the discriminatory acts of their employees but individual employees may also be personally liable. This can act as a good deterrent for unwanted conduct. Finally we briefly consider liability for instructing, causing, inducing and aiding discrimination in the workplace (**6.3.3** and **6.3.4**).

6.1   HARASSMENT

6.1.1   Background to disability-related harassment

Disability-related harassment was not legislated for in the original DDA 1995. It became a form of unlawful conduct from 1 October 2004 when the Disability Discrimination Act 1995 (Amendment) Regulations 2003, SI 2003/1673 introduced s.3B.

Sadly harassment related to disability remains prevalent in our society. The prohibition on harassment found at the Equality Act 2010, s.26 applies to the employment context and is examined below.

6.1.2 Equality Act 2010, s.26 definition

Harassment, for all the protected characteristics to which it applies (disability, age, gender reassignment, race, religion or belief, sex and sexual orientation) is defined by the Equality Act 2010, s.26 as follows:

(1) A person (A) harasses another (B) if–

(a) A engages in unwanted conduct related to a relevant protected characteristic, and

(b) the conduct has the purpose or effect of–

(i) violating B's dignity, or

(ii) creating an intimidating, hostile, degrading, humiliating or offensive environment for B.

For brevity in this chapter we refer to hostile environment to include environments which are intimidating, degrading, humiliating and offensive. In practice if a claim of harassment is brought, thought should be given to the precise effect of the conduct in question. Relying, without thought, on all the possibilities can weaken an otherwise reasonable case.

We can see from the definition that the conduct must:

- be unwanted;
- be related to disability;
- have the purpose or effect of violating the dignity of the disabled worker; or
- have the purpose or effect of creating a hostile environment.

Once a claimant establishes a *prima facie* case of harassment it is for the employer to show that there is a non-discriminatory explanation for the conduct. This is the point at which the burden of proof shifts to the employer.

6.1.3 Unwanted conduct

The Code describes unwanted conduct as conduct which is unwelcome and uninvited. The Code gives a number of examples of matters which may be considered unwanted conduct.

Examples of unwanted conduct from the Code, para.7.7

- Spoken or written words or abuse
- Imagery
- Graffiti
- Physical gestures
- Facial expressions
- Mimicry, jokes and pranks
- Acts affecting surroundings
- Other physical behaviour

Unwanted does not mean that express objection must be made to the conduct before it is deemed to be unwanted. Although an objection will make it easier for the tribunal to find that the conduct was unwanted, it is not necessary to evidence an objection in order to establish that the conduct was unwanted.

There is no need for the conduct to be repeated or part of a series of events. A one-off incident can also amount to harassment.

The conduct need not be directed specifically or on purpose towards the person alleging harassment. It can still constitute harassment if the effect satisfies the test in s.26(1)(b).

Sometimes unwanted conduct arises without any intention on the part of the perpetrator. What matters with disability harassment, and indeed other harassment related to the relevant protected characteristics, is that there is conduct which causes a violation of dignity or which creates a hostile environment. The *result* is key, not the intention.

Example

If there is general banter in the office and a practice of referring to clumsy people as 'spastics' and people who make a lot of mistakes as 'retarded', this could be disability harassment if it produces the purpose or effect of violating dignity or creating a hostile environment for an individual. This will be so even if the conduct is not directed at the individual.

6.1.4 'Related to' disability

The conduct must be linked to disability. The link may be in name only, as in the example given above, or it may be specifically directed at a disabled worker. It is for the person alleging disability harassment to demonstrate that there is a link between the unwanted conduct and the disability. 'Related to' is given a broad meaning and does not mean that the conduct must be *because of* the disability.

The meaning is sufficiently broad to include inadvertent conduct or remarks or treatment not specifically directed at a disabled employee.

It also extends to a non-disabled employee who finds the conduct offensive. An environment where there is general banter and abuse around disability will therefore be captured even if none of the employees are in fact disabled.

There may be a false perception that a person is disabled. For example, a worker is off work with a stress-related condition which, although acute at the time, does not meet the statutory definition of disability. On the worker's return to work he or she is teased by colleagues for being 'mental'. The worker is not mentally disabled but the worker's colleagues think he or she is and subject the worker to abuse. This amounts to disability harassment.

There must be a connection with disability but there is no need for the complainant to be disabled or for the treatment to be because of a particular disability.

In the key case on perception discrimination of *Coleman* (**2.2**), Ms Coleman suffered disability harassment. Ms Coleman was not disabled but her son was. She had to endure comments from her colleagues that amounted to harassment and related to the fact that she had a disabled child. There was a finding of disability harassment.

Given the broad meaning attributed to harassment, employers must be mindful that implementing equal opportunities policies and diversity training is vital to establishing a healthy culture in which harassment on the basis of any protected characteristic is eliminated. If employers do not take such steps they expose themselves to the risk of claims. Remember, it is not enough to have a policy. Policies need to be implemented and policed.

6.1.5 Purpose or effect of violating dignity or creating a hostile environment

The offending conduct must have the *purpose or effect* of either violating the dignity of the person alleging harassment or creating an intimidating, hostile, degrading, humiliating or offensive environment at work.

If the person alleging harassment can demonstrate that there has been deliberate conduct, there is no requirement to establish that the effect is as alleged. If the effect can be demonstrated then, regardless of the intention of the harasser, harassment is established.

There is little guidance given to tribunals about the meaning of violating dignity or any of the elements of a hostile environment. It is a matter of common sense and individual circumstances.

6.1.6 Factors to be taken into account

The Equality Act 2010 tells us that, in order to determine whether conduct violates dignity or creates a hostile environment, the following factors must be taken into account (s.26(4)):

(a) the perception of the person alleging harassment;
(b) the other circumstances of the case; and
(c) whether it is reasonable for the conduct to have that effect.

The test in s.26(1)(b) is partly subjective. It is the impact on the person alleging disability harassment which lies at the heart of any claim. However, the person alleging harassment must have a reasonable perception and not be unusually sensitive. Complaints which are without proper foundation can be rejected by tribunals if it can be shown that no reasonable person could have been harassed in the manner alleged.

Slack v. Weldcare Ltd (2008) ET/2603076/08

Mr Slack was employed as a welder on a three-month contract. On expiry of his contract his employment was not renewed because Weldcare found him to be incompetent. A letter from Weldcare following termination of Mr Slack's employment criticised him for not declaring that he was epileptic. His epilepsy presented a health and safety risk. Mr Slack claimed that the letter was disability harassment. The letter was only addressed to him personally. Mr Slack's complaint was rejected by a tribunal. On the facts it could not amount to harassment.

Tribunals are entitled to look at the overall circumstances of any case and at the background to any claim for disability harassment. Every case is fact specific. This involves an assessment of the personal circumstances of the worker in question, the nature of the work environment, any history of harassment and the culture of the workplace.

A tribunal must consider whether the conduct in question is reasonably capable of producing the effect of harassment. If the tribunal thinks the claimant is being hypersensitive and does not have good reason, the claim will not succeed.

Stuckey v. Daido Industrial Bearings Europe Ltd (2008) ET/1700302/08

Mr Stuckey claimed disability harassment because he suffered abuse as a result of severe dyslexia. He had a reading age of nine and a half years old. He alleged that throughout his employment he was called a 'numpty'. He was constantly the butt of practical jokes such as having his locker locked with superglue, having his work gloves filled with ink and so on. The fact that Mr Stuckey took longer than normal to process information led to the way he had been treated. Daido, in defending the claim, said that Mr Stuckey's dyslexia only affected his ability to read and write. On this basis there was no connection between the harassment alleged and the disability.

The tribunal upheld Mr Stuckey's claim. The conduct did emanate from his disability. He was treated the way he was because of his severe dyslexia. Indeed his dyslexia made him more than usually sensitive about banter and teasing, therefore exacerbating its effect. When he reacted badly, this encouraged the bullies to bully him more. The necessary link and the proscribed effect had been established.

6.1.7 Third party harassment

Employers may be liable for acts of harassment carried out by third parties such as suppliers and customers. This is a high burden on employers because they have limited control over such third parties. There is a three strikes rule. An employer is not liable until the third act of harassment has been committed. The employer must also have failed to take reasonable steps to prevent the recurrence of the harassment.

Example

An employee working in a warehouse depot has daily contact with drivers of lorries coming to collect goods. These drivers are employed by a third party supplier. Following an accident at work the employee sustains a serious injury and loses his hand. His employer makes reasonable adjustments which allow him to return to work. He is subjected to taunts and abuse by the drivers coming to the depot on a constant basis. The employer is obliged, once on notice of this harassment, to take it up with the third party employer. If the third party employer fails to take steps to address the conduct and it continues, the employer will be liable, on the third occasion, for disability harassment.

The Code, para.10.24 sets out reasonably practical steps an employer can take to protect itself from third party harassment:

- notify third parties that disability harassment is unlawful and will not be tolerated. This could be by way of a public notice;
- include a term in all contracts with third parties notifying them of the employer's policy on harassment and requiring observance;
- encourage employees to report third party harassment so that appropriate steps can be taken; and
- take action on every complaint of third party harassment.

In certain circumstances employers might wish to cease dealing with third parties that do not share their values on equal opportunities and diversity. This is one sure fire way to take steps to avoid liability for third party harassment.

In *Sheffield City Council* v. *Norouzi* [2011] IRLR 897 (EAT) the council was held liable for the racism of a third party. The council appealed the decision on the basis that it should only be liable where its inaction was itself motivated by racial grounds. The EAT rejected this argument. It was established that race discrimination had occurred on a number of occasions. This had been reported to the council but the council did nothing to safeguard Mr Norouzi, an Iranian, from further abuse. The council was liable despite the lack of any racial intent on its part.

At the time of writing, clause 58 of the Enterprise and Regulatory Reform Bill removes Equality Act 2010, s.40(2) to (4), meaning employers will no longer be liable for third-party harassment when the Bill becomes law.

6.1.8 Justification

Once established, harassment can never be justified. It is a strict liability offence.

6.2   VICTIMISATION

6.2.1   Section 27

The Equality Act 2010, s.27 defines victimisation as follows:

(1)   A person (A) victimises another person (B) if A subjects B to a detriment because–

    (a)   B does a protected act, or
    (b)   A believes that B has done, or may do, a protected act.

(2)   Each of the following is a protected act–

    (a)   bringing proceedings under this Act;
    (b)   giving evidence or information in connection with proceedings under this Act;
    (c)   doing any other thing for the purposes of or in connection with this Act;
    (d)   making an allegation (whether or not express) that A or another person has contravened this Act.

(3)   Giving false evidence or information, or making a false allegation, is not a protected act if the evidence or information is given, or the allegation is made, in bad faith.

(4)   This section applies only where the person subjected to a detriment is an individual.

(5)   The reference to contravening this Act includes a reference to committing a breach of an equality clause or rule.

The essence of the definition is that victimisation may be established if an employee has suffered a detriment for doing or proposing to do a protected act.

A tribunal will assess the reasons for the conduct of the alleged victimiser when considering whether victimisation has occurred. These could be conscious or subconscious reasons but they are relevant to determining whether victimisation can be established. It is the same test as the 'reason why' test for direct discrimination (**2.1.4**).

6.2.2   Protected acts

Protected acts are listed in the definition. They comprise:

- bringing a claim under the Equality Act 2010;
- giving evidence or providing information in relation to a claim under the Equality Act 2010 (for example being a witness to a colleague's claim) unless giving false evidence or providing information in bad faith;
- making any allegation that an employer has breached the Equality Act 2010, provided the allegation is made in good faith; and
- alleging or doing anything in relation to an allegation that an employer is committing or has committed a breach of an equality clause or rule;
- doing any other thing for the purposes of or in connection with the Equality Act 2010 (a mop-up clause).

Example

An employee is put on a performance improvement plan and then subjected to disciplinary proceedings for performance and eventually dismissed for capability. This employee has previously assisted a colleague in bringing a disability discrimination claim by providing witness evidence at a tribunal hearing. The employee has a previously excellent performance record which has never before been brought into question. She alleges that she has been victimised for assisting with the claim, a protected act. The detriment she has suffered is dismissal. The burden is on the employer, once the employee raises the allegation of victimisation, to demonstrate that the reason for the treatment is fully justified on performance grounds and bears no relevance to the tribunal proceedings she has been involved in.

An example of a successful disability victimisation claim is set out below.

Hudson v. *Home Office* (2009) ET/2301061/09

Mr Hudson started work as an immigration officer in 1993. He had a heart condition which affected his mobility. He was also prone to bruising easily. In 2004 he was told his job was coming to an end. His place of work was to close. There were some issues moving him to another position because of his disability but a vacancy arose at Gatwick. Mr Hudson refused to move to the new post, claiming it was too far for him to travel and was ultimately dismissed. He brought a number of discrimination claims, most of which were rejected. He did succeed, however, in his claim for disability victimisation. His employer had at one point during proceedings accused him of presenting a grievance which was vexatious and malicious. The tribunal found that this was intended to be a threat against Mr Hudson and was an act of retaliation for the bringing of his grievance.

6.2.3 Detriment

Detriment should be given a similar interpretation to unfavourable treatment under s.15 (**3.2.3**). The ultimate detriment is dismissal but there are many forms of detrimental treatment an employee might wish to avoid, for example being refused promotion or permanently rostered to work at weekends. The definition of detriment in Equality Act 2010, s.212(1) specifically provides that detriment does not include conduct which amounts to harassment. If conduct *is* harassment, it should be pleaded under s.26. If there is any doubt as to whether conduct will amount to harassment, it should be pleaded in the alternative.

The Code, para.9.8 says that a detriment is 'anything which the individual concerned might reasonably consider changed their position for the worse or put them at a disadvantage'.

Detrimental treatment will amount to victimisation if one of the reasons for the treatment, but it need not be the only reason, is the doing of the protected act.

6.2.4 Other relevant factors

6.2.4.1 Comparators

There is no requirement to establish a comparator or compare the way an employee has been treated in relation to others. The worker needs only to show they have suffered a detriment because of a protected act or because the employer rightly or wrongly believes they have done one.

6.2.4.2 Time limits

There is no time limit from the time of the protected act to the act of victimisation. A claimant will have to establish a link between the detriment and the protected act but there is no requirement that they occurred at the same time or are even closely linked in time. The Code, para.9.12 gives the example of someone who is rejected for promotion some three years after doing a protected act. They have evidence of the connection – a note on their personnel file which says 'tribunal case'. Despite the time gap this can still amount to victimisation. The longer the gap between the protected act and the act of alleged victimisation the stronger the evidence will need to be of the link.

6.2.4.3 Bad faith

If an employer can demonstrate that an employee has acted in bad faith, the claim will fail. Maliciously giving false evidence or making false allegations of discrimination are cited in the Code, para.9.13 as examples of acting in bad faith. It is for the employer to adduce evidence of this and for the tribunal to decide whose version of events it prefers. Where a worker gives evidence or makes an allegation in good faith which later turns out to be incorrect, they will still be protected from victimisation on the basis that they have not acted in bad faith but have simply been innocently mistaken.

***Martin v. Devonshires Solicitors* [2011] ICR 352 (EAT)**

Ms Martin worked for Devonshires as a legal secretary. She brought claims of sex and disability discrimination including discrimination by way of victimisation. Her allegations were made as a result of illness but Ms Martin refused to accept they were untrue. On medical advice Devonshires were told there was a risk of recurrence. Ms Martin was ultimately dismissed and alleged that her dismissal was an act of victimisation.

The EAT held that dismissing an employee who had raised multiple false discrimination allegations did not amount to victimisation. The tribunal considered the substantive and operative reasons for the dismissal and found several factors which contributed to Ms Martin's dismissal but which were unrelated to her discrimination claims.

> As with every case the decision is very fact specific. It is the job of the first instance tribunal to determine the facts based on the evidence before it. The tribunal was keen to stress that it would only be in *very limited* cases where dismissing an employee in similar circumstances would not amount to victimisation.

6.2.5 Post-termination victimisation

The Equality Act 2010, s.108 makes post-termination harassment and discrimination unlawful but it specifically does not apply to victimisation.

Prior to the Equality Act 2010 post-termination victimisation was protected by virtue of the joined cases of *Rhys-Harper* v. *Relaxation Group plc; D'Souza* v. *London Borough of Lambeth; Jones* v. *3M Healthcare Ltd* [2003] UKHL 33. The House of Lords held in these cases that even though the legislation in force at the time did not expressly protect ex-employees, nonetheless discrimination laws *did* apply to ex-employees.

In a recent case under the Equality Act 2010, *Jessemey* v. *Rowstock Ltd* (2011) ET/2701156/11, a first instance tribunal held that victimisation of an ex-employee is no longer unlawful even though it established that victimisation had occurred. Mr Jessemey appealed and the EHRC intervened on his behalf. The EAT upheld the decision although it stated that it is highly unlikely that Parliament intended to legislate away post-employment victimisation (*Rowstock Ltd* v. *Jessemey* (2012) UKEAT/0112/12). Read literally, s.108(7) does precisely that. This means UK law is not compliant with the Directive and an amendment is required. The position is likely to be reversed so that post-termination victimisation is protected. See our website for further updates (details are given in the Preface).

6.2.6 Justification

As with harassment, once established, victimisation can never be justified.

6.3 LIABILITY FOR DISCRIMINATORY ACTS

6.3.1 Vicarious liability

The Equality Act 2010 attributes liability to employers for any acts of discrimination carried out by employees during the course of their employment (s.109(1)). It is irrelevant whether the employer knew or approved of the acts (s.109(3)). This concept, which is known as vicarious liability, lays employers open to considerable risk. The only defence available to the employer is to show that all reasonable steps have been taken to ensure that no discriminatory acts will take place. For this reason equal opportunities policies and diversity training are indispensible to employers seeking to protect their position.

Employers can also be liable for acts carried out by their agents, for example, recruitment consultants or contractors. Again it is vitally important for employers to ensure they are working with partners who share their values on disability and who have policies and procedures in place which can help to eliminate discrimination. See 'Third party harassment' (**6.1.7**).

6.3.2 Individual liability

An individual employee may be joined as a defendant in tribunal proceedings and may be personally liable for acts of discrimination and harassment pursuant to s.110.

Employees will contravene s.110 where they commit an act of discrimination which creates liability for their employer under s.109 and by committing that act the employer falls foul of the Equality Act 2010. Where an employer succeeds in showing it took all reasonable steps to avoid the discriminatory act, the employee will not automatically be absolved of responsibility but will remain liable. Employees will not be caught by s.110 if they innocently, and reasonably, rely on the employer's word that the act they are committing is not a discriminatory act (s.110(3)).

It is not uncommon to see managers or members of staff joined as defendants in discrimination proceedings. Wise employers will draw this to the attention of staff as a useful and powerful means of implementing their anti-discrimination policies.

6.3.3 Instructing, causing, inducing discrimination

The Equality Act 2010, s.111 makes it unlawful to:

- instruct someone to discriminate;
- cause someone else to discriminate; or
- induce another person to discriminate.

It is unlawful to knowingly help someone discriminate against another, to harass them or to victimise them.

Example

An employer who *instructs* his HR manager not to progress any disabled applicants is unlawfully discriminating. If she carries out this instruction knowing it to be discriminatory the HR manager is personally liable and the employer will be vicariously liable for her acts of discrimination.

If the HR manager reasonably believes the instruction not to be discriminatory, she will not be personally liable, although her employer will remain liable. The HR professional would have a claim against the employer if she suffered any detriment arising from implementing the employer's instructions. A disabled applicant would also have a claim against the employer if he discovered the instruction not to hire a disabled person.

Example

The Code, para.9.18 gives an example of inducing discrimination where, in a scenario similar to the one described above, the manager does not issue any direct instruction but suggests that he thinks the recruitment of a disabled person is a bad idea and would reflect poorly on him. He is *inducing* discrimination, which gives rise to similar claims to those discussed in the first example.

As well as potential liability for an employer from an employee, the Equality and Human Rights Commission (EHRC) has the power to bring proceedings against an employer under s.111.

6.3.4   Aiding discrimination

The Equality Act 2010, s.112 also makes it unlawful to *aid* another person to contravene the provisions of the Equality Act 2010. A person who helps another in this way is treated as if he or she performed the act of discrimination him or herself. This provision extends beyond the end of the employment relationship.

Example

A company manager wants to ensure that a disabled applicant is not hired for a role. The company's HR department does not ask questions about health or disability in competitive interviews. Job offers are made subject to satisfactory health clearance. A disabled candidate, who looks promising for the role, is denied a job offer following enquiries made by the company manager of the occupational health manager which reveal a hidden disability. The occupational health manager has *aided* the discriminator in discriminating. If he knows that the end result of the company manager's actions will be discrimination, his actions in aiding the discrimination will give rise to personal liability on him.

6.4   CONCLUSION

It is clear from this chapter and those that precede it that the ambit of the disability discrimination legislation is far reaching. Both harassment and victimisation, once established, cannot be justified by employers. It is important for employers to take proactive steps to address harassment in the workplace. It is equally important for employees to bring matters of concern to the attention of management while there is still some prospect of them being addressed. We now turn our attention to some of the other legal aspects of managing disability in the workplace.

CHAPTER 7

Other legal aspects of disability in the workplace

In this chapter we will examine other legal aspects of disability in the workplace, from recruitment and promotion (**7.1**) to obtaining medical records (**7.2**). We will also explore adjustments which may be required to employment policies during employment (**7.3**) and contractual provisions which apply to sickness and disability (**7.4**). We then look at issues around pay, long-term absence and disability (**7.5**). This chapter addresses many of the issues arising during the course of employment.

7.1 RECRUITMENT AND PROMOTION

7.1.1 Pre-employment health questions

The Equality Act 2010, s.60 contains a new provision relating to disability discrimination which is the ban on asking pre-employment health questions. Only once a formal job offer has been made is it acceptable for questions to be asked about health. Employers must ensure the responses to health questions do not influence their decision on whether or not to employ the applicant. Unfortunately, in practice, fear of discrimination is usually the reason job applicants will not disclose disability unless it is obvious and they cannot hide it. This is particularly so in the case of people with mental health disabilities such as depression since there is still a lot of stigma and misunderstanding attached to mental health disabilities. Legislation and various campaigns from interested charities are trying to change perceptions around mental health issues but at present, on the ground, it is still very much an issue. We focus on this further in **Chapter 9**.

It is common sense and good business sense that any applicant for a job should be selected on the basis of their skills, attributes and aptitude, not on whether they have a disability or not.

It is unlawful for an employer to ask any job applicant about their health or disability, including questions relating to previous sickness absence, unless a formal job offer has been made. There are, however, six circumstances when health questions are permitted.

The exceptions on asking health questions, which are to be narrowly construed, are as follows:

1. To determine whether reasonable adjustments are required during the recruitment process. It is acceptable to have an application form which states 'If you are disabled and require any adjustments for interview please let us know'. Note that questions about reasonable adjustments required for *doing* the job itself must not be asked until *after* an offer is made.
2. To enable participation of the disabled applicant in a job assessment. The example given in the Code, para.10.31 is of an outdoor activity centre that is recruiting play workers. The employer can ask the applicant about health to determine if they are able to take part in a practical test which requires mobility.
3. To establish whether a disabled applicant can do the job. If the applicant is mobility impaired an employer is entitled to determine whether they can, for example, scale a ladder or do any other activity which is an intrinsic part of the job.
4. To monitor diversity. This information must be kept separate from application forms so as to avoid influencing recruitment decisions.
5. To implement positive action. The example given in the Code, para.10.33 is a guaranteed interview scheme for disabled applicants operated by an employer whose workforce is under-represented by disabled employees.
6. To fill a job which requires the applicant to be disabled. For example, an employer wants to recruit a deaf blind worker who has personal experience of this disability. It is lawful for the employer to ask about the disability on the application form in such a circumstance.

The safest course of action, unless obtaining health information is absolutely vital to the job or the application process, is not to ask health-related questions at all. Even if one of the exceptions above applies, employers and recruiters should refrain from asking further questions about disability other than what they strictly need to know. If a disabled applicant volunteers information, an employer or recruiter should not view this as carte blanche to start asking lots of questions. The rules as to not asking still apply. Let the candidate say as much as he or she wants but avoid probing as this could give rise to unlawful discrimination even if it arises from the best possible intentions.

It is lawful to make a job offer conditional upon satisfactory responses to pre-employment health enquiries or health checks. However, employers must be careful not to discriminate on the basis of the response to such checks and enquiries. If the employer rescinds the offer because a disability is revealed, this may be unlawful direct discrimination (**Chapter 2**). When a disability is revealed, it is time for the employer to consider reasonable adjustments which can be made as opposed to dismissing the candidate's application out of hand because of a disability (**Chapter 4**).

If an employer has pooled a selection of candidates but is not yet in a position to offer a job, it is lawful for it to ask health questions at this stage. Note that this applies to the unusual situation where individuals are interviewed and accepted into a pool to be given a job when a vacancy arises, effectively a waiting list. The individual has a standing job offer and it is therefore permissible to begin health assessments.

The s.60 rules apply to any person recruiting, including a third party recruiter working on an employer's behalf. They also apply to recruiting for contract work, enlisting the services of a barrister and analogous situations. The provision is to be widely applied.

In practice employers need to devise job application forms, assessments and policies which steer clear of making any health-related enquiries unless absolutely necessary and intrinsic to the role in question. This is the safest course of action.

If an applicant thinks an employer has acted unlawfully by asking health-related questions, they are entitled to complain to the EHRC which can use enforcement powers against the employer. Even if the person concerned is not actually disabled but there is a perception that they are, they can complain to the EHRC. Asking health-related questions is not a ground for bringing a claim in the employment tribunals unless the questions have led to unfavourable treatment amounting to discrimination. The burden of proof on an applicant complaining that they have been refused a job on disability grounds is, however, considerable.

7.1.2   Reasonable adjustments in the recruitment process

The reasonable adjustments duty arises during recruitment so the rules in **Chapter 4** apply as they would in any other circumstance. We have seen that it is acceptable to ask health questions for the purposes of making reasonable adjustments in the recruitment process. So what do these adjustments look like? For the most part it will not be difficult to determine what kinds of adjustments will be required. Disabled applicants will have the best idea about their needs. Some examples might be as follows:

Examples of reasonable adjustments in the recruitment process

- Providing a Braille version of an application form for sight impaired applicants
- Arranging to hold interviews in a suitable location for mobility impaired candidates
- Holding interviews late in the day for applicants who suffer from depression and for whom mornings are a challenge
- Arranging for alternative forms of assessment to take place for an applicant with a heart condition where the standard form of assessment day includes an assault course

- Providing software and extra time for a severely dyslexic candidate where the recruitment process includes a written test

---

7.1.3   Career advancement, training and promotion

The Equality Act 2010, s.39(2) provides that:

An employer (A) must not discriminate against an employee of A's (B)–

...

(b)   in the way A affords B access, or by not affording B access, to opportunities for promotion, transfer or training or for receiving any other benefit, facility or service;

...

Employers need to be mindful of any adjustments which can be made to the terms of employment of disabled employees in order to allow them to fully participate in their careers and enjoy access to advancement, training and promotion similar to that available to non-disabled employees. There may be aspects of the promotional process which might unfairly disadvantage a disabled employee and therefore employers need to consider adjustments. For example, if promotion access takes account of attendance record, any absences related to disability may need to be discounted.

It is important to avoid making assumptions about whether a disabled person would wish to be promoted. For example, if a disabled employee has previously asked for shorter hours, an employer may assume they do not want to take on any additional responsibilities at work and therefore exclude them from consideration for promotion. This would give rise to potential discrimination claims. As ever employers are encouraged to discuss such matters with the employees in question so as to avoid inadvertently giving rise to discrimination.

In relation to training, consideration should be given to any adjustments which will facilitate full participation by disabled employees. For example, if a severely dyslexic employee is participating in a group training session, the trainer will need to consider what can be done for that employee to ensure maximum benefit from the training. This might include providing a copy of the presentation being used in advance of the training to allow them to pre-read it and thereby afford them fuller participation in the training session. Similarly, providing a specialist computer screen and/or software are but two examples.

7.2   OBTAINING MEDICAL RECORDS

In managing disability several situations will call for a letter to a medical adviser. We will now look at some of these scenarios, providing an overview of the purpose and a sample letter. We will start with a note summarising an employee's rights under the Access to Medical Reports Act (AMRA) 1988 (**7.2.1** and **Appendix A1**).

We then look at a letter requesting employee consent to access their medical records (**7.2.2** and **Appendix A2**) and the accompanying consent form (**Appendix A3**). We also provide an alternative letter and consent form when the employee is asked to attend a medical assessment (**Appendix A4** and **Appendix A5**). Finally we look at a letter to the medical adviser requesting records or a report on the employee's medical condition (**7.2.3** and **Appendix A6**).

7.2.1 Access to Medical Reports Act 1988

An employer cannot obtain medical records from employees without their explicit written consent, even where a term in the employment contract purports to allow it. It is therefore essential that written consent is obtained from employees before the employer makes any approach to the medical adviser. The request for consent must make it clear to employees that they can refuse consent, request to see the report before it is sent to their employer or simply consent. Sample wording for a note to explain to employees what their rights are under AMRA 1988 can be found at **Appendix A1**. Since a similar note is appropriate where an employee is asked to see a doctor appointed by their employer this explanation covers both. The wording in the introductory passage will just need to be amended to explain the purpose for which the consent is sought. AMRA 1988 is set out at **Appendix C4**.

7.2.2 Requesting consent

Consent must be sought for:

- a medical examination;
- a medical report; and
- access to a copy of medical records.

Where possible the request should be discussed with the employee before the letter is sent so that it is part of an agreed course of action. If access to records is sought confining access to the current condition rather than to all the employee's records, it is more likely to produce a productive response from the employee. An example of such a letter is provided at **Appendix A2**.

Two enclosures should accompany this letter. The first is the AMRA 1988 summary (**Appendix A1**) and the second is a form for the employee to indicate their preference (**Appendix A3**). Sometimes the letter itself incorporates the form. There is no prescribed format for this correspondence so employers have a degree of flexibility. The letter can be adapted to suit the situation.

Where the employee is asked to attend a medical assessment, the AMRA 1988 note should be edited to reflect this (**Appendix A1**). An appropriate request letter (**Appendix A4**) and consent form (**Appendix A5**) should also be supplied. These documents should be tailored to the particular circumstances of the case.

7.2.3 Writing to GP, consultant or medical adviser

Once consent has been obtained from the employee it is necessary for the employer to write to the appropriate doctor or medical adviser for the report. It is prudent to discuss with the employee who the appropriate person is to provide the report as GPs may have limited day-to-day input into care once a specialist is involved. Similarly, a surgeon may not be involved in the post-operative treatment of the condition. Ensuring that the questions are asked of the right professional saves time, money and frustration.

A request for medical records should be appropriately restricted so as to avoid any unnecessary invasion of privacy. It might, for example, be appropriate to ask to see all records from a particular date, or all records relating to a particular condition or event. An open-ended request is less likely to meet with consent than one which is confined to the specific condition or event. It is appropriate to seek information in relation to any related condition so that the full picture is available.

As well as making the request for the report or records, the letter must also notify the medical adviser that the employee has given consent and a copy of the consent form should be enclosed. If the employee has indicated that they wish to see the report before it is sent to the employer then they should also be copied into the letter to their adviser. It is good practice to copy in an employee in any event in case they change their mind, but also to ensure that the process remains open, transparent and collaborative.

If information is needed in relation to possible adjustments or alterations to allow an employee to return to work or remain in work, it will be necessary to set out some details of what the employee does in their day-to-day role.

Examples of information to supply in describing the job role

- How much time is spent standing or sitting?
- Are there any special features of the work environment, e.g. low head height, narrow corridors, specially adapted chairs, etc.?
- Does the job involve lifting? If so, what do they lift, how often and how far? Is there any equipment available to assist?
- Does the employee have to travel? If so, where, how often and by what means?
- Does the employee have to drive? If so, how often and how far?
- Does the employee work alone or with others?
- Is communication oral or in writing?
- Does the employee have to use a telephone? If so, how often? What sort of phone do they have? Does it have speakerphone or hands-free facilities?
- Does the employee need to use a computer? If so, how often? What type of computer is supplied, laptop or desktop, single screen, multiple screen, wireless mouse or keyboard?
- Does the employee work with members of the public? If so, how often, in what capacity and is it with any particular segment of society, e.g. the elderly or children?
- What hours does the employee work? If there is a shift pattern, what is the usual pattern?

It will certainly not be necessary in every case to consider every point on this list and, on the other hand, this is far from being an exhaustive list. The reason for including these examples is to highlight the sorts of issues which might arise. If a person has a mental health condition which does not affect them physically then it will not be necessary to outline the desk and chair available to them, how far they walk or how much they lift. If, on the other hand, a person has a difficulty lifting because of a back injury then these enquiries will be relevant. If the process is being carried out in collaboration with the employee then it is very often possible to agree a description of the role and the particular issues upon which the medical opinion is sought.

As well as setting out relevant elements of the role, it is also necessary to identify what the medical adviser is being asked to advise on. At this stage it is presumed that the report is sought during the course of employment, in the context of discussions with the employee rather than in the context of litigation. Reports sought from medical experts in the context of litigation are considered in **Chapter 15**.

Examples of matters a medical report may address

- What is the current diagnosis?
- When did the symptoms start?
- How long is it likely to last?
- What treatment is being undertaken?
- Can treatment alleviate the difficulties permanently?
- What is the effect of the condition on the employee?
- Is any medication being taken and, if so, what and for how long?
- Have there been any discussions with the employee about any changes which would enable him or her to return to work or remain in work? If so, consider explaining these discussions to the doctor and seek his or her views on whether or not the changes would assist.
- Any other matters which the medical adviser considers may assist the employee or the employer in managing the situation.

7.3 ADJUSTMENTS TO POLICIES DURING EMPLOYMENT

The duty to make reasonable adjustments is explored in detail in **Chapter 4**. There are, however, further aspects to the duty in relation to adjustments to employer policies during employment which warrant special mention. In practice issues often arise with disabled employees when employers fail to adjust their internal policies to reflect the special circumstances around disability.

7.3.1 Disciplinary proceedings

When a disabled employee is off sick for a disability-related reason, it is generally unreasonable for an employer to write to the employee advising of the risk of disciplinary proceedings arising from such absence. The procedure might be an appropriate and proportionate measure for dealing with a person who is taking persistent short-term absences which are not medically authorised. It is entirely inappropriate in the case of an individual who is disabled. An employer is of course entitled to receive notification of absence and to ask the disabled employee to provide a medical form from his or her GP sanctioning the absence. Once again it is the *manner* in which such a situation is handled, with sensitivity and tact, which will lead to a better outcome and one which sees the parties co-operating rather than litigating with one another.

If there are disciplinary sanctions outstanding when a disabled employee goes off sick, it may be tactful to wait until the medical condition is determined and stabilised before taking any further steps. The importance of up-to-date medical evidence cannot be underestimated and the process outlined in **7.2** should be followed.

Nothing that has been said here means that employers are unable to pursue disciplinary proceedings where there is good cause. The caveat is that such proceedings should not be pursued where they arise from absence related to disability which has not been properly investigated. In **Chapter 8** we address the situation where ending the employment relationship is contemplated.

7.3.2   Grievance procedures

Adjustments may also be required in relation to internal grievance procedures. Where a disability has arisen due to issues at work, or where it has been exacerbated by issues at work, a disabled employee may wish to raise a formal grievance. In some circumstances it may be appropriate for employers to adapt grievance policies to accommodate disabled employees. For example where an employee who is disabled by depression wishes to raise a grievance but cannot cope with the stress of a meeting with the company, an adjustment to the grievance procedure may be appropriate. This might mean that in order to avoid a meeting the grievance can be conducted on paper in the following stages:

1.   The employee sends a letter of grievance to the employer.
2.   The employer acknowledges receipt of the grievance and sends a list of clarifying questions to the employee to ensure the correct issues will be investigated.
3.   The employee provides fuller information so that the employer can conduct an investigation.
4.   The employer conducts an appropriate investigation.
5.   The employer notifies the employee of the outcome of the grievance investigation and any corrective measures, sanctions or apologies.

In the event that a grievance is not upheld, a similar process may also be used for the appeal stage in order to avoid a face-to-face meeting if the disabled employee is unable to meet with the employer on health grounds.

7.3.3   Flexibility in policies

A degree of flexibility in applying employment policies to disabled employees may be one way to avoid ending up in a tribunal. Employers should bear in mind that the way in which sensitive issues around disability are managed is key to avoiding litigation. One area in which flexibility is not advised, however, is in relation to pay which is dealt with at **7.5**.

7.4   CONTRACTUAL PROVISIONS AROUND SICKNESS AND DISABILITY

Most employment contracts and employee handbooks will contain contractual provisions around sickness and disability. Such policies will include details of pay arrangements in relation to long-term sickness and requirements in relation to sickness absence reporting. All employers will require the provision by the employee who is absent on sick leave of a GP's Fit Note so that they can operate statutory sick pay (**7.5.1**).

Some contracts will include a specific contractual provision that the employee is required to attend a medical examination where the cost will be met by the employer. The provisions of AMRA 1988 (**7.2**) still apply. If employers are considering inserting a provision in their contracts of employment to provide for a medical examination, they need to be sure to make them subject to a time trigger, i.e. an absence of more than three months. Otherwise they may incur the cost of medical examinations for everyone who is off sick short term.

A persistent refusal to provide medical evidence so that the employer can assess the true position could ultimately be a disciplinary matter. Disciplinary proceedings should not take place until all diplomatic options have been exhausted.

Examples of provisions which may be found in employment contracts and handbooks in relation to sickness absence and disability

- Sickness absence reporting: when, how and to whom to report sickness
- Provisions around pay: contractual or statutory sick pay (**7.5.1**)
- Disability or equal opportunities policy
- Reasonable adjustments policy
- Arrangements for contact during long-term absence
- Any provisions around private medical insurance
- Availability of permanent health insurance
- Provisions relating to pensions contributions during sickness absence
- Disability retirement provisions related to the company pension scheme

---

7.5 PAY ARRANGEMENTS

7.5.1 Sick pay

All employment contracts should incorporate terms relating to pay arrangements during sickness absence. Some employers will operate a contractual sick pay scheme, others will offer only statutory sick pay (SSP) at the prevailing rate which is set by the government annually. See **Appendix D** for the links to information on SSP.

Employers operating SSP will require a Fit Note from employees who are off sick in order to operate the scheme. A letter from a consultant will not suffice. Employees should pay attention to ensuring they provide Fit Notes to cover their absence. A failure to provide one may inadvertently put them in breach of contract.

Where employers operate a contractual scheme, details of the scheme will normally be set out in the contract of employment or employment handbook. Most schemes of this kind are time limited, whereby full salary is payable for a defined period, followed by decreasing levels of pay, at a percentage of normal pay, until contractual sick pay is exhausted and SSP becomes payable. Note that employers may recoup SSP from the government to offset against contractual sick pay in accordance with scheme rules. A typical scheme might look like this:

- one month's full pay;
- one month's pay at 75 per cent of pay;
- one month's pay at 50 per cent of pay;
- SSP only after an absence of three months up to the statutory limit (currently 28 weeks in any one period of incapacity for work).

Employers are sometimes tempted to show some discretion around sick pay to valued members of staff. Caution should be exercised to state that any such discretion may be withdrawn at any time and also to time-limit this provision. Sometimes employers will inadvertently alter the original contract of employment and tie themselves into onerous pay arrangements. When they attempt to stop any such arrangements, they may lay themselves open to charges of discrimination or breach of contract. The safest and clearest approach is to stick to the company policy on sick pay. Where employers wish to provide more generously, the terms should be set out in a letter and agreed with the employee to avoid any misunderstanding and to avoid giving rise to a dispute.

7.5.2 Reasonable adjustments and pay

There is no obligation on an employer to pay full pay to a disabled person who is off work or who is working reduced hours. A disabled person should be paid for the hours they work in the same way as anyone else working full or part-time. The case law has held that, although this might in principle be discriminatory, it can be justified (*O'Hanlon* v. *Commissioners of the Inland Revenue* [2007] EWCA Civ

283 (**4.10**) and the EAT's judgment in *O'Hanlon* v. *Revenue and Customs Commissioners* [2006] ICR 1579 (EAT)).

There is a common misconception among employers that stopping or reducing pay to a disabled employee who is off work is discriminatory. The law is quite clear on this following *O'Hanlon*. The Court of Appeal said:

> it will be a very rare case indeed where the adjustment said to be applicable...giving higher sick pay than would be payable to a non-disabled person...would be considered necessary as a reasonable adjustment. (para.67)

In a later case, *Fowler* v. *London Borough of Waltham Forest* [2007] UKEAT/0116/09, the EAT reiterated Elias J's comments from *O'Hanlon* that the purpose of the disability discrimination legislation is to:

> recognise the dignity of disabled individuals and require modifications which will enable them to play a full part in the world of work. It is not to treat them as objects of charity. (para.60)

It will therefore very rarely be discriminatory to alter, reduce or stop pay in accordance with the employer's policies on pay and sickness absence, although there is nothing to suggest this will prevent employees from presenting it as a disability discrimination claim.

The only circumstance in which it will be a reasonable adjustment to pay a disabled employee who has exhausted sick pay is where it is the employer's failure to implement reasonable adjustments which is responsible for the absence (*Meikle* v. *Nottinghamshire County Council* [2004] EWCA Civ (**4.10**)).

A recent case, *Newcastle Upon Tyne Hospitals NHS Trust* v. *Bagley* [2012] Eq LR 634 (EAT) confirms that *O'Hanlon* remains the standard position (**4.10**).

For more detail on the reasonable adjustments duty and pay, see **4.10**.

7.5.3   Permanent health insurance

Some employers will offer permanent health insurance (PHI) to employees as a benefit. Employees can take out a scheme of their own volition should they wish, although they will have to meet the premiums personally. A PHI scheme operates where an employee, on becoming incapacitated, will be entitled to receive a fixed percentage of salary for the duration of their illness and incapacity. The definition of incapacity differs depending on the provider of the cover. Some insurers define incapacity as an employee's inability to do their normal job. Others define it as an inability to do *any* job. Most commonly PHI payments are deferred, meaning that they are only triggered once a period of absence has elapsed. This period is typically, but not always, six months. PHI insurers may require employees to undergo medical examination and consent will be requested for access to medical records to assess the level of incapacity (**7.2**).

In *Aspden* v. *Webbs Poultry and Meat Group (Holdings) Ltd* [1996] IRLR 521 (QBD) the EAT implied a term into the employment contract of an employee who was receiving PHI benefits so that the employer was not permitted to terminate his employment and deprive him of this benefit. The more recent decision of *Lloyd* v. *BCQ Ltd* [2010] UKEAT 0148/12/1211, UKEAT/0239/12 clarifies that it had been necessary to imply such a term in *Aspden* because of the facts of that case, but generally, unless there is an express contractual term in the employment contract, receipt of PHI benefit will not preclude an employer from making a capability dismissal (**8.4**).

An employer cannot lawfully dismiss specifically in order to remove the PHI benefit (*Briscoe* v. *Lubrizol Ltd (No. 2)* [2002] EWCA Civ 508). It is possible to dismiss for cause even where this leads inevitably to the removal of the benefit, for example where the employee is in breach of contract.

Employers are advised to carefully review the terms of any PHI policy before making a decision to dismiss an employee who is in receipt of cover. If in doubt, take advice to avoid a breach of contract scenario. Inserting an express term into contracts of employment which entitles an employer to dismiss even if disentitlement to PHI will follow is one way to avoid an issue.

7.5.4 Holiday pay during sickness absence

The case of *HMRC* v. *Stringer* [2009] UKHL 31 determined that an employee who is absent on long-term sick leave accrues holiday during their absence. In practice this can be dealt with in a number of ways. An employee must be allowed to carry forward any accrued unused leave into a subsequent holiday year irrespective of an employer's policy on not allowing carry forward. Employees may only be paid for this accrued leave on termination of employment. Another way of dealing with it is for the sick employee to ask to take leave during the holiday year and to be paid for it. This latter option may be particularly attractive to employees who are only in receipt of SSP. It has the advantage for employers that it does not allow an excessive amount of holiday pay to accrue.

Following *NHS Leeds* v. *Larner* [2012] EWCA Civ 1034, an employee does not have to specifically request to carry forward accrued leave to be entitled to payment in lieu on termination.

In *Associacion Nacional de Grandes Empresas de Disribucion (ANGED)* v. *Federacion de Associacions Sindicales* Case C-78/11 (21 June 2012) (ECJ), the ECJ held that where an employee falls ill before or during their annual leave they are entitled to interrupt their annual leave, have the absence treated as sickness absence and retake their annual leave at a later date. The repercussions of this decision in the UK are still being assessed but this is potentially important for disabled individuals with fluctuating conditions.

7.5.5 Bonus payments during sickness absence

Bonus schemes may be capable of founding a disability discrimination claim if employers act perversely or irrationally. For example, where a disabled employee goes off sick part way through a bonus year, employers operating a discretionary bonus scheme and making awards to all other staff should consider including the disabled employee in the bonus pool, at least on a pro rata basis. The bonus will relate to work done during the part of the year when the employee was working. Clearly if no bonuses are payable in the year in question there can be no suggestion of discriminatory treatment if the disabled employee is treated in the same way as everyone else.

7.5.6 Notice pay for sick employees

Specific rules apply to notice for employees who have been off sick and who have exhausted their right to contractual sick pay or SSP. The Employment Rights Act (ERA) 1996, ss.86–91 provide the legislative detail.

The normal rule is that employees who are unable to attend work because of sickness or disability are entitled to receive full pay for their statutory notice period. The exception to this rule is where the notice given by the employer to terminate is at least one week more than the notice provided by s.86(1). In this case no notice pay may be due. Two examples will help to illustrate this point.

Example

An employee who is entitled to statutory minimum notice and who has exhausted sick pay will be entitled to full pay for his or her notice period. A has worked for B for four years. Her statutory minimum notice is four weeks. Her notice does not exceed the statutory notice and she is therefore entitled to four weeks' full pay in lieu of notice at her contractual rate of pay.

Example

Employee C has worked for D for two years but is entitled to contractual notice of 12 weeks. He has exhausted his sick pay. His statutory minimum notice is two weeks. His contractual notice of 12 weeks exceeds the statutory notice by more than one week and he is therefore not entitled to any contractual notice pay.

Where it is the employee who gives notice, eligibility to receive full pay during notice is still governed by the notice the employer would have to give. Note, however, that SSP is still payable during the notice period.

7.6 CONCLUSION

Disability affects every aspect of life and every aspect of the employment relationship. If the Paralympics 2012 showed us anything, it is that disabled individuals of every kind have a great deal to offer. Employers do need to be aware of the issues which arise in relation to managing disabled employees, but if they do manage them correctly they stand to gain considerably for their efforts. In this chapter we have explored how disability issues arise during the life of the employment relationship. It is hoped that the matters discussed here will give employers and employees confidence in maintaining a mutually beneficial relationship. We do, however, recognise that in practice things do not always end well. In the next chapter we consider specific issues around ending the employment relationship.

CHAPTER 8

Termination of employment

In life there is always a balance between the competing interests of affected parties. In the employment field disabled employees are entitled to dignity, respect and reasonable adjustments to allow them to fully participate in working life. On the other side of the scale employers are entitled to seek to run their businesses in a cost effective and efficient manner. At some point the issue of termination of an individual's employment in order to further the interests of the business may arise. When the individual in question is disabled, special considerations are triggered. In this chapter we consider the duty to make reasonable adjustments in the context of termination of employment (**8.1**). We then consider discrimination and dismissal generally (**8.2**) and in relation to redundancy (**8.3**), capability (**8.4**) and ill health retirement (**8.5**). Finally we briefly consider payments on account of disability (**8.6**).

8.1 REASONABLE ADJUSTMENTS AND TERMINATION

There was a time when it was considered that the reasonable adjustments duty did not apply to dismissal (*Clark* v. *TDG Ltd t/a Novacold* [1999] ICR 951 (CA) (**3.1.1**)). This is no longer considered to be good law (*Stockton-on-Tees Borough Council* v. *Aylott* [2010] EWCA Civ 910 (**2.1.4**)). The Code, para.6.8 is clear that the s.20 duty applies to *all* stages of employment, including dismissal.

Employers must ensure, prior to taking steps to dismiss, that all reasonable adjustments have been considered and implemented. Dismissal should be a last resort. The case of *Archibald* v. *Fife Council* [2004] UKHL 32 demonstrates this in practice (**4.2**). The adjustments sought were possible and reasonable and would have enabled Mrs Archibald to remain in work. This case demonstrates the lengths to which employers may be obliged to go to preserve employment for disabled employees. If, however, there were no other opportunities within the council, taking into consideration retraining and other steps, the council would have been entitled to lawfully dismiss Mrs Archibald on capability grounds, subject of course to following an appropriate lawful dismissal procedure (**8.4.1**) and obtaining up-to-date medical evidence.

An employer is not under a duty to create a job where none exists. If there is only one aspect of a disabled employee's job that they are no longer able to perform, consideration should be given to changing the job specification so that this one aspect is no longer part of their job. Failure to address this may give rise to an unfair dismissal claim (*Garricks (Caterers) Ltd* v. *Nolan* [1980] IRLR 259 (EAT)). In *Nolan* the employee could no longer do any heavy lifting. It would have been no inconvenience to the employer to remove this aspect of the job. The consequent dismissal was unfair.

As well as considering alternative roles within the organisation, the employer must also consider alternatives such as enabling the employee to claim under a PHI scheme (**7.5.3**) or ill health retirement (**8.5**).

8.2 DISCRIMINATORY DISMISSALS

Dismissals *because of* a disability will be discriminatory and unfair. In *Taylor* v. *OCS Group Ltd* [2006] EWCA Civ 702 at para.72, the Court of Appeal held that if there was more than one reason for a dismissal, it is necessary to prove that the disability reason was present in the employer's mind when the decision was taken:

> if the disability-related reason had a significant influence on the employer's decision, that would be enough to found the conclusion that the dismissal was for a reason related to the employee's disability.

Note, however, that the discriminatory reason does not have to be the principal or only reason leading to the dismissal. As long as the claimant can establish it is *a* reason, the employer will be liable for discrimination (*Logan* v. *Celyn House* [2012] UKEAT/0069/12).

In cases of dismissals related to disability, claimants are sure to rely, henceforth, on a s.15 claim for discrimination arising from a disability (**Chapter 3**). If a person is dismissed for long-term absence and that absence arises from a disability, this may be a discriminatory dismissal. Clearly the burden on employers is heavy if they are to be able to show that the dismissal was not related to disability, or if it was, that it is justified. This probably means in practice that employers will have to go through more hoops to be able to show that the dismissal is reasonable in all the circumstances. Capability dismissals are discussed further at **8.4**.

8.3 REDUNDANCY

The effect of the reasonable adjustments duty considered in **Chapter 4** is that special considerations arise when a disabled employee is being considered for redundancy (**8.1**).

Employers are required to fully explore alternatives to redundancy before making a disabled employee redundant. This duty goes beyond the duty applied to other staff. For example, in a large corporation where a division is being dissolved, an employer will need to be able to demonstrate that there are no other vacancies within its organisation before terminating a disabled person's employment for redundancy. In smaller organisations there may simply be no alternative; however, the disabled employee should be given preferential treatment to assist them in obtaining any available alternatives. This may include removing the requirement for competitive interviews per *Archibald* (**4.2**).

Any redundancy selection criteria using attendance as a part of their matrix will need to be adjusted in respect of disabled employees who have absence related to disability. If there are other criteria which will adversely prejudice disabled employees, for example speed of output, these should also be adjusted.

8.4 CAPABILITY

Capability is a potentially fair reason for dismissal (ERA 1996, s.98(2)(a)). Capability comprises the employee's skill, aptitude, health or any other physical or mental quality (s.98(3)(a)). In cases where ill health and disability are a barrier to the employee being able to do their job, dismissal may be considered but should be the last resort.

8.4.1 Fairness of procedure

Employers are required to show that in addition to ill health capability being a fair reason for dismissal, a fair procedure has been followed. The Advisory, Conciliation and Arbitration Service (ACAS) Code of Practice 1, Disciplinary and grievance procedures, does not apply to genuine ill health dismissals which are not disciplinary in nature. Note, however, that the non-statutory guidance from ACAS, *Discipline and Grievances at Work* (ACAS, 2011), deals with ill health issues at Appendix 4 and may provide useful guidance (**Appendix D**). Procedural fairness is important but there can be no statutory uplift to compensation for a failure to follow the ACAS Code in an ill health capability dismissal.

Procedural fairness for ill health dismissals will therefore fall to be determined by the case law which is examined below. The leading case is *East Lindsey District Council* v. *Daubney* [1977] ICR 566 (EAT).

East Lindsey District Council v. Daubney [1977] ICR 566 (EAT)

Mr Daubney, who worked for the council as a surveyor was dismissed one day short of his 57th birthday. He had worked in various capacities since 1959, initially for the Rural Development Council, which ceased to exist, and subsequently for East Lindsey District Council. Since 1975 Mr Daubney had experienced a series of illnesses comprising two mild strokes, general debility and anxiety. As a result of his medical issues Mr Daubney lacked confidence generally. The council took the view that he would not be fit to return to work and, without proper examination of the medical position, retired him on grounds of ill health.

The EAT was critical of the respondent leading the medical adviser in the questions asked about retirement. The EAT was also critical of the lack of consultation or discussion with Mr Daubney before his dismissal. The council had acted on its own assumptions without properly examining the position. The decision provides useful guidance on matters that must be taken into consideration by employers when contemplating an ill health dismissal:

> While employers cannot be expected to be, nor is it desirable that they should set themselves up as, medical experts, the decision to dismiss or not to dismiss is not a medical question, but a question to be answered by the employers in the light of the available medical advice…Unless there are wholly exceptional circumstances, before an employee is dismissed on the ground of ill health it is necessary that he should be consulted and the matter discussed with him, and that in one way or another steps should be taken by the employer to discover the true medical position…if in every case employers take such steps as are sensible according to the circumstances to consult the employee and to discuss the matter with him, and to inform themselves upon the true medical position, it will be found in practice that all that is necessary has been done.

The *Daubney* guidelines provide essential guidance for employers when contemplating the fairness of the procedure around ill health dismissal. If these factors are not observed, the dismissal is unlikely to be fair. The factors to consider in assessing the reasonableness of a decision to dismiss on disability grounds are:

- the nature of the illness/disability;
- the prospect of a return to work;
- the likelihood of recurrence of the illness or disability;
- the employer's need for someone to do the work;
- the effect of the employee's absence on other employees;
- the extent to which the employee is aware of the position and has been consulted; and
- the employee's length of service.

A more recent case on ill health dismissal is *Dundee City Council* v. *Sharp* [2011] UKEATS/0009/11. Largely following *Daubney* the EAT restated the relevant questions which must be asked in the case of ill health dismissal.

Dundee City Council v. _Sharp_ [2011] UKEATS/0009/11

Mr Sharp worked for the council as a joiner for 35 years. He had been absent from work due to depression and anxiety for about a year prior to his dismissal. The council believed that Mr Sharp would not be able to return to work in the short term or the foreseeable future. This was confirmed by Mr Sharp to the council and contributed to its decision to dismiss.

The tribunal found that Mr Sharp's dismissal was not in the range of reasonable responses and was unfair. The decision was overturned on appeal to the EAT. The EAT held that the tribunal had set the bar too high for the employer who had actually done all that could reasonably be expected. A series of guidelines and relevant questions for employers to ask emanate from this case and are useful in practical terms.

The EAT held in _Sharp_ that:

- there is no absolute rule that dismissals for ill health capability will be unfair unless the employer has sought and obtained _all_ relevant facts;
- there is no rule that an employer is not entitled to accept an employee's own account of the state of their health;
- length of service is not relevant to assessing the employee's state of health. The same level of investigation is required for an employee with two years' service as for one with 35 years' service; and
- the employer was incurring costs due to Mr Sharp's absence and this was a factor relevant to the decision.

Mr Sharp had been on sick leave for in excess of one year with depression and anxiety and there was no imminent prospect of recovery. The EAT found the decision to terminate fair.

The EAT stated in _Sharp_ that the relevant questions should simply be:

1. Has the employer consulted with the employee?
2. Has the employer carried out a reasonable investigation?
3. Has the employer reached a reasonable view on whether it is reasonable to wait longer before deciding to dismiss?

These questions should be asked by every employer contemplating a capability dismissal on disability or ill health grounds. In _Sharp_ the EAT stated:

> the issue becomes whether or not it is reasonable for the employer to decide, in effect, that matters have gone on long enough and the stage has been reached at which he can reasonably decide that the time has come to take the employee 'off his books'. (para.19)

8.4.2 The _Burchell_ test

The test formulated in the case of _British Home Stores Ltd_ v. _Burchell_ [1980] ICR 303 (EAT) in relation to misconduct dismissals applies to ill health dismissals. Employers must be able to show:

- that ill health was the true reason for the dismissal;

- that they had reasonable grounds for believing this; and
- that they had carried out a reasonable investigation.

Note that no higher standard of investigation is required in the case of ill health dismissal than for a misconduct dismissal.

8.4.3 The band of reasonable responses

Employers will be judged according to the band of reasonable responses test. This test recognises that there is a range of reasonable responses for an employer to take. It is a commonly held misconception that disabled employees can *never* be dismissed. If an employer has discharged its duties and there is no alternative, or if after a considerable period of time there is no prospect of an employee returning to work, it can be reasonable to dismiss on grounds of capability.

8.4.4 Employer responsibility for ill health

Even in circumstances where the ill health of the employee can be attributed to the employer, it may still be reasonable to dismiss for capability.

McAdie v. Royal Bank of Scotland [2007] EWCA Civ 806

In this case the employer mismanaged the grievance process and an employee of 21 years' service was unable to return to work. The tribunal concluded that the respondent had gone through the motions but had never properly addressed Ms McAdie's complaint. The tribunal went on to find that the fact that an employer has caused incapacity cannot preclude it forever from effecting a fair dismissal.

In this case the medical evidence was unequivocal that Ms McAdie was not fit for work and there was no prospect of recovery. The reasonableness of the employer's conduct is to be judged on the basis of what was known or believed at the time of the dismissal. The crucial point was that neither the doctors nor Ms McAdie suggested any possibility of continuing employment. The EAT said: 'There was in truth no alternative to dismissal'. The argument that because the employer was responsible for the incapacity meant it could not dismiss was unsustainable. Concluding, the EAT said:

the bank's culpability in bringing about the appellant's incapability is plainly not a basis upon which it can be said that her dismissal was unfair.

8.4.5 Consideration of alternatives

Before reaching a decision to dismiss on capability grounds an employer *must* consider alternatives to dismissal. Dismissal should be a last resort and can only take place once the reasonable adjustments duty has been explored and exhausted (**8.1**). Other factors such as consultation with the affected employee, the availability of permanent health insurance cover and/or the possibility of ill-health retirement must also be taken into account.

8.4.6   Evidence of discrimination

If an employee is able to demonstrate by direct evidence that the primary motivation for the dismissal is discrimination, that no efforts have been made to ascertain the nature of the disabled employee's ill health and that no consideration has been given to making reasonable adjustments, the dismissal will almost always be unlawful.

The Equality Act 2010, s.15 is going to make it harder for employers to justify the ultimate in unfavourable or detrimental treatment, dismissal (**Chapter 3**). The key for an employer is to take care to ensure that reasonable decisions are reached and documented, the employee is consulted and reasonable adjustments and all possibilities as to alternatives to dismissal are explored. Appropriate up-to-date medical evidence *must* be obtained to inform these decisions.

8.5   ILL HEALTH RETIREMENT

An employer's duty to make reasonable adjustments does not extend to taking steps to facilitate an application for ill health retirement (*Tameside Hospital NHS Foundation Trust* v. *Mylott* [2010] UKEAT 0399/10/1304). The purpose of the reasonable adjustments duty is to take all reasonable steps to *maintain* employment. Ill health retirement is a form of compensation for having to leave employment and is therefore incompatible with the reasonable adjustments duty.

However, a capability dismissal of a disabled employee will be unfair where an employer operates a pension scheme which provides for ill health retirement and the employer fails to *consider* whether the employee might be eligible before taking the decision to dismiss (*First West Yorkshire Ltd (t/a First Leeds)* v. *Haigh* [2008] IRLR 182). The EAT said that in addition to the usual steps of consultation, obtaining medical advice and considering alternatives to dismissal, employers should also address the issue of ill health retirement before dismissal:

> where, however, an employer provides an enhanced pension on retirement through ill health, it seems to us that an employer will also be expected to take reasonable steps to ascertain whether the employee is entitled to the benefit of ill health retirement. (para.41)

8.6   PAYMENTS ON ACCOUNT OF DISABILITY

Where a dismissal is contemplated on capability grounds linked to disability, employers may consider the tax status of any termination payments so as to maximise the benefit of such payments for the departing employee. Under the Income Tax (Earnings and Pensions) Act 2003, s.406 a termination payment on account of disability may be paid free of tax and National Insurance contributions

(**Appendix C6**). This is irrespective of the amount of the payment, as opposed to the standard £30,000 exemption under s.403. The Equality Act 2010 definition of disability does not apply. The HMRC test for disability applies instead and involves:

> an incapacity to fulfil the duties and responsibilities of an office or employment...due to a sudden affliction or the culmination of a process of deterioration of physical or mental health caused by a chronic process (but not due to the normal process of aging) (HMRC Statement of Practice 10/81)

Mr Justice Lightman held in *Horner* v. *Hasted (Inspector of Taxes)* [1995] STC 766 (ChD) that for an employee to be able to benefit from the s.406 exemption it must be shown:

- that the disability constitutes a total or partial impairment in the employee's ability to work (the objective limb of the test); and
- that the payment is made on account of disability and not just in relation to termination of employment and claims arising from it (the subjective test).

In practical terms this means that if part of the payment being made by the employer does in fact relate to settling employment claims, this should be split out and expressed to be by way of compensation for settling those claims – the exemption does not apply to that portion. Failure to do so puts the balance of the payment at risk of being assessed as not meeting the conditions arising under s.406.

8.7   CONCLUSION

In termination, as in employment, communication is key. Employers acting on assumptions risk liability for discrimination claims. Employers taking reasonable steps to consult and understand the position will find tribunal support when difficult decisions have to be made. In our final chapter in this Part of our book we consider particular issues arising in relation to mental health disabilities.

CHAPTER 9

Mental health disabilities

One of the key motivations for both authors in writing this book is a desire to see mental health disabilities better understood and better managed in the workplace. We have tried to address particular difficulties associated with mental health disability as we have explained the law. In this chapter we seek to wrap up a few related points on the subject before looking at our case study in **Part 2** which deals with two mental health disabilities. We start by considering current attitudes and the need for sensitive management (**9.1**) and then address some specific case management issues around mental health disability (**9.2**). We address these issues further in **Part 3** Litigation Case Management.

9.1 ATTITUDES AND SENSITIVE MANAGEMENT

9.1.1 Prevailing attitudes

Mental health disabilities present special problems for employees and employers. There remains a tremendous amount of stigma in our society. A great deal of excellent work is being carried out by organisations like the Mental Health Foundation and Mind, yet for many people mental health illnesses are not understood unless and until they have some personal experience of them.

Since mental health disabilities are not visible, many people do not believe they are really disabilities. A person with cancer can generally be expected to receive much better treatment at work than someone with depression and anxiety or bipolar disorder. Unless people have personally suffered or witnessed first hand the truly debilitating nature of serious mental illness, they simply do not understand. They equate 'Monday morning blues' with a depressive disorder. This attitude causes employees who suffer to be afraid to declare their disability to their employer or to discuss it with their colleagues. Fear of ridicule and misunderstanding is prevalent. This in turn causes many people with mental health disabilities to feel unsupported in the workplace and causes distress. In extreme cases the fear of the impact of a diagnosis on their career can prevent people seeking treatment in the first place. This reluctance to disclose disability reinforces the problem.

Employers frequently run into difficulties dealing with employees with mental health issues. In many cases people who declare mental health disability simply will not get a job. For those in situ who become ill or suffer a relapse of symptoms, all too many employers will be interested in only one thing: managing that person out of the business. Sometimes it will be difficult for employers to establish open dialogue with employees with mental health disabilities because of their conditions.

Another prevalent attitude which is seen in relation to mental health illness is that the individual is 'making it up' or exaggerating their condition. Sadly, a number of people do exploit the ambiguity in the diagnosis of conditions to obtain a medical certificate recording, for example 'stress at work', when the reality is a disinclination to deal with a problem at work. This can lead to cynicism among managers and in turn has repercussions for those genuinely suffering from stress-related issues which have led to illnesses like depression and anxiety.

It is also true that common misconceptions arise from over use of medical terms. Many people will use the word depression to mean that they feel upset, sad or disappointed. A radio commentator recently described the timer on an automatic toothbrush as depressing. When challenged by the co-presenter he readily confirmed that really he meant demoralising. No criticism is made of the comment but it is repeated here to demonstrate the way in which the illness of depression is trivialised by society's flippant use of the term.

Some of this attitude is due to ignorance and misunderstanding. Some of it is due to erroneous assumptions being made about the likely reliability and attendance at work of a mentally disabled person. There is much research to show that disabled employees make better employees because they are loyal to organisations which give them the opportunity and often want to prove that they will not be a problem by working with great dedication and commitment. Sadly, all too often they do not get the opportunity.

9.1.2 Communicating with care

The long-term absence of a mentally disabled employee *must* be handled with tact and sensitivity. If it is not, a breakdown in communication will ensue. It then becomes very difficult for the employment relationship to recover from this position and the parties become entrenched. This is to be avoided at all costs because it leads only to one thing: litigation.

Some general tips which the authors recommend considering are as follows:

- Where a manager is implicated in a person's ill health, it is entirely inappropriate for that person to manage the absence. This is not a judgement on the manager but simply reflects the care needed for the employee. Clear and careful discussions are key, as is keeping the lines of communication open.

- Care must be taken not to expose the disabled employee to unnecessary stress and anxiety which may feed into his or her condition.
- Contact should be guided by medical professionals.
- Sometimes disabled employees who are off sick cannot cope with any contact from work for a period of time. Trying to rush this process and force the person to have contact is counter-productive and may delay progress towards a return to work or entrench the employee so that he or she will not communicate.
- Tact, diplomacy and understanding are critical.
- Appropriate treatment and deviations from company policy will assist in preventing the matter becoming litigious.
- Understanding the employee's preference as to communication and next steps enables constructive dialogue.
- Communicating through a friend or relative of the employee may provide the buffer needed while therapeutic treatment is received.
- Think about the particular individual and the situation he or she is in. In the experience of the authors it is very common to hear the complaint, 'they just sent me a standard letter, they didn't even ask how I am and made me feel like they don't even believe that I am ill'.

Most often disability discrimination claims around mental health are about how matters were handled, not necessarily the issues that arose in the first place. With thought and care these situations can be properly managed.

Assistance in developing a good understanding of mental health difficulties among managers and the workforce is available from a number of excellent resources (**Appendix D**).

9.2   CASE MANAGEMENT ISSUES

Many of the matters we raise in this part are addressed elsewhere. We have brought them together here to provide a useful reference source for those specifically addressing mental health issues in litigation.

9.2.1   Establishing disability

Employees presenting claims for disability discrimination on mental health grounds face a first hurdle, which is to demonstrate that their disability meets the statutory definition (**Chapter 1**). Often this is far less straightforward than assessing other physical disabilities in spite of the fact that most mental health disabilities present physiological changes and physical impacts and are categorised in medical texts.

Judges in the tribunal will need to be satisfied that a mental health disability amounts to a disability pursuant to the Equality Act 2010 definition and is not what has been referred to in some cases as simply a case of 'Sunday night syndrome' or 'Sunday blues'. In recent years medical understanding of mental health illnesses has increased significantly. Understanding among the general population and non-medical practitioners is not as high (**9.1**). Some judges have a detailed understanding of mental health issues from their own experience or from previous cases they have been involved in. Others may have very limited knowledge or understanding of these complex conditions. Claimants seeking to establish a mental health disability should assume that the judge has no knowledge of the condition and provide all the evidence and information needed to understand the illness.

A major issue for many mental health disability claimants is the unpredictability of diagnosis and prognosis in the field of mental health. One professional may legitimately conclude that an individual does not meet the Equality Act 2010, s.6 threshold for disability while another may consider him or her to have exceeded it. This uncertainty can increase anxiety for the claimant during the tribunal process.

There have been a number of key cases in this area. We will examine two in order to demonstrate the particular issues which may arise in relation to mental health conditions. In most cases around mental health disabilities, medical evidence will be crucial in determining whether or not there is an impairment capable of satisfying the s.6 definition.

Morgan v. Staffordshire University [2002] ICR 475 (EAT)

Mrs Morgan worked in the catering facility at the University. She had been assaulted by her female supervisor at work. She was offered alternative positions within the University's employ but there could be no assurance that she would not again encounter her former supervisor. Mrs Morgan returned to work for a short time before going off sick with stress and anxiety which had been caused by the assault. She subsequently resigned, claiming that the University had forced her into this by failing to recognise the mental effect on her of the assault. She brought claims of constructive unfair dismissal and disability discrimination.

At a preliminary hearing it was held that although the other necessary components of disability within the then Act, DDA 1995, were met, Mrs Morgan did not have a mental impairment within the meaning of the definition of disability. The tribunal was apparently reluctant to reach this decision but in her IT1 (now ET1) Mrs Morgan alleged only stress and anxiety rather than a formal mental illness such as a depressive disorder. One of the key issues for Mrs Morgan's case was that she provided no medical evidence, orally or by way of a report, which could address the requirements of the legislation. She relied only on her general medical notes which used terms such as 'feeling depressed', 'very low', 'nervous debility' and 'anxiety'. Regrettably for her, Mrs Morgan could have perhaps persuaded the tribunal of her mental impairment had the medical evidence she provided been more robust.

Morgan sets out useful guidance for claimants on what they are required to prove in relation to mental disability and also how they can assist the tribunal in reaching a positive determination:

- The onus is on the claimant to prove mental impairment on the conventional balance of probabilities.

- Tribunal members have nothing more than a layman's rudimentary familiarity with psychiatric classification. Things therefore need to be spelled out.
- A loose description such as 'anxiety', 'stress' or 'depression' will not suffice. A report must be obtained from a suitably qualified medical practitioner.
- Where the World Health Organization's International Classification of Diseases (WHOICD) is relied on, the medical expert should indicate which of the symptoms identified in its diagnostic guidelines are present. A bare statement that does no more than identify the illness is unlikely to dispel doubt.
- A full report by a consultant psychiatrist is not required in every case and there will be cases where the illness is sufficiently marked for the claimant's GP to provide a letter in terms which satisfy the legislation. The existence or not of a mental impairment is very much a matter for qualified and informed medical opinion.
- If a GP's letter is relied on and there is dispute, further medical evidence may be necessary.
- The medical evidence will need to cover not merely a description of the mental illness but when, over which periods and how it can be expected to have manifested itself, either generally or to the employer, in the course of the claimant's employment.
- The dangers of the tribunal forming a view on mental impairment from the way the claimant gives evidence on the day cannot be overstated. Aside from the risk of undetected, or suspected but non-existent, play acting by the claimant and that the date of the hearing itself will seldom be a date at which the presence of the impairment will need to be proved or disproved, tribunal members will need to remind themselves that few mental illnesses are such that their symptoms are obvious all the time and that they have no training or, as is likely, expertise in the detection of real or simulated psychiatric disorders.
- The tribunals are not inquisitorial bodies charged with a duty to see to the procurement of adequate medical evidence (*Rugamer* v. *Sony Music Entertainment UK Ltd* [2001] ICR 381 (EAT)). It is for the claimant to provide the evidence and the respondent to rebut it with its own evidence. The tribunal has a discretion to consider adjournment in appropriate cases so that such evidence can be obtained.

Often in tribunal proceedings, the tribunal will make orders and give directions as to the obtaining of medical evidence necessary to dispose of the proceedings (**Chapter 15**). The case of *De Keyser* v. *Wilson* [2001] IRLR 324 (EAT) is instructive in this regard (**15.4**).

The more recent case of *J* v. *DLA Piper LLP* [2010] IRLR 936 (EAT) reiterates some of the issues around establishing mental impairment that arose in *Morgan*.

J v. DLA Piper LLP [2010] IRLR 936 (EAT)

J was a barrister who had applied to work for DLA Piper as a professional support lawyer (PSL). An offer was made subject to satisfactory references and medical clearance. J disclosed a history of depressive illness which was managed with medication and would not prevent her from fulfilling the role. DLA Piper subsequently withdrew the offer on grounds that its requirements for a PSL had diminished and it did not have work for J. J presented a claim on disability discrimination grounds.

A tribunal found that J did not meet the statutory definition of disability. The diagnosis recorded in her GP's notes was of 'mild to moderate depression' on the Beck scale (Beck Depression Inventory) which increased to moderate. There was some evidence that the depression originated in the breakdown of a relationship. She was prescribed Sertraline, an antidepressant. She also consulted a psychotherapist. One of her doctor's reports stated:

> I think it is very difficult to differentiate between a fundamental mental illness and a sense of despondency, de-motivation and anxiety which can be a natural response to negative appraisal feedback.

He stated that there seemed to be a strong reactive component to J's mood. She did, however, have some biological symptoms of depression such as tiredness, inability to concentrate, being tearful and finding everything an effort. A report from the respondent's doctor prepared for the tribunal stated:

> Overall, it seems possible that this is a case where what are in fact employment problems have been as it were medicalised and the diagnosis of some form of mild depression has been reached.

J failed to establish that there was a substantial adverse effect on her normal day-to-day activities or to demonstrate that there was a mental impairment having such effect.

Very recently the need for medical evidence was confirmed by the EAT in *Royal Bank of Scotland plc* v. *Morris* [2012] Eq LR 406 (EAT) where the claimant's failure to adduce medical evidence of the long-term nature of his condition led to a failure to establish disability.

For claimants seeking to establish mental impairment the focus of medical evidence should therefore be on providing a clinical diagnosis together with an examination of the impact on their lives of their illnesses. The tribunal is primarily interested in the *effect* on the claimant of the disability. For further information on meeting the s.6 definition, see **Chapter 1**.

9.2.2 Adjustments during litigation

The other area where claimants with mental health disabilities require particularly careful thought and consideration is in relation to adjustments to the tribunal process. We consider adjustments to the tribunal process generally at **17.2**.

The key point to consider in relation to claimants, or indeed witnesses, with mental health illnesses is that the adjustments required cannot be selected from a standard list. Every individual is different and the symptoms which arise from his or her disability are unique. The only way to ensure that the right adjustments are made for the individual in question is to discuss adjustments with the individual and any relevant medical adviser and friend or relative who is able to speak on the individual's behalf. If an individual's reaction to treatment at work has led to particular triggers affecting his or her condition then care should be taken to avoid those triggers during the tribunal process. Examples might include a reaction to particular individuals or a reaction to certain locations. Adjustments might include the use of screens in the tribunal room to prevent eye contact with trigger individuals or a change in tribunal location.

As with the more general adjustments seen at **17.2**, the key is to plan ahead and make the arrangements in advance so that at the tribunal hearing all necessary measures are in place and no additional delay or anxiety is caused.

9.2.3   Managing the stress of litigation

For many mental health disabilities, being exposed to stress or anxiety leads to deterioration in the health of the individual. Litigation is a stressful process but there are steps which can be taken to minimise stress. These apply to all tribunal proceedings but particularly when individuals suffer from mental health illness.

9.2.3.1   Understanding the process

Stress is particularly prevalent in unfamiliar situations. For many individuals the tribunal process is unfamiliar and daunting. Early steps should be taken to ensure that individuals have the information they need to understand the process. As ever this needs to be bespoke. For some people detailed information from the outset addressing every stage of the process is helpful. For others, receiving the information in manageable stages is more useful. Advisers need to be aware of what is needed for the individual and should plan to provide the information accordingly.

9.2.3.2   Changes in the process

As well as being inherently stressful, the tribunal process is also inherently unpredictable. In practice this means that the only certainty is change. At some stage during the process there is likely to be a delay, a change to the timetable or an unexpected development. Change is one of the most stressful things for any of us to deal with. Very often this is exacerbated by mental health disabilities. The impact of changes and in particular those taking place at short notice is best managed by providing support and certain fixed elements. For example, it may be more important for those with mental health illnesses to ensure continuity of representation, to have a friend or relative supporting them or to have regular breaks with their representative to understand the change and the developments during the hearing. Experienced representatives can help take some of the stress out of the process as they are able to adapt quickly to change and explain it clearly to the claimant.

9.2.3.3 Delays

Another cause of stress in the tribunal process is delays. Delays in preparatory steps should not cause great anxiety if properly managed by representatives. Delays at the tribunal can be very difficult to deal with as the environment is unfamiliar and often not especially relaxing. Waiting rooms are often communal and there can be several cases all being discussed by nervous witnesses in a room which can never be comfortable for everybody present.

One way to manage this part of the process is to seek a private consultation room. This might be required as a reasonable adjustment or simply something which is preferable on the day, if possible. Another important way to reduce anxiety caused by delay is to ensure that individuals bring a distraction with them for the waiting room hours. This might be a paper, a book, crosswords, knitting, whatever it is that will help them pass the time without watching the clock.

9.2.3.4 Looking after physical health

As well as a diversion, individuals should also consider their physical needs for the time at tribunal. Facilities between the different hearing centres of the tribunals vary enormously. It is always wise to ensure that appropriate snacks or refreshments are brought if they are likely to be necessary. There are no guarantees that there will be the time or opportunity to buy such things. Familiarity with the different tribunals can help with this issue and again an experienced representative will be able to offer some assistance as to the facilities around the tribunal.

Feeling as comfortable as possible will help reduce distress and keep the proceedings progressing smoothly. This also extends to ensuring that appropriate clothes are worn. It is impossible for the temperature of the tribunal to be right for all participants throughout the day. The best way to ensure personal physical comfort is to have different layers so that adjustments can be made as necessary.

9.3 CONCLUSION

Much of managing mental health disabilities in the workplace and in litigation is consideration or common sense. The key is to stop and think and not to be afraid to ask for more input when required. Even with limited resources, the tribunals will always do their best to assist if special arrangements are required, especially if they have been given notice in advance. We have provided some examples of how issues can be addressed and the sorts of issues which may arise. This chapter concludes the Part of our book looking at the law and introduces case management, which is considered in more detail in **Part 3**. Some of the practical aspects of managing disability and some of the legal issues which arise are explored next in a case study which we hope helps bring the law to life.

PART 2

Case study

CHAPTER 10

Managing disability in the workplace: case study

HOW TO USE THIS CASE STUDY

The purpose of this case study is to demonstrate how the provisions of the Equality Act around disability apply in practice and how they can impact on the workplace. The information here is not intended to be a full examination of the law, which we have considered in **Part 1**. We use this case study to demonstrate the practical issues which arise around disability in the workplace and to put the law in context. Our aim is that you will use this case study to assist you in managing disability issues in the workplace. The short numbered paragraphs provide the facts for the case study. The checklists between ruled lines are designed to alert you to the kinds of issues you should be considering. References in bold are cross-references to other paragraphs or chapters within this book. Remember that this is only an illustration. The facts of your situation might demand a different approach. There is no substitute for formal legal advice.

10.1 RECRUITMENT AND INTERVIEW

1. John Dixon is 34 and is an experienced senior salesman. He has decided to look for a new job. John is severely dyslexic but this does not affect him when interviewing unless the process involves any form of written assessment. If it does, he asks for extra time to deal with written questions and uses his adapted laptop computer.

2. John applies for a role with XYZ Inc, an American company with a branch in the UK. John is offered a role following a competitive interview with 15 candidates.

3. John is sent a series of forms from the HR department of XYZ Inc. His job

offer is conditional on receipt of two satisfactory references and clearance from XYZ Inc's internal occupational health department that he is fit to work.

4. John provides two satisfactory references. When he goes to his occupational health appointment he tells the occupational health specialist nurse that he is severely dyslexic. He explains that this makes no difference to his ability to work to a high level.

Issues to consider

1. An employee or prospective employee is under no legal obligation to declare a disability.
2. If adjustments are needed to the application process then an employee may need to make sufficient declaration to obtain the adjustments.
3. There are restrictions on what an employer can ask at interview (**7.1.1**).
4. The obligation to make reasonable adjustments arises when the employer has actual or implied knowledge of disability (**4.8**).
5. Not hiring someone because of a disability may lead to claims of direct discrimination (**2.1**). In certain limited circumstances an employer may be able to justify its decision (**2.1.5**).
6. HR and occupational health are required to address any adjustments so confidentiality can be maintained in relation to the knowledge of the employer (**4.8**).
7. Sometimes an employer may want to hire someone because he or she is disabled. This is permitted by law (**2.4.2**).

10.2 REASONABLE ADJUSTMENTS

5. John tells occupational health that he has had a workplace assessment for dyslexia at a previous employer so he does not need another one. He gives occupational health a copy of the workplace assessment report.
6. John needs a dictaphone or other digital recording device to record instructions from his boss so he doesn't have to write them down. This helps him to process instructions. He also needs an anti-glare screen filter for his PC at work and to change the colour of the background screen from white to green. The final item which John needs is assistive text software such as ClaroRead or TextHelp.
7. Occupational health is happy to agree to the adjustments. Bob, John's future line manager, has told the nurse that she must give clearance to this candidate because he is just what is needed to turn around the sales progress of XYZ Inc. The occupational health nurse tells John that she will arrange for the reasonable adjustments to be made. They are not very costly to XYZ Inc but make the world of difference to John.
8. The occupational health nurse informs John that she will be giving him clearance. He will be able to start work shortly. To maintain patient confidentiality the occupational health nurse does not inform Bob that John is dyslexic.

There is no need for him to know because John can function perfectly well with the adjustments in place. The nurse actions the adjustments ready for John's first day.

Issues to consider

1. Employers are required to implement reasonable adjustments once the duty is triggered (**Chapter 4**).
2. Usually the employee will have the best idea of what adjustments would help but the reasonable adjustments duty is not a blanket duty (**Chapter 4**).
3. Some adjustments will be reasonable (**4.7.2.1**), others not (**4.7.2.2**).
4. It may assist both parties to arrange a workplace assessment to determine appropriate adjustments (**4.9**).
5. Early, clear and open discussions between the parties will constructively move matters forward even if the adjustment is not possible. If the issue is properly managed, it need not end up in a legal claim.
6. Occupational health should keep knowledge of a disability confidential unless the employee consents to the information being shared with his or her manager. If the employee wants to volunteer the information to his or her boss, that is a decision for the employee.

10.3 KNOWLEDGE

9. John is hugely relieved that he has health clearance because he did not give occupational health the full picture on his health. He has learned from past bitter experience that he should not declare his other disability of rapid cycling bipolar disorder.
10. On the one occasion that John declared his bipolar to a prospective employer after being offered a job the offer was rescinded. John is sure that the real reason for the job being rescinded is that he had declared a mental health disability.
11. John takes lithium on a daily basis and has to undergo regular blood tests to check the level of lithium in his blood. He can fit this into his daily work life when making field sales without telling his employer. John's bipolar does not interfere with his life as long as he keeps taking lithium.
12. Rapid cycling bipolar disorder means that John usually suffers four or more episodes per year of mania, hypomania (a less severe and shorter-lived form of mania), depression and sometimes a mixture of all three. In recent years John has become skilled at managing his bipolar and has not had any episodes which have required him to take time off work. In his last two jobs (spanning a total of four years) John did not declare his bipolar nor did he take any time off work because of his disability.

Issues to consider

1. For a disability which has not been declared from the outset, when circumstances change it may be necessary to declare the disability and for the parties to follow up with a discussion about any work impacts and any requirement to make adjustments. Constructive dialogue is key to a successful outcome.

2. When circumstances change a reference to occupational health for an assessment may assist. A further workplace assessment may be required so that the employer knows what it should be doing for the disabled employee (**4.9**).

3. The employer must make relevant enquiries, approaching the employee with tact and sensitivity so that the full medical position can be established.

4. In some circumstances an employer may have reason to believe there may be an underlying health issue, for example where a previously reliable employee starts to take a lot of time off sick or shows signs of distress at work. Employers must investigate the position. They might be fixed with implied knowledge even if they do not have explicit knowledge of a disability (**4.8**) and this could result in an inadvertent reasonable adjustments failure.

5. Managers will need to give careful consideration, upon discovering that there is a disability, as to how the issue will be addressed in the workplace. There may be a need for training for the disabled employee, for those they work with or those who manage them. Sensitive management is critical. Managers need to consider whether they need to inform others.

6. Employers must consider whether any medical evidence is required to assist them in considering what their obligations are under the Equality Act 2010 (**7.2** and **Appendices A1–A6**).

7. When there is a change of management, employers should consider the impact on the employee and what the new manager needs to know in relation to his or her disability, if anything. The employee may not consent to disclosure of the disability but those who manage the employee should be advised about any adjustments they must implement.

10.4 NEW MANAGEMENT

13. John gets off to a flying start in his new role at XYZ Inc and gets on well with his manager, Bob, who thinks highly of him. John is reliable and always at work earlier than his start time of 9 am. He regularly leaves the office after 6 pm and as time goes on starts to work longer and longer hours. His disability does not impact on his work at all as long as he is taking lithium and getting regular blood tests.

14. John's results speak for themselves. He regularly exceeds his sales targets and has brought in a number of new clients, much to Bob's delight. John has very quickly become a real asset to XYZ Inc and Bob and John have an excellent relationship.

15. Throughout his first 18 months at XYZ Inc John's feedback through the firm's

appraisal system is outstanding. He is being groomed for a higher role in the business due to his performance. John has not taken any sick leave since he started.

16.   After almost two years Bob tells him that he is leaving the company and John will now be working for a new manager, Bill. John learns quickly that Bill is quite demanding as a manager and once Bill has been in situ for a few weeks things start to change. Bill openly criticises the way the sales department has been run by Bob and decides that more formal systems of work are needed to track and generate sales.

17.   Bill is more bureaucratic than Bob and starts implementing a new method of reporting which requires John to regularly complete forms. This increase in reporting adds work to John's day, which in itself is not an issue but with his dyslexia John finds it difficult to manage the reporting on top of his other responsibilities. John decides that he cannot raise this with Bill who has already started bullying some other members of the sales team, who have complained about it to John. John does not have the same confidence in Bill that he had in Bob and starts to become quite stressed.

18.   Keeping up with the written reports is causing John a lot of extra work. Some nights he takes the reports home and works on them until 2 am. It takes John so much longer to do this work because of his dyslexia. He begins to be late in submitting his reports which makes Bill more heavy-handed with him. Bill starts to criticise him openly in front of his team. John feels as though he is being mocked and humiliated.

19.   John's dictaphone breaks. He asks Bill if he can authorise a replacement. Bill tells John he doesn't see why he needs a dictaphone when no one else does and refuses to sanction the purchase of a new one.

20.   This is the last straw for John because he knows he cannot work without this aid. The next day John does not arrive for work. This is the first time in more than two years that he has not attended work.

Issues to consider

1.   If employers do not make adjustments which are reasonable once the duty has been triggered, employees may choose to raise a grievance.

2.   It may be appropriate to follow a formal grievance procedure (**7.3.2**). Best practice is for employees to raise the issue first with their line manager on an informal basis. If this yields nothing, a formal process may be required. If this yields nothing, an employee may present a claim to the tribunals for failure to make reasonable adjustments.

3.   Employees can bring claims for disability discrimination while still employed. If they issue a claim in the tribunals following unsuccessful attempts to resolve via the grievance procedure, the employer is not permitted to victimise them for bringing a claim or raising a grievance (**6.2**). If employers do victimise them, employees can either present a further tribunal complaint or make an application to amend the existing one (always within time limits).

4.   Employees who have issues with their direct manager should consider involvement of

115

HR and/or occupational health in any discussions with their manager. Alternatively it might be appropriate to discuss the matter first with another senior manager.

5. The obligation to make reasonable adjustments applies to the grievance process (**7.3.2**).
6. As an outcome of the grievance it may be appropriate to consider workplace mediation to repair the employment relationship (**14.5**).
7. Employees need to be aware of the three-month time limit if submitting a claim to the tribunals (**12.2**).

10.5 OBTAINING MEDICAL RECORDS

21. John suffers a major depressive episode as a result of which he is admitted to a psychiatric hospital.
22. During his admission to hospital Bill keeps trying to contact John. He calls him and leaves messages on his mobile phone telling him he needs to call work. He sends a text message when he doesn't get any answer. Bill then starts to send emails demanding contact from John. John finds this all very distressing during the peak of his symptoms and asks his consultant to write to Bill and HR asking them to cease contact while his symptoms are acute. HR takes note but Bill continues to make inappropriate contact, mostly by email.
23. After four weeks of absence and while he is still an inpatient, John receives a letter from occupational health asking him to provide a Fit Note to cover his absence. They also ask for his consent to apply to his doctor for a medical report so that they can understand the medical position.

Issues to consider

1. Employees must provide Fit Notes from their GP to cover their absence. This enables their employer to reclaim SSP subject to the terms of the government scheme. A note from a consultant will not suffice. Employers require the government form (**7.4**).
2. Persistent refusal or omission to provide a Fit Note might give rise to a breach of contract by the employee and/or disciplinary proceedings.
3. Employees are encouraged to co-operate at all times with the sickness absence reporting procedures in their employment contract or employee handbook.
4. Employers should avoid raising disciplinary proceedings when the employee is acutely ill unless it is absolutely necessary. This conduct may amount to disability harassment (**6.1**).
5. Employers are entitled to contact employees who are off sick but the contact should be kept to a minimum and should more appropriately be managed by occupational health or HR. If there is medical advice against contact, employers must respect this otherwise they may expose themselves to a claim for disability harassment (**6.1**).
6. Occupational health, HR or line managers should have discussions with the employee about diagnosis, prognosis and likely length of absence at an appropriate time once the employee is able to have direct contact. Best practice is to ask those treating the employee when contact can be made.
7. Co-operation from both sides is essential to avoid a deterioration of the situation or a

breakdown of the employment relationship. From the employer's perspective, best results will be achieved with patience and understanding. Employers have a duty to protect the health and safety of employees. Any measures which might endanger the employee must be avoided.

8. Tone and nature of communications are particularly important where the disability is related to mental health. It is critical that employers show sensitivity and do not exacerbate the issues. With mental health issues the way the matter is managed will largely determine the success of the outcome (**9.1**).

9. It will never be a good strategy for employers to pressurise disabled employees to try to force them to leave. This will certainly lead to a legal claim. As will dismissing for another reason, such as redundancy, which is not the real reason (**8.2**).

10.6 SICK PAY

24. John is advised by a letter from the company that he is entitled to receive full pay for the first three months of his sickness absence. After that he will only receive SSP. He will continue to be entitled to the other benefits he receives from the company which include pension contributions, season ticket loan, private medical insurance and private dental insurance.

Issues to consider

1. Employees who are off sick will be entitled to receive statutory sick pay, contractual sick pay or a combination depending on the terms of their employment contract (**7.5.1**).

2. Once sick pay has expired, it will never be a reasonable adjustment to pay someone in the usual way while they are off work for a disability reason unless the employee is prevented from returning to work by the employer's failure to make reasonable adjustments (**7.5.2**).

3. Holiday pay continues to accrue during sickness absence (**7.5.4**).

4. Disabled employees who are on long-term sick leave are entitled to their benefits in the usual way. The position on bonus payments may not be straightforward (**7.5.5**).

5. If a disabled employee is going to be off sick on a long-term basis, it may be possible to obtain PHI (**7.5.3**). Not all employers provide this benefit. Employees might make enquiries as to their own private scheme but none might be available if they already have a diagnosed medical condition.

10.7 MEDICAL EVIDENCE

25. John remains a psychiatric inpatient for two months but remains off work for a total of four months, after which he and his doctors feel he is ready to return to work. John will remain on a new medication for 18 months. He will also need to continue psychotherapy and group therapy sessions for a considerable period.

26. Having determined that the reason for John's major depressive episode was work-related stress, his psychiatrist recommends that he cannot return to work under Bill. Bill's management style will not suit John. Steps must be taken to avoid a relapse. John's psychiatrist recommends that John be moved to another team under a different manager.

Issues to consider

1. It seems from the medical evidence that John will meet the definition of disability (**Chapter 1**).
2. Employers have a choice whether to accept the medical evidence and concede that the employee is disabled. Some employers choose instead to let the tribunal decide if the matter becomes litigious.
3. If it is obvious that the definition is met, employers should turn their thoughts and actions to the obligations they are required to comply with, specifically reasonable adjustments (**Chapter 4**).
4. Any failure to act reasonably or implement adjustments which are reasonable will give rise to possible claims in the tribunal for disability discrimination.

10.8   MANAGING A RETURN TO WORK

27. HR begins a dialogue with John's consultant psychiatrist to find out what John is going to need to get him back to work. The doctor says John is ready to return on a phased timetable. He will begin by working three hours per day for two days a week for two weeks and build up over a period of two months back to full time. He should not work any overtime for at least six months.
28. John will need to leave at 3 pm every Wednesday and at 4 pm every Thursday so that he can pursue psychotherapy and group therapy. He will also need two hours off every eight weeks for follow up by his psychiatrist. These arrangements are anticipated to continue for at least 18 months.
29. John gets off to a shaky start. He lacks his former confidence and it is noticed by his colleagues that he is a changed man. They assume that he has had a mental breakdown but they do not ask. People in the office who have had cancer and kidney problems are more open about their health issues.

Issues to consider

1. Employers must address the reasonable adjustments that may be required to get a disabled employee back to work (**Chapter 4**). The involvement of appropriate medical practitioners is invaluable.
2. A phased return to work is common after long-term sickness absence. In cases of mental health illness it is almost always going to be necessary.
3. Some employers may consider giving a period of disability leave to an employee who has been sick long term (**4.11**).

4. As a reasonable adjustment for disability, employers must allow time off for medical appointments and treatment.
5. Employees are not entitled to be paid for time they do not work (**4.10**).
6. Sensitivity is required when reintroducing someone back into work after a long absence. The longer the absence the harder this becomes. It is advisable to agree with the employee what colleagues are told. Employees with mental health disabilities may be especially sensitive about how this is managed.

10.9   VICARIOUS LIABILITY

30. HR shares the consultant's letter with John's manager, Bill. Bill is annoyed that the medical report is critical of his management style. When he reads the word 'lithium' and realises that John has a long-term mental health condition, this sets alarm bells ringing. He tells HR he will not have John back in his team because this 'maniac' is a danger to other staff.
31. HR is shocked by Bill's prejudice and his reaction to the psychiatric report. HR tells Bill that it has legal duties around disability and getting John back to work. HR is unable to find an alternative team for John to join and Bill is told to toe the line.

Issues to consider

1. In the case of mental health disabilities which are often misunderstood, special care should be given to sensitive management of information.
2. HR will be alert that a disciplinary issue might arise with Bill. His attitude does not bode well. HR should takes steps to get Bill some training around managing mental health disability. If HR is on notice following remarks like Bill's, it needs to take steps to protect the business from legal claims arising from Bill's attitude and likely conduct. It also needs to take steps to protect John from discrimination.
3. The company must remember that it is legally liable for the acts of its employees (**6.3.1**).
4. HR might advise Bill that he also has a potential personal liability (**6.3.2**). This might act as a deterrent to unwanted conduct.

10.10   HARASSMENT

32. John notices that Bill is even more unpleasant to him than before he went on sick leave. He does not say hello in the morning but he does greet other staff. Bill also makes inappropriate remarks within John's earshot. He refers to John as a 'lunatic' – 'ask that lunatic John to help you with it' and makes it known that he has an issue with the fact that John is bipolar.
33. Bill decides to put John on a PIP because his performance has declined since he has been ill. John asks him to hold off on the PIP until he is fully integrated

back into work but Bill refuses. Bill also tells John that if he raises a grievance against him he will make his life hell.

Issues to consider

1. A key responsibility for HR and management is to protect disabled employees from harassment because of their disability. Failure to do so may give rise to a disability harassment claim (**6.1**).
2. A harassment claim can be brought during employment. If a claim is brought during employment the employer must not victimise the employee for bringing it (**6.2**).
3. The reasonable adjustments duty applies to all stages of employment. On returning to work it would have been a reasonable adjustment to defer any decision to put John on a PIP (**Chapter 4**).
4. If John's sales targets were not being met for disability-related reasons, it would be a reasonable adjustment to alter his targets so that they are achievable.
5. If Bill's motivation for the PIP is to wear John down so that he leaves, this will be an act of disability discrimination and harassment. Bill's general attitude to John is unprofessional, inappropriate and discriminatory.

10.11   DISMISSAL

34. John's persistent failure to meet the objectives of the PIP leads to Bill disciplining him. John raises the fact of his disability as a reason for his not achieving the objectives but Bill refuses to make allowances for this.
35. Bill dismisses John for performance. The real reason is that Bill does not want someone with bipolar on his team. He assumes, based on prejudice, that John will take a lot of sick leave in the future.

Issues to consider

1. Capability can be a lawful reason for dismissal (**8.4**).
2. Employers must ensure that the real reason for the dismissal is capability and not a discriminatory reason giving rise to a legal claim (**8.2**).
3. The reasonable adjustments duty applies to dismissal (**8.1**). Employers need to consider any adjustments that would avoid dismissal and any available alternatives to dismissal. This is a high duty to discharge (**4.12**).
4. If there is a dismissal on capability grounds which relate to disability, it is essential to obtain an up-to-date medical report before taking a decision to dismiss. Failure to do so will render the decision unfair (**8.4**).
5. If there is a disability reason for dismissal, consideration needs to be given to PHI (**7.5.3**), disability retirement (**8.5**) and payments on account of disability (**8.6**).
6. If the real reason for John's dismissal is Bill's prejudices about mental health, this may give rise to a liability for XYZ Inc on a number of counts:

    (a) direct discrimination (**2.1**) (Bill's conduct towards John is because of John's disability);

     (b) discrimination arising from disability (**3.2**) (there is a link between the PIP and John's disability);

     (c) indirect discrimination (**5.2**) (applying the PCP of a PIP);

     (d) reasonable adjustments failure (**4.12**) (for failing to delay or cancel the PIP, make changes to John's targets or consider alternatives to dismissal);

     (e) disability harassment (**6.1**) (Bill's unreasonable conduct); and

     (f) victimisation (**6.2**) (Bill's conduct because of John's protected act).

7.   Bill may also have personal liability for disability discrimination (**6.3.2**).

See **Appendices A1–A6** which comprise precedents for correspondence which will be required in relation to obtaining medical consents, records and reports.

10.12 CONCLUSION

We can see from this case study that a wide range of considerations come into play when managing disability in the workplace. Properly managed, the duties need not be onerous. It is obvious to see how easily it can go wrong without sensitive management. It is also pertinent to note the extent of an employer's legal liability for disability discrimination.

You will note that throughout the references to our chapters on the law around disability one issue comes up time and time again: reasonable adjustments (**Chapter 4**). As we have said, this is the backbone of the disability discrimination legislation. It must be fully understood by employers. Managers need to be trained around it. This is the area of most legal claims and where a breakdown in the employment relationship is most likely to occur. It requires proper and thorough consideration.

In the next section, **Part 3** Litigation Case Management, we show how a claim for disability discrimination may be brought and defended in the employment tribunals. **Part 3** also contains samples of many of the key documents you will need to bring or defend a disability discrimination claim.

PART 3

Litigation case management

CHAPTER 11

The tribunal process

We sincerely hope that with a proper understanding of disability and good communication, disability will not be an issue which need reach the tribunal. That is our aspiration. We recognise however that the reality of life means that disputes will happen. In this chapter we start with an overview of this part of the book (**11.1**). We then consider the steps before litigation is engaged (**11.2**) and consider reasonable adjustments before the tribunal process begins (**11.3**). Finally we set out a timeline for the tribunal process (**11.4**). In the following chapters we will consider the different stages in more detail.

11.1 OVERVIEW OF THIS PART

This Part of the book contains the following chapters:

- Bringing a claim (**Chapter 12**)
- Responding to a claim (**Chapter 13**)
- Settlement (**Chapter 14**)
- The process for determining disability including medical evidence (**Chapter 15**)
- Preparation for a hearing (**Chapter 16**)
- The hearing (**Chapter 17**)

In addition, reference should be made to sample documents including an Employment Tribunals Claim Form (ET1) at **Appendix B1**, an Employment Tribunals Response Form (ET3) at **Appendix B2**, an impact statement at **Appendix B3**, a letter of instruction to a medical expert at **Appendix B4**, a schedule of loss at **Appendix B5** and a Scott Schedule at **Appendix B6**.

11.2 STEPS BEFORE THE TRIBUNAL PROCESS

Before a claim is brought, two things should have happened: an act which is relied upon as an act of discrimination and an attempt to resolve the dispute without the intervention of the tribunal. This will usually involve an internal grievance process. Many companies have written grievance procedures for employees to comply with. In the absence of a company-specific written procedure, the ACAS grievance procedure should be used and can be found on the ACAS website (**Appendix D**). Such procedures usually involve:

- the employee setting out the complaint in writing;
- the employer investigating the complaint including meeting with any necessary witnesses or alleged perpetrators;
- the employer providing the outcome to the employee and explaining any next steps, including how to appeal if the employee is dissatisfied with the outcome; and
- if the employee appeals, a new manager investigating and hearing the appeal and subsequently providing the outcome in writing.

This process is common to any grievance within the workplace. Of particular significance for employees with disabilities is the issue of adjustments to the process to permit them to fully participate.

11.3 ADJUSTMENTS BEFORE TRIBUNAL PROCEEDINGS

Depending on the particular alleged disability, it may be necessary to permit adjustments to the usual grievance process. If an employer is disputing disability then it may wish to refer to such adjustments as gestures of goodwill rather than reasonable adjustments which might imply acceptance of the legal obligations arising from disability and acceptance that the employee is disabled.

Remember that even if disability is accepted, reasonable adjustments are only required if they alleviate the particular disadvantage suffered by an individual. In other words, if an employee has a bad back, allowing him or her to be accompanied by a family member or friend is unlikely to alleviate the pain. Instead consideration might be given to alternative chairs, meeting in the employee's home or taking regular breaks. On the other hand, a person suffering from stress and anxiety may well benefit from having a companion who falls outside the strict legal provisions for a colleague or union representative.

One of the most common adjustments for people on long-term sick leave is to allow the grievance or disciplinary process to be conducted in writing so that they do not need to attend the office and can respond when they are able.

It is also frequently the case that time limits need to be extended to permit an employee an opportunity to participate.

As with all of these issues, very often the most important thing to do is to talk. It is an enormous help to be clear about what the adjustment is that is sought and why it will alleviate the difficulty. Clarity at this stage may avoid a tribunal, but if it does not it will at least define the issues. In many of the cases we have seen, the problem is a lack of understanding on both sides regarding expectations and intentions.

When internal processes are exhausted it may be that the tribunal process is required to resolve the differences between the parties. We look at this in more detail in the following chapters. It is important to note that time limits in the tribunal process begin from the date of the alleged discriminatory act, not the date of the completion of the grievance process, so employees may need to issue protective tribunal proceedings to bring the claim in time and then seek to agree with the employer and the tribunal a stay of proceedings while the internal process is completed.

11.4 OVERVIEW OF THE TRIBUNAL PROCESS

In the event that it has not been possible to resolve the issue through a grievance procedure, the tribunal process may be used. The diagram which follows sets out the different stages of an employment tribunal claim. Each step is considered in further detail in the following chapters.

At the time of writing considerable amendments are being proposed to the Employment Tribunals Rules of Procedure (see Employment Tribunals (Constitution and Rules of Procedure) Regulations 2004, SI 2004/1861, Sched.1), which may make changes to several parts of the tribunal process. When the rules are finalised we will provide an update on our website (details are given in the Preface).

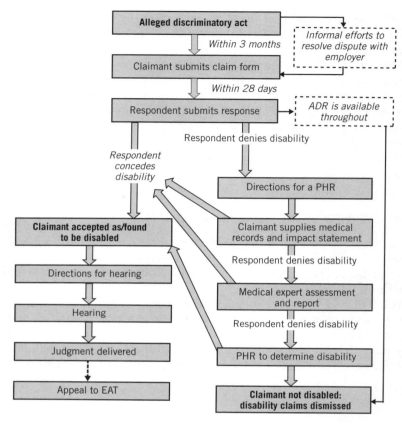

Figure 11.1 Disability claim flowchart

CHAPTER 12

Bringing a claim

In this chapter we look at the purpose of the ET1 (**12.1**), when it needs to be submitted (**12.2**), the form (**12.3**), the heading for a grounds of complaint (**12.4**) and the content of the claim form (**12.5**). A draft grounds of complaint can be found at **Appendix B1**.

12.1 PURPOSE OF THE ET1

Before providing some pointers on the content of an ET1 it is perhaps worth considering the purpose of the document. The ET1 is the first document that appears in the case. It is often the first thing read by the tribunal and it is the first opportunity for claimants to present their case. Therefore a good ET1 does the following:

1. It sets out the legal claims being brought.
2. It sets out the factual allegations relied upon in support of those claims.
3. It provides a concise and persuasive account of the claimant's complaints.

A failure to provide the correct information may lead to claims not being accepted by the tribunal and will almost certainly lead to requests for further information. Such requests increase costs for the claimant and can cause unnecessary delay.

12.2 TIMING OF THE ET1

The ET1 must be submitted within the appropriate timescale. Ordinarily this is within three months of the act of discrimination relied upon. If there is a series of events which is relied upon, the ET1 must be submitted within three months of the last of that series. Three months means three months less a day, so if the alleged act of discrimination or the last act in a series occurred on 10 July, the claim must be submitted no later than 9 October.

Claims submitted outside the time limits may be accepted if the tribunal considers it just and equitable to do so. Factors which may be relevant if the tribunal is considering whether or not to exercise its discretion and extend time include:

- the reason for the delay in submitting the claim. Delay may reasonably be caused by discovering matters relevant to the claim at a later date or a period of ill health which has prevented the claimant from giving instructions or dealing with the case for a time. Where the latter is relied upon, it is sometimes helpful to obtain medical evidence on the point. Delay on the part of legal advisers is not a valid reason for delay;
- the availability of legal advice;
- the speed with which the claim was submitted once the claimant was aware of the right to bring the claim and the relevant matters giving rise to the claim; and/or
- any prejudice caused to the respondent by the delay.

12.3 THE ET1 FORM

The ET1 form provided by HM Courts and Tribunals Service can be completed online or printed out and submitted by fax, post or email. The form is available online on its website (**Appendix D**) under 'claims' and 'forms'. Increasingly tribunals prefer email and online submissions. When the form is submitted in this manner, they do not want to receive a further copy by fax or post. Electronic submission guarantees that the tribunal can track the receipt of the ET1 so that even if it is mislaid in the tribunal administrative system it is possible to prove when it was submitted.

The current ET1 form is included at **Appendix B1**. The form is predominantly self-explanatory. Sections marked with an asterisk (*) must be completed. This includes the equality monitoring questionnaire. Key parts of the form include identifying the correct respondent and the details of the claim in section 5.

The correct respondent is usually the employer, but where it is alleged that an individual has personally discriminated against the claimant, the individual can also be named as a respondent. He or she should be inserted in the 'additional respondent' section of the form. If the employer is not clear, it is often best to look at who is named in the employment contract and then set out any particular confusion in the details of the claim so that the issue is raised at the earliest opportunity. If, for example, the employer has changed due to a Transfer of Undertakings (Protection of Employment) Regulations 2006, SI 2006/246 (TUPE) transfer, the new employer post-transfer should be included but the history of employment including the transfer should be recorded in the details of claim.

In most cases the part of the ET1 which demands closest attention is the details of claim section. Section 5 requires the claimant to select from fixed options the nature of the claim and also to provide details of the claim. It is important that all legal complaints are set out. An application to amend is possible but it is not always granted. For this reason it is imperative to state all elements of the claim in the details of claim part of the form.

It is often neater and clearer to set out the details of the claim in a separate attachment known as Particulars of Claim, ET1 Rider or grounds of complaint. We will refer to this as a grounds of complaint throughout but any of the terms may be used in practice. The ET1 form and the grounds of complaint together form the pleadings for a claimant. We will now consider the contents of such a document.

12.4 HEADING

The customary heading for a grounds of complaint is:

Example

IN THE [*] EMPLOYMENT TRIBUNAL

Case No.

BETWEEN

[NAME OF CLAIMANT]

Claimant

-and-
[NAME OF RESPONDENT]

Respondent

GROUNDS OF COMPLAINT

---

* It is necessary to insert the name of the tribunal where the claim is brought. The correct tribunal can be found on HM Courts and Tribunals Service website (**Appendix D**) where a list of tribunals by postcodes covered can be found. This does change from time to time. The claim is brought in the tribunal which covers the respondent's postcode.

12.5 CONTENT

The basic structure of an ET1 for a disability discrimination claim is:

1. Introduce the parties (**12.5.1**).
2. Summarise the legal complaints brought (**12.5.2**).
3. Provide details of the claimant's disability (**12.5.3**).
4. Provide relevant factual background (**12.5.4**).
5. In relation to each claim set out the matters relied upon (**12.5.5**).

Tribunals prefer to see the document set out with short numbered paragraphs and double spaced for ease of reference.

12.5.1 Introduction of the parties

The introduction of the parties can be very brief but in the employment context it is usual to say when the claimant became an employee of the respondent, the job which the claimant was employed to do and, if the employment has ended, when it ended and how, i.e. by resignation or dismissal. It may be appropriate at this stage to set out other matters such as the branch or office in which the claimant was employed or details of the claimant's team or immediate management. If these are important to events later, it can be helpful to set them out clearly from the outset. Any issue over who is the correct respondent should also be included at this stage.

12.5.2 Summary of legal complaints brought

Since the ET1 is often the first document that the tribunal considers, it is helpful to headline the document with early details of the claims being pursued. If the introduction to the parties is complicated, for example with a number of TUPE transfers to explain before the current respondent is reached, then consider putting this summary of complaints before the introduction to the parties.

The summary of complaints can be very brief, for example:

Example

The Claimant brings claims of unfair dismissal contrary to section 98 of the ERA 1996, direct disability discrimination contrary to section 13 of the Equality Act 2010, and harassment on grounds of disability contrary to section 26 of the Equality Act 2010.

It can be helpful to include in your summary the statutory sections relied upon. If there are a large number of claims then a numbered list is very often the clearest way of setting out the claims. It also acts as a useful checklist as you proceed through the rest of the document.

12.5.3 Details of the alleged disability

In any disability discrimination claim the claimant must prove their disability. It is important that this is clearly set out at this stage. If the disability is a deemed disability such that there can be no dispute about whether or not it meets the statutory definition, it is also good practice to plead this so that time is not wasted on the point.

Example

The Claimant was diagnosed with lung cancer in May 2010. In accordance with paragraph 6 of Schedule 1 to the Equality Act 2010, the Claimant is a disabled person.

If the disability is not a deemed disability, it is necessary to set out in outline the elements of the definition.

Example

In May 2010 the Claimant was diagnosed with depression. The Claimant has suffered from depression continually from 2010 and receives medication in order to help her cope with her disability. The Claimant's condition has a substantial adverse effect on her ability to carry out normal everyday activities including, by way of example, processing post, preparing meals, getting up in the morning, washing and getting dressed. In the circumstances it is averred that the Claimant is a disabled person within the definition set out at section 6 of the Equality Act 2010.

The date of disability is often crucial. Not only will it arise in the context of whether or not the claimant meets the long-term element of the definition of disability, but it may be relevant to questions of the respondent's knowledge and whether the treatment complained of was because of the alleged disability. It is therefore important to set out the date from which it is alleged the claimant was disabled. Remember, disability is assessed at the time of the alleged discriminatory act (**1.6**).

12.5.4 Relevant factual background

An ET1 is not the same as a witness statement and therefore detail can appropriately be reserved for witness evidence. Since, however, the ET1 is the first opportunity to set out the case for the claimant, it is important that a coherent and engaging narrative is set out. Getting the right balance is not easy but a helpful way to check whether a detail needs to be included is to consider which element of a claim it relates to. If there is no relevant element then it can be reserved for witness evidence.

The most effective way to structure this section is very often to adopt a chronological approach. If the narrative becomes very lengthy consider using headings to address the issues in a clear manner.

This section should state in relation to relevant events what happened, where and when it took place, who was present and what was said or done.

12.5.5 The matters relied upon in relation to each element of the claim

It is very important that in relation to each claim brought the matters relied upon for each element of the claim are set out clearly. To the extent that particular allegations or comments have already been set out in the factual background, there is no need to repeat them at this stage. It is appropriate simply to refer back to the relevant parts of the factual background.

If there are a number of claims, it is best to set them out under separate headings of direct discrimination, failure to make reasonable adjustments and so on. If you did not provide statutory references in the initial summary, be sure to include them at this stage. This section of the ET1 very often forms the basis of the list of issues which will be used later by the parties and the tribunal at the hearing. The clearer you are able to be, the less time will be occupied by these matters at a later stage.

12.5.5.1 Elements of direct discrimination

For a claim of direct disability discrimination under the Equality Act 2010, s.13, the following must be set out:

(a)   who is alleged to have discriminated against the claimant;
(b)   that the alleged perpetrator knew or ought reasonably to have known of the claimant's disability;
(c)   the less favourable treatment relied upon;
(d)   any comparator relied upon, actual or hypothetical; and
(e)   that the less favourable treatment was because of the claimant's disability.

Example

The Claimant informed her line manager of her disability during a one-to-one meeting on 12 June 2012. From this point on the Claimant's line manager subjected her to direct discrimination by removing her from all client facing work. This was less favourable treatment as the Claimant was prevented from earning commission or obtaining promotion as she was prevented from meeting her billings targets. None of the Claimant's non-disabled colleagues were removed from client facing work.

12.5.5.2 Elements of discrimination arising from disability

For a claim of discrimination arising from disability under the Equality Act 2010, s.15, the following must be set out:

(a)   who is alleged to have discriminated against the claimant;
(b)   that the alleged perpetrator knew or ought reasonably to have known of the claimant's disability;
(c)   the unfavourable treatment relied upon; and

(d)   that the unfavourable treatment was because of something arising in consequence of the claimant's disability.

Example

The Claimant was discriminated against by his team leader in that, while aware of the
Claimant's dyslexia from his application form, his team leader criticised the Claimant's
spelling, shouted at the Claimant for taking too long to read and respond to emails and placed
the Claimant on a PIP because he was not able to understand training on the first occasion.
The team leader's conduct was because of the symptoms of the Claimant's dyslexia. The
Claimant relies on the matters set out in paragraphs X to Y of the factual background for full
particulars of the dates and comments made by his team leader.

12.5.5.3   Elements of indirect disability discrimination

For a claim of indirect disability discrimination under the Equality Act 2010, s.19,
the following must be set out:

(a)   who is alleged to have discriminated against the claimant;
(b)   the PCP relied upon;
(c)   the particular disadvantage that the PCP places a disabled person at;
(d)   the disadvantage suffered by the claimant; and
(e)   any comparators, actual or hypothetical relied upon.

Example

The Claimant was unlawfully discriminated against contrary to section 19 of the Equality Act
2010 because the Respondent operated a practice of conducting all sales by telephone. This
practice places individuals with a hearing impairment at a particular disadvantage. This
includes the Claimant. As a result the Claimant was prevented from obtaining her sales
targets and failed to obtain commission at the level of her non-disabled colleagues.

12.5.5.4   Elements of a claim of a failure to make reasonable adjustments

For a claim of a failure to make reasonable adjustments under the Equality Act 2010,
ss.20 and 21, the following must be set out:

(a)   which of the three requirements is relied upon, i.e. a PCP, a physical feature or
the provision of an auxiliary aid;
(b)   details of the PCP, physical feature or auxiliary aid which is relied upon;
(c)   the substantial disadvantage that it is alleged the claimant suffered;
(d)   any comparators, actual or hypothetical, relied upon; and

(e)   the reasonable adjustments which it is alleged should have been made which would have alleviated the substantial disadvantage suffered.

Example

The Respondent's practice of conducting all sales by telephone placed the Claimant at a substantial disadvantage because her hearing impairment meant that she found it difficult to hear the caller and had to ask them to repeat themselves a lot. This affected her ability to complete sales and earn her commission. The Respondent failed to make any reasonable adjustments to assist the Claimant including, but not limited to, providing a phone on which the volume could be adjusted, providing a quieter place for the Claimant to take the calls or providing text support for the calls.

12.5.5.5   Elements of disability harassment

For a claim of harassment under the Equality Act 2010, s.26, the following must be set out:

(a)   who is alleged to have discriminated against the claimant;
(b)   the unwanted conduct which is relied upon;
(c)   the fact that the unwanted conduct was related to disability;
(d)   that the unwanted conduct had the purpose or effect of violating the claimant's dignity or creating an intimidating, hostile, degrading, humiliating or offensive environment for the claimant; and
(e)   any circumstances which might be relevant to considering the effect of the unwanted conduct, for example the claimant's perception, whether the conduct was in public or private, the reaction of any witnesses and similar.

Example

The Claimant was harassed by his team leader in that, while aware of the Claimant's dyslexia from his application form, the team leader criticised the Claimant's spelling, shouted at the Claimant for taking too long to read and respond to emails, and placed the Claimant on a PIP because he was not able to understand training on the first occasion. The team leader's conduct was unwanted and related to the Claimant's disability. The purpose and/or effect of the team leader's comments were offensive and degrading, particularly as his comments were made in the open plan office. The Claimant was humiliated by the team leader on a daily basis with many members of the team offering sympathy, although they were too afraid to speak up because of the intimidating environment which the team leader's conduct had created. The Claimant relies on the matters set out in paragraphs X to Y of the factual background for full particulars of the dates and comments made by his team leader.

12.5.5.6   *Elements of disability victimisation*

For a claim of victimisation under the Equality Act 2010, s.27, the following must be set out:

(a)   who is alleged to have discriminated against the claimant;
(b)   the protected act relied upon (including a reference to the relevant subsection of s.27(2));
(c)   that the protected act was done in good faith;
(d)   the detriment relied upon; and
(e)   that the detriment was because of the protected act.

Example

The Claimant complained about her removal from client facing roles on 20 July 2012. The Claimant's complaint was made orally to the production manager and was followed up with an email to HR on the same day. The Claimant's complaint was made in good faith with a view to resolving the situation. Instead of investigating the Claimant's complaint of discrimination, the production manager and HR officer simply informed the Claimant's line manager that she had complained of disability discrimination. As a result the Claimant was treated even more poorly than before by her line manager.

The Claimant's complaint was a protected act within the meaning of section 27(2)(d) of the Equality Act 2010. As a result of the Claimant's protected act the Claimant's line manager changed the Claimant's duties again such that she was effectively demoted to an administrator, setting up the room for meetings, making teas and coffees and covering reception. The Claimant claims that this amounts to victimisation contrary to section 27 of the Equality Act 2010.

12.6   CONCLUSION

This is a book looking specifically at disability discrimination. It is often the case that there will be overlap with other claims, perhaps for unfair dismissal, for breach of contract or unpaid wages. We do not address the elements of these claims here. Adopting the same approach as set out above for those claims will ensure that the necessary information is provided to the tribunal.

Where there are multiple acts, protected acts or detriments relied upon, these may be best set out by way of a numbered list.

To illustrate how the different elements come together, we have produced a sample grounds of complaint to accompany an ET1 or to insert at section 5.2 of the form. The facts are based on a fictitious scenario. It is impossible to provide a template as such but we hope that you find the sample useful in understanding how to write a grounds of complaint. The example can be found at **Appendix B1**.

In this chapter we have broken down the elements of an ET1 and the different types of claim relating to disability discrimination. In the next chapter we look at the response to a claim, the ET3 and grounds of resistance.

CHAPTER 13

Responding to a claim

In this chapter we will mirror **Chapter 12** on bringing a claim and look at the purpose of the response (**13.1**), the timing of the response (**13.2**), the form to be used (**13.3**), including the heading (**13.4**) and content (**13.5**). The response form is called an ET3 and in this chapter we will use 'ET3' or 'grounds of resistance' interchangeably. An example of a complete grounds of resistance is at **Appendix B2**.

13.1 PURPOSE OF THE ET3

Having considered the purpose of the ET1 previously, it will be apparent that for an employer the ET3 is its first opportunity to present its case to the tribunal. It is the first chance for it to set out its defence and to respond to the allegations raised by the claimant.

A good ET3 therefore does the following:

1. It raises any jurisdictional issues or barriers to the claim.
2. It sets out the defence to the legal claims being brought.
3. It sets out the factual background necessary.

As with the ET1, a failure to provide the correct information may lead to requests for further information or, more seriously, a defence being rejected.

13.2 TIMING OF THE ET3

The ET3 must be submitted within 28 days of the employer being provided with the ET1 by the tribunal. A failure to submit an ET3 in time can lead to the defence being rejected and the claim succeeding without the employer having an opportunity to defend it. This process is known as default judgment. It is possible to challenge a decision to reject the defence through the process known as review (**17.5**).

13.3   THE ET3 FORM

As with the ET1, the ET3 can be completed electronically and submitted online or it can be printed out and submitted by fax, post or email. The tribunal will notify the employer of the claim, the timescale in which to respond and indicate the appropriate form with which to do so. The employment tribunal should also supply the employer with the claim or case number.

The majority of the form is fairly self-explanatory. Details of the employee's wages, job title and dates of employment, etc. should all be readily available from the employer's personnel records. The part which warrants most careful attention, and sometimes external drafting, is the grounds of resistance, response or defence. We will use grounds of resistance throughout but the terms are interchangeable in practice. This can be either included in the form at section 5 or attached as a separate document. When the grounds of resistance are in a separate document from the ET3, the ET3 and the grounds of resistance together form the pleading for the respondent. A copy of the current ET3 form has been included at **Appendix B2**.

13.4   HEADING

If the grounds of resistance are attached as a separate document then the heading is very similar to the ET1 heading. The employer should include the name of the tribunal which has conduct of the claim and the case number allocated to the case. See **12.4** for a precedent document heading.

13.5   CONTENT

In cases where there is a well-drafted ET1, the ET3 will often follow a similar structure, admitting parts of the ET1 which are correct and denying, with reasons, those parts which are in dispute. Where the ET1 is not well structured it may be unhelpful to follow it through paragraph by paragraph at the outset and it may be clearer to provide a structured response followed by detailed denials if necessary. This decision is one which requires the author of the document to consider the audience and the best way to provide them with the information which they need as quickly and concisely as possible.

A basic structure would be as follows:

(a)   introduce the parties (**13.5.1**);
(b)   summarise the response to the legal complaints brought (**13.5.2**);
(c)   set out any jurisdictional issues (**13.5.3**);
(d)   admit or deny the claimant's disability and/or the employer's knowledge of it (**13.5.4**);
(e)   provide relevant factual background (**13.5.5**); and
(f)   respond to each of the claims brought (**13.5.6**).

13.5.1 Introduction to the parties

If the claimant has accurately set out the parties and their roles then this may be as simple as accepting their descriptions. If there is a misleading description which needs correcting then it will be appropriate to provide any necessary correction before accepting the rest of the claimant's description. If the claimant has missed relevant parties or failed to describe the business and this is relevant to the defence, it may be that the paragraph needs expansion. It might be necessary, for example, to make clear the size of the business for the purposes of considering a reasonable adjustments claim.

13.5.2 Summarise the response to the legal complaints brought

The response to the legal complaints at this stage might be as simple as saying that the claimant's claims are denied. Alternatively it might be preferable to set out a more general denial, particularly where the precise complaints are unclear.

Example

It is denied that the Respondent has discriminated against the Claimant whether in the manner pleaded or otherwise.

The detailed response should come after the relevant factual background so at this stage the purpose is simply to make clear to the tribunal whether the claims are admitted or denied.

13.5.3 Set out any jurisdictional issues

If the respondent wishes to raise any barriers to the tribunal's jurisdiction, these should be raised clearly in the ET3. For example, it might be that the employer wishes to limit the claim to acts within the last three months and does not accept that there has been a continuing act. If that is the case then this issue should be clearly flagged in the ET3 to be considered by the tribunal hearing the claim or, in certain circumstances, by an earlier tribunal at a pre-hearing review.

Example

The Claimant submitted her claim on 1 December 2012. It is therefore averred that any act or omission prior to 2 September 2012 is out of time and should not be considered by the Tribunal unless it is persuaded that it is appropriate to extend time in the circumstances of the case. The Respondent disputes that there is a continuing act and asserts that the allegations must be considered individually.

Again it can be helpful to include any statutory provisions relied upon.

13.5.4 Admit or deny the claimant's disability and/or the employer's knowledge of it

It may be that it is accepted that the claimant is disabled. If so, this should be made clear at the earliest opportunity. Disputes over disability add significantly to the tribunal timetable and can substantially increase the costs to the parties. If the claimant has a prescribed condition such that he or she is deemed to be disabled then failing to admit it may be unreasonable conduct and leave the employer open to potential penalties in relation to costs.

If the information with which to decide whether or not to admit disability is not yet available then the most practical approach is to set out the information which is required and to deny disability at this stage.

Example

At present the Respondent has not seen any medical evidence, either from the Claimant's GP or from any treating specialist. It is therefore not admitted that the Claimant is disabled. The Claimant is required to prove the same.

It is often necessary to establish when the employer became aware of the alleged disability. Conduct cannot be because of a disability if the employer does not know there is a disability. Similarly an employer is not under an obligation to make reasonable adjustments unless it is aware of the employee's disability. It may be that the employee has expressly declared his or her condition in relation to sick leave or when applying for the role. If so, the date of knowledge should be clearly set out. If the employee has not made his or her position plain then it might be that the employer was completely unaware of the alleged disability or that it only became aware at a very late stage. Whatever the situation, the ET3 should set out the employer's case in relation to whether it knew of the alleged disability and, if so, when.

13.5.5 Relevant factual background

The chronology provided by the claimant will often favour his or her version of events. Meetings or emails may well have occurred on the days pleaded but the content of the communications may be very different. It is helpful to keep to a chronological approach and, where meetings or documents are addressed which were mentioned in the ET1, cross-reference to the relevant paragraph so that the tribunal can see clearly the dispute on the document.

Example

It is admitted that the Claimant emailed the Respondent's HR on 8 October 2011. The email read, 'I continue to have problems with my manager, this is not fair'. In the circumstances it is denied that this was an email requesting a meeting or raising a formal grievance as pleaded at paragraphs X and Y of the ET1. It is averred that this was a further example of the Claimant's unhelpful and combative approach to the issue.

13.5.6 Respond to each of the claims brought

The response should address each element of the different claims brought. Tactically it can be very beneficial to consider appropriate concessions so that the focus of the tribunal claim is not on weak points but on stronger arguments. For example, it might be appropriate to concede that a PCP was applied but deny the substantial adverse effect or that the adjustments would alleviate the substantial adverse effect.

As with the ET1, examples are given below in relation to the different types of disability discrimination claims.

13.5.6.1 Elements of direct discrimination

In defending a claim of direct disability discrimination under the Equality Act 2010, s.13, the response must address:

(a)   whether the alleged perpetrator carried out the acts complained of;
(b)   whether the alleged perpetrator knew or ought reasonably to have known of the claimant's disability;
(c)   the less favourable treatment relied upon;
(d)   any comparator relied upon, actual or hypothetical; and
(e)   whether the less favourable treatment was because of the claimant's disability.

Example

It is admitted that the Claimant informed her line manager of her disability during a one-to-one meeting on 12 June 2012. At the same meeting the Claimant informed her line manager that she no longer wished to perform client facing work as she wished to develop more back office experience with a view to changing her role internally in the future. It is accepted that from this point on the Claimant's line manager removed her from all client facing work. It is accepted that none of the Claimant's colleagues were removed from client facing work. It is denied that this amounts to less favourable treatment as the change was agreed following the Claimant's request. It is denied that this amounts to disability discrimination. The Claimant was removed from client facing work in order to further her career as requested. None of the Claimant's colleagues made such a request. If they had done so they would have been treated in the same way as the Claimant.

13.5.6.2   Elements of discrimination arising from disability

In defending a claim of discrimination arising from disability under the Equality Act 2010, s.15, the response must address:

(a)   whether the alleged perpetrator did the acts complained of;

(b)   whether the alleged perpetrator knew or ought reasonably to have known of the claimant's disability;

(c)   the unfavourable treatment relied upon;

(d)   whether the unfavourable treatment was because of something arising in consequence of the claimant's disability; and

(e)   whether the treatment was a proportionate means of achieving a legitimate aim.

Example

It is denied that the Claimant was discriminated against by his team leader. The Claimant's team leader was not aware of the Claimant's alleged disability. The Claimant's team leader joined after the Claimant and did not see the Claimant's application form. As to the matters raised in the claim form:

1.   It is accepted that the team leader provided feedback to the Claimant in relation to his failure to use the spell check function on the computer software. This feedback was given to all staff.

2.   It is denied that the team leader shouted at the Claimant for taking too long to read. As set out above, this incident relates to an occasion when the Claimant and his colleague were not reading the document the team were asked to consider but were instead watching videos on YouTube.

3.   It is admitted that the Claimant was warned about his failure to respond to emails. For the reasons given this was raised and resolved in July 2012 and was not related to the Claimant's alleged disability.

4.   The Claimant was not placed on a PIP because he was not able to understand training on the first occasion. As set out above, the Claimant was given a first verbal warning for disruptive behaviour during a training session run by an external provider.

The Respondent will say that any treatment of the Claimant was a proportionate means of achieving a legitimate aim, namely the appropriate training of staff and maintenance of professional standards in written communication.

13.5.6.3   Elements of indirect disability discrimination

In defending a claim of indirect disability discrimination under the Equality Act 2010, s.19, the response must set out:

143

(a)   whether the alleged perpetrator did the acts complained of;

(b)   whether the PCP was applied;

(c)   whether the PCP places a disabled person at a substantial disadvantage;

(d)   whether the claimant suffered that disadvantage;

(e)   any comparators, actual or hypothetical, relied upon; and

(f)   whether the treatment was a proportionate means of achieving a legitimate aim.

Example

It is denied that the Respondent operated a practice of conducting all sales by telephone. The Claimant applied for a particular role within the Respondent's telesales team. This role required the Claimant to conduct sales by phone. There were also roles within the Respondent's stores or via the website, all of which were available to the Claimant. The Claimant could earn her commission from such sales. The Respondent avers that having a dedicated telesales team is a proportionate means of achieving a legitimate aim, namely maximising sales through optimal client service.

13.5.6.4   Elements of a failure to make reasonable adjustments claim

In defending a claim of a failure to make reasonable adjustments under the Equality Act 2010, ss.20 and 21, the response must address:

(a)   whether the pleaded PCP, physical feature or auxiliary aid applied to the claimant;

(b)   whether the claimant suffered the substantial disadvantage alleged;

(c)   any comparators, actual or hypothetical, relied upon; and

(d)   whether the reasonable adjustments, which it is alleged should have been made, would have alleviated the substantial disadvantage suffered.

Example

It is denied that there was a practice of conducting all sales by telephone, as set out above. Furthermore, it is denied that the Claimant suffered a substantial disadvantage as she was able to complete sales and earn commission via web chat sales, email orders, store roles and website transactions. The Claimant failed to follow the approved sales technique and therefore failed to complete sales. In the circumstances it is averred that the proposed adjustments would not have alleviated her alleged substantial disadvantage as she would still have been unable to complete sales. In any event it is averred that providing text support is prohibitively expensive.

13.5.6.5   Elements of disability harassment

In defending a claim of harassment under the Equality Act 2010, s.26, the response must address:

(a)   whether the alleged perpetrator did the acts complained of;

(b)   the unwanted conduct which is relied upon;

(c)   whether the unwanted conduct was related to disability;

(d)   whether the unwanted conduct had the purpose or effect of violating the claimant's dignity or creating an intimidating, hostile, degrading, humiliating or offensive environment for the claimant; and

(e)   any circumstances which might be relevant to considering the effect of the unwanted conduct, for example, the claimant's perception, whether the conduct was in public or private, the reaction of any witnesses, etc.

Example

It is denied that the Claimant was harassed by his team leader. In particular, for the reasons set out above, the Claimant's team leader had fair and reasonable grounds for his conduct towards the Claimant which did not relate to the Claimant's disability. The effect of the team leader's comments cannot reasonably be considered to be offensive and degrading in the context in which they were made. It is denied that the Claimant was humiliated on a daily basis. The Claimant is required to provide proper particulars of any such conduct so that this can be addressed.

13.5.6.6   Elements of victimisation

In defending a claim of victimisation under the Equality Act 2010, s.27, the response must address:

(a)   whether the alleged perpetrator did the acts complained of;

(b)   whether the protected act relied upon amounts to a protected act;

(c)   whether the protected act was done in good faith;

(d)   the detriment relied upon; and

(e)   whether the detriment was because of the protected act.

Example

It is denied that the Claimant complained about her removal from client facing roles, whether on 20 July 2012 or otherwise. The Claimant did speak to the production manager and HR on this day to complain that she had too much work to do since the change in her role. The Claimant did not mention discrimination, whether related to her disability or otherwise. The appropriate HR representative discussed with the production manager the Claimant's complaint and the production manager agreed to reduce her workload while she adjusted to the new role.

In the circumstances it is denied that the Claimant's comments or email were a protected act within the statutory provisions. It is admitted that the Claimant's role changed following the comments but for the reasons set out above it is denied that the changes amount to victimisation. It is averred that the changes were an appropriate response to the Claimant's concerns.

13.6 CONCLUSION

To illustrate how all the parts of an ET3 come together we have produced at **Appendix B2** both the form and accompanying grounds of resistance to respond to the ET1 at **Appendix B1**. It is impossible to provide a template ET3 which will meet every possible permutation of claim; however, we hope that by seeing an ET1 and ET3 together, the information provided in this section can be understood in context.

The ET1 and ET3, including the grounds of complaint and grounds of resistance if separate, form the pleadings in a tribunal claim. The documents are at the centre of everything that follows. Having considered their content and purpose we now turn our attention to what happens to the claim as it progresses through the tribunal process. We start with the issue of settlement.

CHAPTER 14

Settlement

Settlement can take many different forms. It is sometimes known as alternative dispute resolution (ADR) to reflect the fact that it covers any method of resolving a dispute without recourse to the courts. The most common methods are considered briefly here. We start with settlement by way of compromise agreement (**14.2**) and then settlement via ACAS and a COT3 agreement (**14.3**). We then consider forms of mediation with judicial mediation (**14.4**) or independent mediation (**14.5**). Finally we consider settlement at court with a consent order (**14.6**). Before we consider each of these in more detail, we consider the benefits of avoiding litigation (**14.1**).

14.1   BENEFITS OF SETTLEMENT

Litigation is an adversarial process. At its heart is one party 'winning' and the other 'losing'; winner takes all. Resolving the dispute out of court can deliver the following benefits:

- The early bird benefit: litigation, especially where disability is disputed, can be a lengthy process taking months to reach resolution. In some cases it can be several years. Throughout this time the parties are drawn back to the dispute and prevented from closing the issue. This can be particularly damaging for people suffering from mental health issues. Settlement can bring matters to an early satisfactory close.
- For your eyes only: resolution of disputes out of court usually involves confidentiality clauses and non-derogatory comment clauses. This means that the parties agree to keep the settlement confidential as between them and they agree not to make derogatory comments about the other party. Keeping an outcome private can avoid bad publicity and, for those companies required to disclose records of claims in tenders and so on, it limits the level of information about the case which is in the public domain.

- Atypical remedies: it may be that really what the former employee needs is a reference to help them obtain a new job. It may be that the current employee needs a mediation session and an apology from the manager in question. It may be that training or retraining would resolve the difficulty in the workplace. Round table discussions allow the parties to discuss all of these options and agree to implement them. These are not solutions which a tribunal can order. If this is what is sought, a tribunal judgment is not going to deliver it.

- Keep the faith: where a claim has been brought by a current employee the relationship of trust and confidence is often damaged by the litigation process. Early resolution in a conciliatory environment is essential if the parties wish to repair and retain trust and confidence.

- Clean break: sometimes the reality is that the relationship has reached a point of no return and actually one of the things that the settlement agrees is how to end the relationship and allow the parties to part ways.

- Avoiding the litigation lottery: no matter how strong the case may appear on the documents and when discussed with the client, unpredictable things happen in court. The evidence does not come out as expected, a new document is produced, the judge and panel place particular weight on one factor – the list is endless. Sometimes these factors will favour a party and sometimes they will turn against it. Settlement provides certainty of outcome.

- Cheaper …: litigation costs money and every step, every delay, every letter and every day at court adds to the bill. Sometimes some of these costs can be recovered but often in the employment tribunal the costs are borne by each of the parties. This can mean that for an employer, even if the claims are dismissed in their entirety, it may cost more to defend the issue than was claimed. For an employee, any compensation may be absorbed by legal costs. Early settlement may well be better than a pyrrhic victory later.

- And more cheerful: it is commonly the case that witnesses and parties emerge from the tribunal process feeling that they have been through the mill. Details of their business practices, of their health, of emails and disciplinary records have been scrutinised and examined in a way which was never intended when the events took place. Many witnesses report sleepless nights before the hearing, loss of appetite and all the classic signs of stress. If this can be avoided it is worth something. This has a particular significance when the witnesses in question suffer from mental health issues which are exacerbated by stressful situations.

Assuming the parties are persuaded to explore settlement, we have set out some of the options available below.

14.2 COMPROMISE AGREEMENT

It is open to the parties at any point to agree a settlement. Any discussions to settle the dispute should be labelled, or expressed to be 'without prejudice save as to costs'. This means that if no resolution is reached, neither party can refer to the discussions during the course of the hearing. The only time when the correspondence or discussions can be raised is in relation to the question of costs. A tribunal may consider whether there has been any unreasonable failure to accept an offer of settlement when they consider whether to make an order as to costs.

Compromise agreements must satisfy the requirements of the Equality Act 2010, s.147. In particular:

- the agreement must be in writing (s.147(3)(a));
- the agreement must relate to the particular complaint (s.147(3)(b));
- the claimant must have received independent legal advice about the terms and effect of the agreement (s.147(3)(c));
- the adviser must have appropriate insurance at the date of advising (s.147(3)(d));
- the adviser must be identified in the agreement (s.147(3)(e)); and
- the agreement must confirm that subsections (c) and (d) have been complied with (s.147(3)(f)).

Further provisions as to who is an appropriate adviser are contained in s.147.

As well as meeting the formalities, it is often the case that parties will set out the terms of their agreement.

Examples of matters which may be addressed in a compromise agreement

- Confidentiality
- Non-derogatory comments
- Terms of any agreed reference
- Terms of any oral reference
- An agreement to continue PHI payments
- A reason for termination
- Arrangements as to notice

The Government is consulting on a new settlement regime to be known as Settlement Agreements. Please see our website for updates (details are given in the Preface).

14.3 ACAS

When a claim is brought in the employment tribunal it will be referred to ACAS who will contact the parties to see whether they are interested in using their services to reach a settlement. A single point of contact will be assigned to the case and the parties can communicate with them about any offers which they wish to make on a without prejudice basis.

If the parties reach an agreement, with or without the assistance of their designated conciliator, ACAS can provide a COT3 agreement, which is a standard form settlement which meets the statutory requirements mentioned above. The parties are able to tailor the agreement to include bespoke terms if these arise.

At the time of writing the government is preparing to introduce compulsory mediation which will be known as Early Conciliation. Please see our website for updates (details are given in the Preface).

14.4   JUDICIAL MEDIATION

The judicial mediation scheme is a new scheme available for specific classes of cases. Practice varies across different regions but the general factors which make a case suitable for judicial mediation are that there must be claims of discrimination and the length of the proposed hearing must meet regional limits. The required length is usually defined by reference to a minimum number of days. At its lowest this is three days but in some of the busier regions the minimum is set at a higher level. Mediation involves all parties attending the tribunal for a day to discuss with a trained judge whether settlement may be possible.

In cases which meet the initial criteria the tribunal will ask the parties to indicate if they are interested in judicial mediation. If both parties indicate interest then the regional chair will review the case and determine whether to offer judicial mediation. Mediation is all about reaching a negotiated solution, so if one party is not prepared to consider it and actively engage in it on a voluntary basis, there is no value in arranging the mediation.

When a case is accepted by the regional chair, a telephone case management discussion is arranged to organise a date and to agree what should be prepared by the parties ahead of the mediation. The mediation itself is provided free of charge although parties may choose to have a representative attend with them and in this case they will need to pay any costs associated with their own representative.

On the day of the mediation an employment judge will try to help the parties reach an agreement to settle the case. They have specific training in mediation of disputes. They will sometimes call everyone together and at other times speak to the parties separately. Should the mediation prove unsuccessful, the employment judge will excuse themselves from further involvement in the case. The same judge will not sit in any full merits hearing to determine issues in the case. If the mediation is successful, an agreement is drawn up and signed by the parties on the day.

14.5   INDEPENDENT MEDIATION

A number of organisations provide independent mediation services. There is usually a charge for the use of a mediator and it may be necessary to arrange a venue for the mediation to take place in. Commonly the cost will fall on the employer as many employees are not in a position to share the bill. If an employee is able to contribute and interested in mediation then the offer to pay some of the cost may be the gesture needed to bring the employer to the table.

The big advantage of independent mediation over judicial mediation is that it can be arranged at a much earlier stage in the proceedings and even before litigation is commenced. If the employee is still employed, this could be the difference between an acrimonious termination with claims for loss of earnings and repairing the relationship so that no claim is even brought.

Another advantage of independent mediation is that it is available even for cases that do not qualify for judicial mediation.

14.6 CONSENT ORDER

Sometimes settlement discussions happen at the tribunal. This can happen at an interim hearing or at the final hearing. Sometimes it happens during the course of the hearing or after judgment on liability and before remedy issues are addressed. Whenever an agreement is reached the parties can draft the agreement between them and sign copies.

They can then seek a consent order from an employment judge to dispose of the case on the terms agreed between the parties. Agreements can be very brief or more lengthy. There is no requirement for an independent adviser but tribunal judges will often explain to a litigant in person the consequences of the order to satisfy themselves that the individual understands the effect of their agreement.

14.7 CONCLUSION

Settlement can take place at any time and in any number of different ways. As we consider the steps in the tribunal process in the following chapters, it should not be forgotten that the process can be terminated at any point by settlement.

CHAPTER 15

The process for determining disability

Disability is a legal concept, therefore unless disability is admitted there will need to be a judicial determination on whether or not the claimant is disabled. In this chapter we look at the process for determining whether a claimant is disabled. If disability is admitted then directions will be set for a full hearing (**Chapter 16**). We start with an overview of the process (**15.1**) and then look at what is meant by a claimant's impact statement (**15.2**). An example impact statement is at **Appendix B3**. We also look at other evidence the parties may adduce (**15.3**). We then look at instructing a joint medical expert (**15.4**).

15.1 OVERVIEW OF THE PROCESS FOR DETERMINING DISABILITY

The issue of disability is usually determined at a separate hearing called a pre-hearing review (PHR). In preparation for this hearing a number of steps need to be completed (see **Figure 15.1**). The tribunal will normally make orders about the steps to be taken and sets dates for compliance.

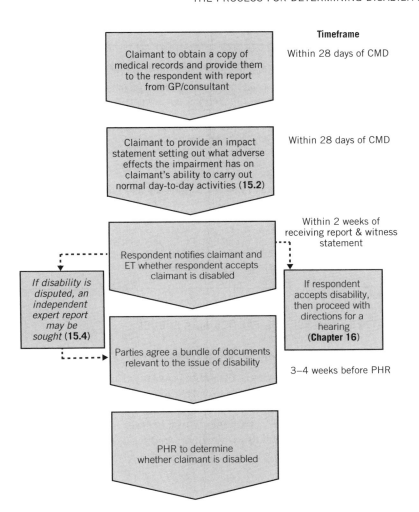

Figure 15.1 Directions for pre-hearing review on the issue of disability

15.2 IMPACT STATEMENT

An impact statement is a witness statement addressing only the impact of the alleged disability on the claimant. It can be tempting to rehearse the claims and complaints at this stage but doing so does not assist the tribunal and merely provides the other side with early notice of the way in which the claimant will put his or her evidence.

Examples of issues which the impact statement should address

- Any significant medical history. Much will be contained in the medical records so it is not necessary to simply repeat the records, but key points, e.g. surgery or changes to medication, should be highlighted
- When symptoms were first noticed and what those symptoms were
- Whether there has been any change or deterioration in the symptoms; if so what the pattern has been
- What the claimant cannot do at all because of the condition
- What the claimant can do but only with difficulty
- What the claimant can do only with adjustments and what those adjustments are
- Any impact which the claimant's condition has on his or her family
- What medication is taken by the claimant or if there are any measures in place to reduce the impact of the condition
- What the impact of any such medication or measures is on the claimant
- How the claimant would be in the absence of such medication or measures
- What the claimant understands to be the prognosis

15.3 OTHER EVIDENCE THE PARTIES MAY ADDUCE

15.3.1 Supporting statement for the claimant

The key evidence on the question of disability is usually from the claimant and any medical expert. It is open to the parties to call evidence from others in relation to the issue of disability. It is not uncommon to have a witness statement from a family member of the claimant. This is particularly true in cases involving mental health conditions because the claimant's own memory and recall may be affected by the condition.

15.3.2 Statement from the respondent

It is sometimes appropriate to have a witness from the respondent. This is particularly the case where it is said on behalf of the claimant that he or she was unable to do something and a colleague saw him or her doing it during the course of the employment. For example, if a person said that he or she was unable to answer the phone due to anxiety about who would be calling and yet in the office was regularly seen taking calls, it would be relevant evidence to put forward. Likewise if a person claims to be unable to stand for more than five minutes due to a back problem and yet danced all evening at the work Christmas party, it may be relevant to put in brief witness evidence. It is important to avoid the temptation to argue the underlying claims so any respondent evidence should be strictly and clearly limited to the issue of disability.

15.3.3 Documentary evidence

Documentary evidence may also be relevant to show how the condition has been reported and categorised in the relevant period.

Examples of documentary evidence which may be called in support

- Medical records
- Sick notes
- Occupational health reports
- Any complaints or correspondence about the condition
- Any medical records or reports which the employer sought to assist it in managing the claimant during employment (**Chapter 7**)

15.4 MEDICAL EVIDENCE

Medical evidence may be required on many different issues and at many different stages of the tribunal process. In **Chapter 7** we looked at obtaining medical reports during employment. Where these reports have been obtained they may be used later as evidence and will be invaluable in showing the tribunal the knowledge and understanding of the parties at the time of the relevant events. They will also provide a contemporaneous record of the employee's condition.

We now look at the use of medical evidence in litigation (**15.4.1**), how to choose an expert (**15.4.2**) and the steps in instructing a medical expert (**15.4.3**). We also consider briefly the attendance of any expert at the tribunal (**15.4.4**). We provide a sample joint letter of instruction to a medical expert at **Appendix B4**.

There is no presumption that the tribunal will permit expert evidence to be adduced. Some judges will have strong views on what kind of medical evidence is required. Sometimes a claimant's treating physician will be permitted to stand as the claimant's expert without the need for further evidence. In such a case the respondent may wish to seek its own evidence and the claimant is expected to co-operate with a request to attend a medical examination.

Tribunals will consider the guidelines from *De Keyser* v. *Wilson* [2001] IRLR 324 (EAT) in relation to whether an expert should be permitted and, if so, the directions which should be given.

De Keyser v. *Wilson* [2001] IRLR 324 (EAT)

The EAT set out the following guidelines in relation to expert evidence:

- Is expert evidence necessary? Just because one side wants it does not mean that a tribunal will allow it.
- A joint single expert is preferable in all cases unless one side has already instructed an expert (which should be avoided in the absence of special circumstances).
- When a joint expert is instructed, the parties need to agree joint instructions, what the costs will be and how they will be shared.
- If one side can afford the costs but the other cannot and a single expert is used, the evidence of the single expert can carry more weight if the other side has seen or agreed the terms of instruction.
- Tribunals will fix a time period within which the identity of the joint expert must be agreed and a time deadline for producing the report.
- The letter of instruction should give as much detail as possible as to the answers which the report must address.
- The instructions should be impartial and the expert should be reminded that their overriding duty is to the tribunal and not to either party.
- Where a joint expert is to be used and the parties cannot agree on the expert, the tribunal may be required to assist.
- Tribunals may give formal directions about the questions which the expert is to address.
- If there is no joint expert, there must be a timetable for disclosing or exchanging expert reports, a meeting of experts to settle the areas of agreement and disagreement and for producing a schedule of agreed issues.
- That timetable may allow for supplementary questions.
- Tribunals may consider costs penalties if one side fails unreasonably to comply.

This approach has been endorsed in the specific context of medical reports in *GCHQ* v. *Bacchus* [2012] All ER (D) 151 (Aug) (EAT) and it continues to be the approach adopted by the tribunals in relation to medical evidence.

15.4.1   Use of medical evidence

The method for obtaining medical evidence will depend in part on the reason for which medical evidence is sought. Medical evidence may be relevant to many different issues. It is important to carefully identify the reason for the evidence so that the right questions are asked.

Issues on which medical evidence may be required

- Establishing disability
- Establishing the reasonableness of proposed adjustments
- Supporting issues of remedy including the level of injury to feelings award and the impact of the disability and discrimination on future earnings prospects
- Establishing a claim for personal injury

- Supporting a lack of mitigation due to ill health
- Obtaining adjustments to the tribunal process

It may be that the required evidence can be obtained by the employee simply writing to the medical adviser and asking them to provide a report. If a report is sought in relation to the proceedings, it may become a disclosable document and the claimant may be required to supply it to the other side even if it does not support their case.

The main formalities arise when the medical adviser is jointly instructed.

15.4.2   Choice of medical expert

If an employee has been treated by a particular specialist then very often it is appropriate for that specialist to prepare a report for the tribunal. This is particularly so where the condition has changed since the time of the relevant acts and so any fresh assessment will not be able to consider the impact of the relevant condition on the employee at the relevant time, i.e. the time of the alleged acts of discrimination. Sometimes the employer may want to see a new assessment from an independent professional in order to make its determination. As mentioned, the tribunal expects the parties to co-operate in obtaining the report.

The usual order in the tribunal is to have a joint medical expert rather than permitting a battle of the experts with each party calling their own. This means the expert is jointly selected, jointly instructed and any discussions with the expert should be with both parties present or copied in. The cost of the report may be split between the parties. If the employee has already obtained a report from his or her own specialist then he or she may require the employer to pay for any further report. If the employee does not yet have any medical evidence to support the claim then it is appropriate that the employee pays half the costs of the report as without it he or she is unlikely to establish disability.

15.4.3   Instructing a medical expert

If the decision is taken to instruct a joint expert, the usual orders are shown in **Figure 15.2**.

15.4.3.1   Agreeing the choice of medical expert

There are directories of medical professionals in relevant disciplines from which a specialist may be chosen. Often it will be very useful to speak to other people who have instructed an expert in the field to see whether they have any recommendations.

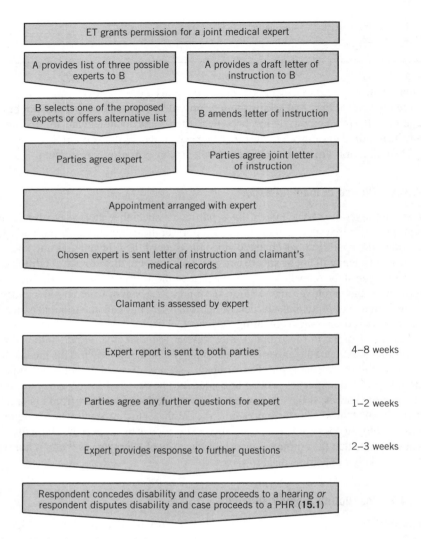

Figure 15.2   Steps for obtaining a medical expert report

Matters to consider in selecting a medical expert

- Does the expert currently practise in the relevant area (i.e. is their knowledge current or dated)?
- Does the expert specialise in the condition which is being considered? This is particularly important for mental health issues. It is tempting to consider any psychologist or any psychiatrist appropriate, but those who specialise in geriatric treatment may not be best placed to address a case of post-traumatic stress disorder or depression associated with addiction.
- How busy is the expert? This is relevant to how quickly he or she can see the claimant and produce the report as well as how soon the tribunal can consider the matter if the expert is called. Some professionals who regularly produce expert reports will have specific spaces in their clinics to conduct assessments so there should not be a significant delay.
- Has the expert given evidence in court before? There is lots of training for experts on the court process and the issues they can address in evidence. There is an advantage in having an expert who is familiar with the tribunal process and the determination of disability.

The usual approach is for one party to shortlist three experts with appropriate expertise and availability and for the other party to select from that shortlist. If none of the proposed experts is considered suitable by the selecting party or there are issues of availability then the selecting party should supply its own shortlist to allow the other side to choose from that list. Tribunals do not like to see too much time spent on this stage of the process since delays inevitably arise with obtaining the report. Parties should work hard to ensure that they check availability before proposing an expert and do not take longer than is necessary in making any selection.

15.4.3.2   Joint letter of instruction

Once the expert has been selected it is then necessary to send a joint letter of instruction. To save time this letter can be drafted and agreed at the same time as the expert is being selected.

The letter needs to set out the issue(s) that the expert is being asked to address. It is usual to include a brief explanation of the legal test for disability and it is important to stress to the expert that he or she is not being asked to determine whether or not the person is disabled. That is a question for the tribunal. The expert's job is to provide information which will assist the tribunal in reaching its determination.

Once instructed, the expert will meet the claimant and assess him or her. The expert will then produce a report. To ensure that the report is as comprehensive as possible it is important that the expert has access to the claimant's medical records. It is sensible to arrange for these to be sent with the letter of instruction or shortly thereafter so that they can be considered by the expert before the claimant is seen.

This way all relevant questions can be asked. It is possible to ensure that the expert does not disclose these records to the respondent other than where the expert needs to refer specifically to the condition(s) in question.

The report can take several weeks to produce and may give rise to further questions on either side. As the expert is a joint one, if further questions are to be asked then the parties should seek to agree a list of additional questions to be put to the expert. The expert should then respond to both parties with an addendum to the report containing the response to the questions.

A sample letter of instruction is set out at **Appendix B4**.

15.4.4   Calling the expert at the tribunal

Very often it will not be necessary to call the expert to give live evidence at the tribunal so the report and any addendum will stand as his or her evidence. If a party wishes to challenge the report then the expert should attend for cross-examination. In these circumstances no separate witness statement is produced but the report and any addendum will be considered as the witness statement on which the expert may then be questioned.

As the expert is jointly instructed it is not appropriate for the individual to sit in either the respondent or claimant waiting room. Arrangements should be made with the tribunal for the expert to have a consultation room for his or her use while waiting to give evidence.

15.5   CONCLUSION

When disability is disputed, medical evidence will be a key part of the evidence in the case. This chapter has looked at how to gather such evidence. In the next chapter we consider the other steps which parties need to take to prepare for a hearing.

CHAPTER 16

Preparation for a hearing

Where disability has been admitted or a tribunal has determined that the claimant was disabled at the relevant time, it will be necessary to prepare for a hearing to determine the disability discrimination claims. In this chapter we look at the orders made by a tribunal to prepare the case for a hearing. We start with an overview (**16.1**) and then consider the steps in a little more detail, including case management discussions (**16.2**), producing a schedule of loss (**16.3**), disclosure (**16.4**), preparation of the bundle (**16.5**), witness statements (**16.6**) and other orders which may be made (**16.7**).

16.1 PROCESS OVERVIEW

Orders for preparation of the case for a hearing are often made at a case management discussion (CMD) (**16.2**). Sometimes, to avoid the cost of a CMD, the tribunal may send standard directions in the post to the parties without consultation. This does not usually happen where disability is disputed.

When the parties receive standard directions with which they do not agree, they should seek to agree a variation between themselves and then make an application to the tribunal to vary the order under rule 11 of the Employment Tribunals Rules of Procedure (Employment Tribunals (Constitution and Rules of Procedure) Regulations 2004, SI 2004/1861, Sched.1). If the parties cannot agree a variation then the party seeking the change should apply to the tribunal under rule 11 and copy the other side if required under the rule. The general rule, under rule 11, is that correspondence with the tribunal should be copied to the other side. The details of the tribunal rules can be found online on HM Courts and Tribunals Service website (**Appendix D**).

If there are no difficulties with the directions set then the parties are each responsible for complying with them to prepare for the hearing. While the litigation process itself is adversarial, the parties should work co-operatively to prepare the case for a full hearing.

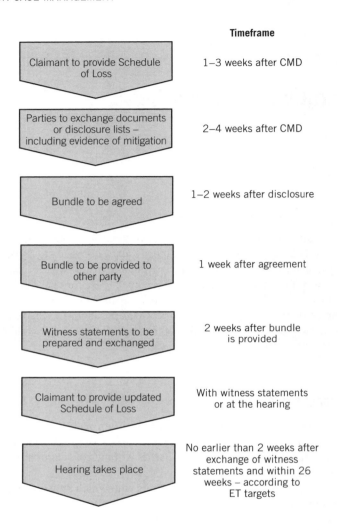

Figure 16.1 Directions from a case management discussion to a hearing

16.2   CASE MANAGEMENT DISCUSSION

A CMD can be listed at any point in the case. It may be conducted in person or by telephone. It may be set to deal with all the matters in the case or only a specific issue, such as the directions for a PHR or an application from one of the parties.

When a CMD is listed, an employment judge, sitting alone, will seek to clarify with the parties what the issues in the case are, both factual and legal. The judge will also seek to set an agreed timetable to prepare for the hearing. The usual steps in such a timetable would include:

- provision of a schedule of loss by the claimant (**16.3**);
- disclosure (**16.4**);
- agreement of the trial bundle (**16.5**);
- exchange of witness statements (**16.6**); and
- an updated schedule of loss at the start of the hearing.

Other orders which may be appropriate in particular cases are:

- orders for further information from either side (**16.7.1**);
- preparation of a schedule of acts relied upon as acts of discrimination, some-times referred to as a Scott Schedule (**16.7.2** and **Appendix B6**);
- an agreed chronology (**16.7.3**); and
- a cast list (**16.7.4**).

Where both parties are represented, it is expected that the representatives will seek to agree a list of issues and timetable before seeing the judge. Where a CMD has been scheduled to take place in the tribunal but a telephone CMD is requested by the parties, a list of issues must usually be agreed before the tribunal will agree to a telephone CMD.

16.3   SCHEDULE OF LOSS

A schedule of loss is a document setting out what the claimant seeks to recover if successful in his or her claim. The tribunal has a broad discretion to award such compensation as is just and equitable. Types of loss which might be claimed in a disability discrimination claim include:

- loss of earnings (**17.4.3.1**);
- injury to feelings (**17.4.3.2**);
- loss of benefits (**17.4.3.3**);
- pension loss (**17.4.3.4**);
- costs of seeking new employment (**17.4.3.5**);
- loss of statutory rights (**17.4.3.6**);
- personal injury (**17.4.3.7**);
- exemplary damages (**17.4.3.8**);

- aggravated damages (**17.4.3.9**); and
- future loss (**17.4.3.1**).

The general principle is to compensate claimants for losses actually suffered rather than to penalise respondents. Other heads of loss arising in the particular circumstances of the case may also be sought and recovered.

The schedule of loss can be updated at any time and must be current at the time of the hearing. We have produced an example schedule of loss at **Appendix B5**. Further detail of the different heads of loss is contained under remedies (**17.4.3**).

The earlier a schedule of loss is served, the easier it is for both parties to take stock of the value of the claim. Often settlement is facilitated by the schedule of loss as it demonstrates the parameters within which discussion ought to take place.

16.4   DISCLOSURE

At an early stage the tribunal wants to ensure that both parties have access to all the relevant documents. To achieve this it will order the parties to exchange copies of all documents by a certain date. Alternatively it can order the exchange of a list of documents in the possession of the parties and the other side is then asked to request copies of any particular items that it wishes to see.

The best approach often depends on the type of documents involved. In a case where most of the documents are correspondence between the parties, both sides might have a fairly full record and the exchange of lists may avoid duplication. Where policies and emails are involved and the claimant no longer has access to the systems then the exchange of copy documents may be preferred.

Documents relevant to the case will include those which assist a party and those which do not assist it. Both must be disclosed. A party holding a document which is unhelpful to its case is still required to share that document with its opponent under tribunal rules. It has a duty to do so.

On consideration of the disclosure provided by the other side, there may be documents which appear to be missing, for example emails which have no reply or, more tellingly, emails which are a reply where the originating email has not been provided. If documents can be identified which appear to be missing, a request should be made to the other side that it provides copies of the same.

If a document is not voluntarily disclosed despite a request then the party seeking specific disclosure may make an application to the tribunal for specific disclosure. Such an application should be made under the Employment Tribunals Rules of Procedure, rules 10 and 11 and should contain sufficient detail to identify the missing document and an explanation as to why the document is believed to be relevant. Any such application should comply with rule 11 in relation to notification to the other side if it is represented.

The duty of disclosure is ongoing. Any relevant document coming to the attention of a party during the course of the proceedings, even as late as when the tribunal has retired to consider its judgment, must be disclosed to the other side.

At the time of writing, the Equality Act 2010, s.138 provides for a questionnaire process to enable a claimant to ask specific questions of the respondent in relation to a discrimination claim. The process obliges the respondent to provide the information or risk an adverse inference being drawn by the failure to do so. The questionnaire procedure is due to be repealed and therefore we have not addressed drafting a questionnaire or its response in this book. The current forms are available on the Government Equalities Office website (**Appendix D**).

It remains a feature of litigation that a party may ask the other party to provide information at any stage. If the party fails to provide the information then a court or tribunal may draw any reasonable inferences from the failure. In the circumstances there is nothing to prohibit an employee writing to an employer and seeking information in relation to, for example, the number of disabled employees, the diversity training available, the number of claims brought against the company, the number of employees on long-term sick leave and so on. If the questions are relevant then a failure to answer may support an inference being drawn by the tribunal.

16.5 PREPARATION OF THE BUNDLE

Once disclosure has taken place the parties are under an obligation to seek to agree the bundle of documents to put in front of the tribunal. This does not need to include all of the documents which have been disclosed and should be limited to relevant documents only. For example, it is not necessary to include the complete employee handbook if the parties agree that only the grievance process is relevant. Taking a pragmatic approach to the preparation of the bundle saves cost and time. If there is a dispute about the relevance of a document then it should usually be included in the bundle. The parties can then address the tribunal on the issue if necessary.

There is a practice in some tribunal regions to place limits on the number of pages which may be included in the bundle. If an order is given to this effect and the bundle will significantly exceed it, efforts should be made to seek to agree with the other side a joint letter to the tribunal explaining the reason. In most situations a tribunal is prepared to consider documents falling outside the limit but if the bundle greatly exceeds the limit and documents are not relied upon in the evidence then the tribunal may address the issue in relation to the question of costs.

16.5.1 Contents of the bundle

A bundle should contain all the agreed documents in chronological order, which should be paginated sequentially. If there are documents which the tribunal will need to refer to on multiple occasions, it is best to make sure that they are accessible, if necessary putting policies and manuals to the back of the bundle to bring emails and grievances to the fore. It is customary to ensure that the ET1 and ET3, including the grounds of complaint and grounds of resistance, are the first documents in the bundle. When inserting emails it is important to include the full trail so there can be no suggestion of any missing parts of the correspondence. If the parties agree, it may be possible to avoid some repetition in relation to email chains.

16.5.2 Bundle index

The bundle should start with a detailed index, usually headed in the same way as the claim (**12.4**) and then containing a table with the first column providing the date of the document in question, the second providing a brief description and the third providing the page number where the document is found in the bundle. Some people also include a document number column as the very first column. It is a matter of personal preference but once the documents are paginated they will usually be referred to by page number and therefore any document number becomes redundant.

Date	Document	Page No.
1 December 2012	ET1	1
27 December 2012	ET3	18
30 March 2002	Claimant's contract of employment	33

16.5.3 Bundle preparation

Preparation of the bundle involves considerable collaboration between the parties or their representatives. It is helpful if one party has conduct of preparing the bundle so that work is not duplicated. Very often the task of preparing the bundle falls to or is given to the respondent, who may have the majority of the documents to begin with and is likely to have access to photocopiers and legal representation to assist with the task.

16.5.4 Bundle costs

The cost of preparing the bundle may be shared between the parties. If this is the proposed approach, it is advisable to divide the task such that both parties prepare an equal number of bundles. The alternative is that one party prepares all the bundles and passes on half of the cost to the other party. On occasion this can lead to unnecessary and frustrating disputes about the costs charged for copying.

Six copies of the bundle are required in total. The simplest approach therefore is for the party with the conduct of preparing the bundle to produce three copies. One copy is for themselves, one for the other side and one for the witness table at the hearing. The other party then makes three copies from their bundle for the three tribunal members to use at the hearing.

If there is a CMD then the issue of preparing the bundles, who will do it and cost distribution may all be agreed at this stage and included in the order issued by the tribunal.

16.6 WITNESS STATEMENTS

16.6.1 Purpose of a witness statement

A witness statement is the record of the evidence which the witness wishes to give in the case. It should be focused on the factual issues which the tribunal will need to decide and it should not stray into opinion or commentary. It is, however, sometimes necessary and helpful to set out some background material which is not directly relevant to the claim but provides important context.

It is common practice that a witness statement is drafted with often significant assistance from a legal adviser. This is understood by the tribunal and does not cause difficulty provided that the witness is happy with the evidence contained within the statement, including the language used.

A witness statement must be prepared by anyone who is going to give oral evidence at the hearing. A statement from a person who is not going to attend and give oral evidence may be read but will not be given much weight as the other party will not have an opportunity to challenge the evidence by cross-examination.

The CMD order will say when witness statements are to be exchanged. It is usual for parties to exchange statements on the same day. This may be a fixed period after the bundle is prepared or a fixed date prior to the hearing. Parties must then bring signed copies of their statement to the tribunal. In discrimination claims the hearing is dealt with by a full three-person tribunal so four copies of statements must be brought to the tribunal. For a pre-hearing review a judge sits alone and therefore only two copies are required.

16.6.2 Format of a witness statement

Witness statements should be double spaced with numbered paragraphs and with the standard document header. Where documents are mentioned which appear in the bundle of documents, these should be referenced by the page number in the bundle. At the end of the statement, the statement of truth should be set out with space for the witness to sign and date it.

IN THE LONDON SOUTH EMPLOYMENT TRIBUNAL

CASE No. 3112012/2012

BETWEEN

MRS ELEANOR TANG

Claimant

-and-
(1) PERFECT PACKAGING LIMITED
(2) MR IAN MORRIS

Respondents

WITNESS STATEMENT OF MRS GLADYS MOFFETT

I, Mrs Gladys Moffett, of Perfect Packaging Limited, Units 2-7 Coningsby Industrial Estate, Lincoln, will say as follows:

1. I am employed by the First Respondent as the HR Manager. I have held this position since 1998.
2. I make this statement in relation to the claims of disability discrimination brought by the Claimant. The facts stated in this statement are within my own knowledge. Where matters are not within my direct knowledge I have set this out and I believe them to be true.
3. I was involved in the Claimant's recruitment and general day-to-day management in terms of processing holiday requests, promotions and so on. In preparing this statement I have reviewed the Claimant's file and see that neither in her application form nor in her pre-employment health questionnaire has she disclosed any disability (pages 24–25 of the bundle).
4. [*Further facts to be inserted as necessary.*]

The matters set out in this witness statement are true to the best of my knowledge and belief.

Signed . . . .

Dated . . . .

16.7 OTHER ORDERS

The tribunal has wide powers under the Employment Tribunals Rules of Procedure, rule 10 to manage the preparation and conduct of hearings. Orders may be made dealing with many different issues. They may be made in response to an application from either side or by the tribunal of its own volition. It is impossible to provide an exhaustive list but examples of common orders include:

- provision of further information (**16.7.1**);
- preparation of a Scott Schedule (**16.7.2**);

- preparation of a chronology (**16.7.3**); and
- preparation of a cast list (**16.7.4**).

16.7.1 Provision of further information

Where an element of the claim or response is unclear, an order may be made to compel the relevant party to provide further details. For example, it may be necessary to identify a comparator or provide details of the legitimate aim that is relied upon. Properly drafted pleadings should avoid this difficulty (**Chapters 12 and 13**).

If the answer to the request for further information is straightforward, it may be supplied in a simple letter or email. If it is more complex then it may be necessary to amend the pleadings or produce a table or schedule of information.

Where extensive further information is provided, it may be that there needs to be provision for the other party to respond, perhaps by amending their grounds of complaint or grounds of resistance.

When documents are amended, steps should be taken to ensure that the changes are made clear. Original text which is to be deleted should remain visible but with a single straight line through it to indicate its deletion. New text should be underlined to indicate that it is new information. Legal representatives refer to this as 'redlining' since changes are usually marked in red. The tribunal does not require participants to comply with legal convention beyond their level of expertise. It will suffice for litigants in person to make clear the changes they have made.

16.7.2 Scott Schedules

Scott Schedules are sometimes ordered when there are a number of allegations and a tabular summary is required for ease of reference and navigation through the claims. In these circumstances it will be usual for the parties to agree the column headings, sometimes with input from the tribunal. The general matters to be included may be:

- a description of the allegation;
- the date of the alleged events;
- the alleged perpetrator(s);
- what type of discrimination is alleged;
- where victimisation is relied upon, what is the relevant protected act; and
- whether the allegation is admitted and, if not, any defence relied upon.

The usual process is for the claimant to start the schedule and send it to the respondent to complete the response. A sample Scott Schedule is provided at **Appendix B6**.

16.7.3 Chronology

In some cases where events take place over an extended period or the timing of allegations is important, an agreed chronology may be ordered. When a chronology is ordered, it is common for the order to state who is to produce the first draft. If items on the chronology are disputed, this should be clearly stated. If the chronology cannot be agreed, it should be set out in such a way that the tribunal can see the areas of dispute.

It is always open to either party to produce a chronology whether or not one has been ordered and consideration should be given to doing so if it will assist the tribunal. A chronology may follow a similar format to the bundle index (**16.5.2**) but it should focus on relevant issues and not get drawn into repeating the index with every email and note recorded.

16.7.4 Cast list

A cast list is a list of relevant individuals along with a brief description of their role. For example, it might state 'Mrs Manager, Finance Manager, heard the Claimant's grievance'. If the list is extensive it would be appropriate to place witnesses at the top and then others in a sensible order, whether alphabetical, in order of seniority or by reference to when they appear in the chronology.

16.8 CONCLUSION

Having considered the various steps necessary to prepare a case for a hearing, in the next chapter we look at what happens at a full merits hearing.

CHAPTER 17

The hearing

When all the preparation is complete, the day of the hearing arrives. In this chapter we look the usual running order (**17.1**), adjustments to the hearing process (**17.2**), adjournments (**17.3**), remedies (**17.4**) and, briefly, the review (**17.5**) and appeal processes (**17.6**). We conclude with a brief mention of costs (**17.7**). This rough guide is no substitute for having an experienced representative at the hearing to conduct cross-examination, make submissions and address any queries from the judge. Litigation is unpredictable and therefore we could not possibly cover all eventualities in a book of this nature. The idea is to provide a general flavour.

17.1 RUNNING ORDER

17.1.1 Reading time

The current practice is for tribunals to take a little time at the start of a hearing to read witness statements and key documents. In a simple case this may be done without seeing the parties first. In more complicated cases there is normally an agreement for a period of reading (sometimes this can last as long as a few days) and a reading list may be agreed between the parties in advance so that the tribunal spends some time familiarising itself with the case before the parties are required to attend. For many cases which fall between these extremes, the tribunal will see the parties and discuss with the representatives the timetable for the hearing and what documents they should read before sending the parties out while they read the appropriate documents. If the documents are brief, the tribunal may ask the parties to wait in the room while they read.

17.1.2 Opening the case

It is rare in the employment tribunal for there to be anything by way of formal opening submissions although some representatives may hand up a written skeleton argument setting out the issues in the case.

It is common for the tribunal judge to go through the issues as agreed at any CMD or, if there has not been a CMD, to agree with the parties the issues to be decided in the case. In **Chapter 12** we looked at the different elements of discrimination claims. These will form a helpful checklist when looking at the issues the tribunal will need to determine.

There may be other issues which need to be discussed with the parties, for example if one side is objecting to a document being included in the bundle, the tribunal might be asked to determine whether the document can be included at the start of the hearing.

17.1.3 Evidence

The next stage in the process is to hear the witness evidence from the parties. In discrimination claims the usual running order of witnesses is that claimants give their evidence first, followed by any witnesses that the claimant may be calling. Then the respondent's witnesses give their evidence.

17.1.3.1 Evidence in chief

Witnesses are asked to stand and affirm or swear a religious oath that they will tell the truth. For the rest of their evidence they are seated. The witness is asked to confirm their statement is truthful. It may then be appropriate to seek the permission of the tribunal to ask a few supplemental questions to address specific issues not previously covered in the evidence. The tribunal orders say that the witness statement should give all the evidence of the witness and therefore if supplemental questions are required it is important to be clear about what needs to be asked and why. Any supplemental questions must be open and not suggest the evidence for the witness to give. The written statement and any supplemental questions form the evidence in chief for that witness.

17.1.3.2 Cross-examination

The other side then has an opportunity to cross-examine on areas of dispute. Cross-examination should be closed questions focused on the issues in the case and must give witnesses an opportunity to respond to the case against them. Either at the end of the cross-examination or at any point throughout the evidence, the tribunal may interject with questions of its own.

17.1.3.3 Re-examination

The final stage of a witness's evidence is re-examination. This is where a party's own representative is given an opportunity to ask any questions arising from matters raised in cross-examination. Re-examination should be open questions. A party cannot lead its own witness. After re-examination the witness should be formally released by the judge, which means that the witness is free to leave the tribunal if he or she wishes.

17.1.4 Closing submissions

When all the evidence has been heard, both sides have an opportunity to make closing submissions on the issues in the case and in particular how these issues should be determined. In cases which run across several days it is common for legal representatives to prepare written closing submissions. It is also not uncommon for the tribunal to request that written submissions are prepared by legal representatives. This can save considerable time during the hearing and allows the tribunal to have a good record of what is said by each party.

If there are cases which are relevant to the proceedings then it is important that the parties raise these during the closing submissions and, if necessary, provide copies of the cases to the tribunal.

In some cases there is not time to hear oral closing submissions. The parties and the tribunal will discuss the best way to provide closing submissions. Sometimes the parties will return for a further day to present oral submissions. Sometimes the parties will supply written submissions by a future date for the tribunal to consider. Where this issue arises, the tribunal will discuss the best approach with the parties and the timetable for actions at the close of the evidence.

17.1.5 Deliberation and reserved judgments

It is usual for the tribunal to retire after closing submissions to deliberate and consider its judgment. If the case has run to time then the parties will adjourn until an agreed time and when the tribunal is ready the parties will be called in to hear the oral judgment.

When the case has overrun and there is no time left in the listing for deliberation, the parties may be sent home. When this happens the tribunal reserves its judgment, sending it out in the post when it is ready. If the tribunal members need to arrange a further time to meet and consider the matter, it can be several weeks or months before the judgment is received by the parties. In this situation the tribunal will arrange a date for further deliberation and inform the parties of the date so that they are aware that no decision will be made before that date. The parties do not attend for deliberations, which are held in private.

17.2 ADJUSTMENTS TO THE HEARING PROCESS

Where a claimant, or indeed a respondent or witness, has a disability it may be necessary to make adjustments to the usual tribunal process to accommodate the disability. The adjustment will depend very much on the individual and the disability.

Examples of adjustments which may be appropriate include

- Statements provided in large font or in braille
- Arranging the room so that the witness and/or claimant is able to lip read all participants
- Arranging for a lip speaker or a lip reader to assist a witness
- Dividing the day into short, manageable chunks
- Permitting a witness to stand or walk around to relieve pain
- Starting late or finishing early to avoid difficulties on public transport
- Allocating a tribunal room which is close to the lift or waiting room so movement within the building is limited
- Allocating a tribunal room with sufficient space for a wheelchair
- Allocating a tribunal room with a loop system
- Hearing the evidence only on every other day or on Monday–Tuesday and Thursday–Friday so that there is recuperation time built in
- Providing more time for adjournments and for taking instructions
- Making arrangements to shield a witness from other individuals

---

Many of these adjustments require the tribunal to plan ahead with the allocation of the room and arrangements for professional assistance. Requests for adjustments should be set out in the ET1, ET3, grounds of complaint or grounds of resistance, and followed up at CMDs so that all arrangements are in place at the start of the hearing. A failure to do so can cause wasted costs and unnecessary delay. It is always possible to write to the tribunal and ask for adjustments to be made. It is the responsibility of the party seeking the adjustment to contact the tribunal to make the arrangements. Tribunals are very accommodating in making adjustments for witnesses and parties with disabilities. The more notice they have, the more they are able to help.

17.3 ADJOURNMENTS

Where a litigant's presence is required for the fair trial of a case but the litigant is unable to attend through no fault of his or her own, an adjournment will usually be granted, however inconvenient it may be to the tribunal or the other parties. The tribunal must be satisfied that the inability of the litigant to be present is genuine. The onus is on the applicant for an adjournment to prove the need for such an adjournment.

The claimant in *Teinaz* v. *London Borough of Wandsworth* [2002] EWCA Civ 1040 was refused an adjournment even though a GP's letter was provided which said that the claimant was unfit to attend work or the tribunal. The EAT overturned the tribunal's decision. The EAT's decision was upheld by the Court of Appeal. The tribunal should have taken notice of the medical evidence that said the claimant was not fit to attend.

If there is some evidence that a litigant is unfit to attend, in particular if there is evidence that on medical grounds the litigant has been advised by a qualified practitioner not to attend, but the tribunal or court has doubts as to whether the evidence is genuine or sufficient, then the tribunal or court has a discretion whether or not to give a direction such as would enable the doubts to be resolved. Thus, one possibility is to direct that further evidence be provided promptly. Another is that the party seeking the adjournment should be invited to authorise the legal representatives for the other side to have access to the doctor giving the advice in question. The advocates on both sides can do their part in assisting the tribunal faced with such a problem in order to achieve a just result.

Andreou v. The Lord Chancellor's Department [2002] EWCA Civ 1192

The Lord Chancellor's Department successfully appealed the EAT's decision to allow Mrs Andreou's appeal against a strike out of her claim. The claimant had failed to produce medical evidence in support of an adjournment application in spite of applying for an adjournment on the basis of ill health. She sent a medical certificate in which her general practitioner signed her off work for 13 weeks with anxiety and stress. The tribunal did not refuse an adjournment outright. They took the view that the medical certificate was inadequate because it did not say that Mrs Andreou was unfit to attend court, but they adjourned for a week ordering Mrs Andreou to produce, in effect, a proper medical report. She did not do that and her claim was struck out.

More recently, in *Ashton & Ashton* v. *Burbage and District Constitutional Club* [2012] UKEAT/0496/11, UKEAT/0497/11 the EAT has overturned the decision of a tribunal which refused an adjournment on grounds of ill health (stress). The claimants needed two months to address their stress before they would be fit for a hearing. They had medical evidence from their GP that they were not fit to attend. The tribunal said it would proceed nonetheless but the EAT overturned the decision and said in the circumstances an adjournment was reasonable.

In some circumstances the tribunal may have reason to postpone, adjourn or vacate a scheduled hearing, for example where another case has overrun or where the judge or a panel member has fallen ill. The tribunal will take steps to notify the parties and ask for any dates to avoid so that the hearing can be relisted. This is not uncommon in some of the busier tribunal centres.

17.4 REMEDIES

The range of remedies available is extensive. We have addressed the most common issues here. Useful guidance can be found on HM Courts and Tribunals Service website (**Appendix D**). What follows is an overview of common issues and steps in the process.

17.4.1 Determining remedy

Tribunals will deal with the issue of liability first and then consider remedy separately. Sometimes this means a completely separate hearing for remedy as there may not be time within the full hearing to address the issue. Sometimes it means that after judgment is delivered in relation to liability there is a brief adjournment and then evidence is taken on the issue of remedy.

17.4.2 Evidence in relation to remedy

The key information considered at the remedy stage is the schedule of loss and supporting evidence (**16.3**). There may be further evidence from the claimant in relation to their efforts to mitigate their loss by searching for a new job and there may be cross-examination on this issue.

If there is a personal injury claim then it may be necessary to hear from the medical expert again in relation to the extent of the injury and the prognosis. To save expert time it is common for all issues involving the expert to be addressed in one go, so questions of causation and severity may all have been addressed during the course of evidence on liability.

17.4.3 Financial claims

The vast majority of remedies in the tribunal are awards of financial compensation. There are a number of different heads of loss including:

- loss of earnings (**17.4.3.1**);
- injury to feelings (**17.4.3.2**);
- loss of benefits (**17.4.3.3**);
- pension loss (**17.4.3.4**);
- costs of seeking new employment (**17.4.3.5**);
- loss of statutory rights (**17.4.3.6**);
- personal injury (**17.4.3.7**);
- exemplary damages (**17.4.3.8**); and
- aggravated damages (**17.4.3.9**).

17.4.3.1   Loss of earnings

If a claimant has lost his or her job then he or she may have a loss of earnings claim. If there has been an unfair dismissal then there is a basic award calculated according to a statutory formula contained in ERA 1996, ss.119–122 and then a compensatory award under s.123. The compensatory award is such as the tribunal considers 'just and equitable'.

It is usual to set out the loss by reference to time periods. The period up to the hearing is one period. If the claimant has obtained a new job then the period prior to the new job should be differentiated from the period after the new job. Where there is a difference in pay between the old job and the new job, there may be a claim for ongoing loss. It is also possible to claim for future loss after the tribunal hearing. Each period in the calculation should be clearly laid out and explained if necessary.

A tribunal will need to be satisfied that the claimant has taken sufficient steps to mitigate their loss, for example by looking for a new job. It is customary for the claimant to produce a diary or witness statement demonstrating his or her efforts to obtain new employment and to support this with printouts of job adverts and application forms. Where the claimant has been unable to actively seek new work due to ill health, medical evidence should be adduced in support. It may also be appropriate to include an explanation in the claimant's witness statement or in a supplementary statement. The burden of showing a failure to mitigate is on the respondent and the tribunals expect to see evidence in support of such a submission. In practice this will often lead to a bundle of job adverts and postings during the relevant time period. These jobs should be jobs which were suitable for the claimant.

There may be a claim for loss of earnings even where the claimant did not lose his or her job but has suffered a reduction in earnings, a lost promotion or a lost bonus payment as a result of the discrimination. It may also be the case that discriminatory conduct has led to a psychiatric illness which prevents the person working. In this scenario the claimant may claim for any difference between sick pay and full pay, as well as injury to feelings and the other applicable heads of loss.

17.4.3.2   Injury to feelings

In discrimination cases the usual remedy for the discrimination is an award for injury to feelings, along with compensation for any loss flowing from the discriminatory act. Injury to feelings is assessed according to three bands. The bands were established by the Court of Appeal in *Vento* v. *Chief Constable of West Yorkshire Police* [2002] EWCA Civ 1871 and updated in *Da'Bell* v. *National Society for the Prevention of Cruelty to Children* [2010] IRLR 19 (EAT). The lowest band is up to £6,000 and is designed to deal with cases involving isolated or limited acts of discrimination. The middle band is £6,000 to £18,000. This is for claims which are not severe enough to feature in the top band and yet are more serious than the lowest category. The upper band is from £18,000 to £30,000. This is reserved for the most serious cases, such as where there has been a lengthy campaign of discriminatory conduct.

In exceptional cases it may be possible to recover in excess of £30,000. However, according to the Employment Tribunal Service statistics from 2011/12, the median award in a claim for disability discrimination was £8,928. It is therefore clear that it is not common to reach the upper band for injury to feelings, let alone exceed it.

The tribunal has a discretion as to the award that is made and may take into account evidence from the claimant as to the impact of the conduct, as well as any mitigating or aggravating features.

17.4.3.3 Loss of employment benefits

Loss of benefits can be recovered in the same way as loss of earnings. Benefits might include private health insurance, dental cover, share benefit schemes, travel concessions, lunch allowances and so on. Efforts should be made to calculate the value of the lost benefit. Reference to the value of obtaining the same benefit on the open market may assist in demonstrating the loss suffered. It is for the claimant to make the relevant enquiries if he or she is asking the tribunal to make an award in this respect.

17.4.3.4 Pension loss

Where claimants have lost their job, they may have also lost out on a valuable pension scheme. Calculating pension loss is a complicated process in tribunal claims. Where the issue arises, parties are referred to the guidelines *Compensation for Loss of Pension Rights* (3rd Edn, 2003) produced on behalf of the HM Courts and Tribunals Service and available on its website (**Appendix D**).

17.4.3.5 Costs of seeking new employment

A claimant who has been seeking new employment and has incurred costs in doing so may seek to recover these costs on the basis that they are costs caused by the unfair treatment. Costs might include printing costs, travel costs to go to interviews and so on. If a claimant intends to seek recovery of these costs then receipts and records of expenditure must be kept. The costs incurred must be reasonable.

17.4.3.6 Loss of statutory rights

Where a claimant's employment has ceased in circumstances which are found to be unfair, the tribunal has a discretion to award a sum to reflect the fact that it will take two years for the employee to accrue full employment rights with any new employer. This sum is usually a nominal sum between £250 and £500 and is awarded at the tribunal's discretion.

17.4.3.7 Personal injury

It is possible to recover compensation for personal injury found to have arisen from issues at work. Where it is claimed that psychiatric harm has arisen as a result of the way in which the employee has been treated at work, it may be appropriate to consider a claim in relation to this injury in the tribunals. A personal injury claim can only be brought in the tribunals if it is ancillary to another employment claim. A stand-alone personal injury claim must be brought in the civil courts.

Medical evidence will be required in order to substantiate not only the fact and extent of the injury but also the causation of the injury. The burden is on the claimant to show the link between the treatment and the injury. This can be a high hurdle to meet in practice.

The compensation for a claim under this head of loss is based on the Judicial College guidance *Guidelines for the Assessment of General Damages in Personal Injury Cases* (11th Edn, 2012). Factors taken into account include:

- the impact on the injured person's ability to cope with life and work;
- the effect on the injured person's relationships with family and friends;
- any medical treatment available and being received;
- future vulnerability;
- prognosis; and
- the nature of any abuse and its duration.

The four categories of award for psychiatric injury are:

1. Severe – where the problems are serious and the prognosis very poor (£39,150–£82,750).
2. Moderately severe – where the problems are significant but the prognosis is better (£13,650–£39,150).
3. Moderate – where significant progress has already been made and the prognosis is good (£4,200–£13,650).
4. Less severe – where the problems are of a limited duration (£1,100–£4,200).

The guidelines suggest that in cases of work-related stress leading to psychiatric injury, where an individual is unlikely to be able to return to comparable employment, the award is likely to fall in the moderately severe category. For many this will also make loss of earnings a more significant claim if their future earnings capacity is limited.

A discount will be given to any award to reflect contributory causes. For example, if severe depression was caused both by discriminatory treatment at work and by a pre-existing condition or, for example, by abusive conduct from a partner at home, the award will be reduced by a percentage to reflect the relative contributions.

17.4.3.8 Exemplary damages

Exemplary damages are an exception to the general rule on compensating the claimant rather than penalising the respondent. They are only awarded in very rare cases: either where there are oppressive, arbitrary or unconstitutional actions by servants of the government or where the respondent's conduct was calculated to make a profit for him or herself. It is difficult to see these requirements ever being met in the private employment context. It will be a rare case where they are met in a public sector employment context.

17.4.3.9 Aggravated damages

Aggravated damages address a situation where the respondent's conduct in committing the discriminatory acts was exceptional conduct that was highhanded, malicious, insulting or oppressive. The reference to exceptional conduct is to recognise that this must be conduct which takes the case beyond the ordinary run of discrimination cases. A summary of the circumstances in which an aggravated damages award may be made was given in *Singh* v. *University Hospital NHS Trust* [2002] UKEAT/1409/01.

There is scope for overlap between an award for injury to feelings and aggravated damages. The tribunals will not award compensation twice for the same conduct. If the injury to feelings award includes an element for the respondent's failure to investigate the complaints then there will not be an award for aggravated damages in relation to this head of loss. The total of both awards should reflect fair compensation for the injury suffered by the claimant. In most discrimination claims this is considered by the tribunal to be adequately covered by the injury to feelings award.

17.4.4 Non-financial remedies

17.4.4.1 Tribunal recommendations

At the time of writing tribunals have the power to make recommendations where discrimination has been found. This provision was due to be reformed by the Enterprise and Regulatory Reform Bill but for now looks safe.

17.4.4.2 Reinstatement or re-engagement

An employee who has lost his or her job may also seek reinstatement or re-engagement. Since both of these remedies involve a return to the workplace where the discrimination occurred, it unlikely that this will be a popular or practical option in all but very large employers. The power to order reinstatement or re-engagement is found at ERA 1996, ss.112–117.

17.5 THE REVIEW PROCESS

Under the Employment Tribunals Rules of Procedure, rules 33–36, tribunals may review their own decisions in certain circumstances. An application for review may be brought on any of the following grounds found in rule 34:

(a) the decision was wrongly made as a result of an administrative error;
(b) a party did not receive notice of the proceedings leading to the decision;
(c) the decision was made in the absence of a party;
(d) fresh evidence has become available and could not have been reasonably known of or foreseen at the time; or
(e) a review is required in the interests of justice.

An application for a review must be made within 14 days of the decision being sent to the parties (rule 35). Where a judgment is being reviewed, it will be referred to the same judge and tribunal that heard the claim. Where a default judgment is being reviewed, it may be considered by any judge.

17.6 THE APPEAL PROCESS

Detailed guidance on the appeal process is available on HM Courts and Tribunals Service website. The details provided here are by way of overview only.

An appeal from a decision of the tribunal is made to the EAT. It is possible to appeal on grounds that there is a mistake of law or that the decision was perverse. It is not possible to appeal simply because the decision is unacceptable to the losing party or because a discretion has been exercised in favour of one party over another. Questions of fact are not appropriate grounds for appeal. It is the tribunal's remit to determine on the facts which party's evidence it prefers and the EAT cannot interfere with this once the facts have been determined.

An appeal must be made within 42 days of the judgment being sent to the parties. This will be the same day of the week as the day the judgment was sent, so if it was sent on a Thursday, the deadline will be a Thursday six weeks later. The EAT strictly enforces the time limit. All parts of the appeal must be received no later than 4 pm on the day of the deadline. An incomplete set of documents or documents received after 4 pm on the day of the deadline will render the appeal out of time.

The documents which must be received by the EAT are:

- a fully completed notice of appeal;
- the judgment, decision, direction or order being appealed;
- any written reasons for the judgment or order;
- the ET1, and grounds of complaint if separate;
- the ET3, and grounds of resistance if separate; and
- any application for a review.

Appeals are subject to a first sift where those determined as having no reasonable grounds for appeal will be dismissed. If this happens the appellant can seek to have an oral hearing to obtain permission for an appeal.

An appeal hearing before the EAT can lead to one of three outcomes:

(a)   the appeal is rejected;
(b)   the appeal is accepted and judgment is substituted; or
(c)   the appeal is accepted and the matter remitted to tribunal for further determination.

When a matter is remitted it may be to the same tribunal or a fresh tribunal, depending on the circumstances of the appeal.

17.7 COSTS

The general rule in the tribunal is that costs are not recoverable by the successful party. Unlike in the civil courts, in tribunal the parties bear their own costs. The exception to this rule is where a party has acted vexatiously, abusively, disruptively or otherwise unreasonably in the bringing or conducting of proceedings, or if the claim was misconceived. This power is contained in the Employment Tribunals Rules of Procedure, rule 40. Under rule 40 costs may also be awarded where the conduct of a party causes an adjournment of proceedings. Costs are still rarely awarded in the tribunal although in recent years there is a growing trend of awarding costs in tribunals where the conduct of either party is unreasonable. In certain circumstances legal representatives may seek an order for wasted costs against their opponent. This is where the unreasonable conduct of a representative has led to increased unnecessary costs for a party. Again such orders are rare. More information can be found on HM Courts and Tribunals Service website (**Appendix D**).

17.8 CONCLUSION

This concludes our discussion of litigation case management. What follows is a number of sample documents based on a fictional scenario. The facts can be found in **Appendices B1** and **B2**. We hope that these sample documents will assist in demonstrating how the case management works. They should also assist in clarifying the various documents common to many tribunal claims for disability discrimination.

Case study: sample correspondence

Summary of rights under the Access to Medical Reports Act 1988

*Sample information to be supplied to an employee when seeking access to medical reports – for more information see **7.2**. If a copy of the employee's medical records or medical report from his or her current physician is sought then this information should be supplied along with the correspondence in **Appendices A2** and **A3**. If the employee is being asked to attend a medical assessment then this information should be supplied along with the correspondence in **Appendices A4** and **A5**.*

ACCESS TO MEDICAL REPORTS ACT 1988: SUMMARY OF EMPLOYEE'S RIGHTS

This is a summary of your principal rights under the Access to Medical Reports Act 1988 which sets out the procedure for obtaining medical reports for employment or insurance purposes from a doctor who has been or is looking after you, usually your General Practitioner (GP) or a specialist consultant responsible for your care. The Act also applies to any report which is prepared by a doctor we ask you to see. The term 'Doctor' is used to refer to your GP, a specialist consultant or a doctor by whom you consent to be examined.

*[We are seeking your consent to apply to your [GP/consultant, [*insert name*]] for [access to your medical records/a report on your current state of health and its effect on the work which we employ you to undertake].]

OR

*[We are seeking your consent to be examined by Doctor [*insert name*] for the purposes of producing a report on your current state of health and its effect on the work which we employ you to undertake.]

You have three options. Please complete and return the enclosed consent form indicating your decision.

Option 1

You may consent to the application and indicate that you do not wish to see a copy of the report before it is supplied to us.

If you change your mind after the application has been made, you will still be able to contact the Doctor in writing to ask to see a copy of the report. If the report has not yet been sent to us, the Doctor must delay sending it for 21 days following receipt of your written request to allow time for you to arrange to see it.

185

Whether or not you decide to see the report before it is sent, you still have the right to ask the Doctor for a copy of the report at any time up to six months after it has been supplied to us. The Doctor is entitled to make a reasonable charge for this.

Option 2

You may consent to the application, but indicate that you wish to see the report before it is supplied to us. If you choose this option, you must contact the Doctor directly to request the report, as it will not be sent to you automatically.

Once we receive your consent form, we will inform the Doctor by letter that you wish to see the report and will copy the letter to you. The Doctor will allow 21 days for you to see it before supplying it to us. You should contact the Doctor directly to make arrangements to see the report after you return the enclosed forms if you have chosen this option. The Doctor is entitled to make a reasonable charge for this. If the Doctor has not heard from you in writing within 21 days of the report being prepared, he or she will assume you do not wish to see the report and that you consent to its being supplied directly to us.

If you arrange to see the report before it is sent to us and there is anything in it that you consider incorrect or misleading, you can write to the Doctor to ask him or her to amend the report. If the Doctor refuses to amend it, you may:

- withdraw your consent for the report to be issued to us;
- ask the Doctor to attach to the report a statement setting out your objections/views; or
- agree to the report being issued to us unchanged.

NOTE: The Doctor is not obliged to show you any parts of the report that he or she believes might cause serious harm to your physical or mental health or that of others. Neither does the Doctor have to show you information about other people without their permission. If the Doctor limits your access to the report for any of these reasons, he or she will tell you.

Option 3

You may refuse your consent to our application.

Please indicate this decision on the enclosed form(**) and return it to us. You are advised to keep this note for future reference.

* Select and amend the appropriate paragraph.

** The enclosed form should be either **Appendix A3** or **Appendix A5** depending on the request made.

APPENDIX A2

Letter to employee requesting consent for medical report or access to medical records

*When an employer seeks a copy of the employee's medical records or a report from his or her treating physician then this letter should be sent to the employee to request his or her consent. This letter should be accompanied by the correspondence in **Appendices A1** and **A3**. This letter does not address the situation where an employee is asked to attend a medical assessment (see **Appendices A4** and **A5**).*

Dear John,

Re: Access to medical records/medical report

We would like to seek your consent to access your medical records and obtain a medical report in relation to your current medical condition.

Under the Access to Medical Reports Act (AMRA) 1988, you can elect to give consent, refuse consent or give consent on the condition that you see the records/report prior to it being sent to us. We enclose a summary of your rights under AMRA 1988. Please read this carefully and indicate your choice on the form (*).

If you want to discuss the contents of this letter or the relevant process please contact human resources.

Kind regards

XYZ Inc

* The form mentioned is **Appendix A3**.

APPENDIX A3

Employee consent to obtaining medical records/report

*This is a letter to be completed by an employee but supplied by an employer giving or refusing consent to the employer obtaining a copy of the employee's medical records or a medical report. This letter would be sent by an employer with the correspondence in **Appendices A1** and **A2**. The employee should complete the options, sign and return it to the employer. Consent to processing sensitive personal information is required pursuant to the Data Protection Act 1998.*

To XYZ Inc

I have read the summary of my rights under the Access to Medical Reports Act 1988 and understand my rights.

Please select one of the following two options and delete as appropriate.

[I consent to my employer applying to my GP or consultant for a medical report and/or my medical records and any verbal or written updates required subsequently and I consent to the processing of sensitive personal data relating to my health for these purposes.]

OR

[I do not consent to my employer applying to my GP or the specialist with responsibility for my care for a medical report and/or my medical records and I do not consent to the processing of sensitive personal data relating to my health for these purposes.]

Please select one of the following two options and delete as appropriate.

[I wish to see a copy of the medical report before it is supplied to my employer. I understand that I must contact my GP or the consultant within 21 days of the date of my employer's application for the report to make arrangements to see it.]

OR

[I do not wish to see a copy of the medical report before it is supplied to my employer.]

Signed: . . . .

Dated: . . . .

Letter to request medical assessment

*When an employer is requesting that an employee should attend a medical assessment, this letter should be sent to the employee to request his or her consent. This letter should be accompanied by the correspondence in **Appendices A1** and **A5**.*

Dear John,

RE: Access to medical records/medical report

We would like to seek your consent to attend an examination with [*specialist's name*] of [*specialist's practice*], in relation to your current medical condition. An appointment has been arranged for [*date*] at [*address and contact details*]. Following the appointment [*specialist's name*] will prepare a report for us on your condition, your prognosis and how this affects the work you do for us. [*Specialist's name*] will address, if appropriate, any adjustments which we may need to make in order to assist you in returning to work.

Under the Access to Medical Reports Act (AMRA) 1988 you can elect to give consent, refuse consent or give consent on the condition that you see the report prior to it being sent to us. We enclose a summary of your rights under AMRA 1988. Please read this carefully and indicate your choice on the form enclosed.

If you want to discuss the contents of this letter or the relevant process, please contact human resources.

Kind regards

XYZ Inc

Employee consent to attending medical assessment

*This is a letter to be completed by an employee but supplied by an employer giving or refusing consent to attending a medical assessment. As part of the assessment consent is sought from the employee for access to his or her medical records and/or a report from his or her GP. This letter would be sent by an employer with the correspondence in **Appendices A1** and **A4**. The employee should complete the options, sign and return it to the employer.*

To XYZ Inc

Please select one of the following two options.

[I agree to attend an examination with [*specialist's name*] on [*time*] at [*location*] and to the production of any subsequent verbal or written report by him for [*company name*]. I consent to the processing of sensitive personal data relating to my health for these purposes.]

OR

[I do not consent to attending an examination with [*specialist's name*].]

If you have consented to attending the examination, please read the options below and select one of the following two options.

[I understand that [*specialist's name*] may wish to apply to my GP for a medical report and/or my medical records. I have read and understood the enclosed summary of my rights under the Access to Medical Reports Act 1988.

I consent to my employer applying to my GP for my medical records and/or a medical report and I consent to the processing of sensitive personal data relating to my health for these purposes.]

OR

[I do not consent to my employer applying to my GP for my medical records and/or a medical report and I do not consent to the processing of sensitive personal data relating to my health for these purposes.]

Finally if you have consented to the examination, please select one of the following two options.

[I wish to see a copy of the medical report before it is supplied to my employer.]

OR

[I do not wish to see a copy of the medical report before it is supplied to my employer.]

Signed: . . . .

Dated: . . . .

Letter to medical adviser requesting assessment

*The facts in this letter are based on the case study (**Part 2**). If the employee gives consent for his or her employer to seek a report then the employer will need to write to the medical adviser and set out what it would like the report to consider. This is an example of such a letter. More detail is provided at **7.2.3**. Medical advice can be sought at any stage. Sometimes it will be purely in relation to reasonable adjustments and sometimes it will relate to the issue of whether or not the employee is disabled. It may be sought during employment or during the litigation process. The questions asked and advice sought should fit the needs of the parties at the time of the request and should not be extended in a disproportionate manner. This letter addresses issues which go to whether or not John is disabled and also what adjustments, if any, may be appropriate.*

Dear Dr Kram,

RE: John Dixon

We employ John as a senior sales manager. John has recently begun to suffer from depression and has had a period of time off work.

We wish to obtain a report from you in relation to his condition and in particular any changes which we should consider to facilitate his return to full duties. John has consented to the production of the report and his signed consent is enclosed. You will note that John has requested that he sees a copy of the report before it is supplied to us and he will be in touch with you to arrange this.

We would particularly like your assistance on the following points:

1. Please provide details of John's condition, including relevant extracts from his medical records as to when he first began experiencing this condition and what treatment and medication he has received to date.
2. Please provide details of the impact of John's condition on his ability to carry out normal day-to-day activities. Please give examples of what John can and cannot do, and what he can only do with difficulty or modification.
3. John's job involves making sales calls and writing related reports. The sales environment is target-focused. The hours vary considerably on a daily basis. Please consider and advise whether John is fit to perform these duties or any part of them.
4. Please also provide information on the appropriate timescale for implementing any changes to John's work arrangements and when John might expect to be able to return to work.
5. Please provide any other information which you think may assist.

We understand that there will be a charge for the production of this report. Please send your invoice to XYZ Inc at the address above for the attention of [*insert name*]. If you have any queries in relation to the content of the request, please contact human resources on the number provided.

Yours sincerely,

[*insert name*]

For and on behalf of XYZ Inc

cc. John Dixon

Litigation case management: sample documents

APPENDIX B1

Sample grounds of complaint

This information can be included at what is currently section 5.2 of Form ET1 (Your claim) or can be submitted as a separate document at the same time as the ET1 is filed. If a separate rider is used, it must be submitted at the same time as Form ET1. Form ET1 is available from HM Courts and Tribunals Service website at www.justice.gov.uk/tribunals/employment.

IN THE LONDON SOUTH EMPLOYMENT TRIBUNAL

CASE NO.

BETWEEN

MRS ELEANOR TANG

Claimant

-and-

(1) PERFECT PACKAGING LIMITED

(2) MR IAN MORRIS

Respondent(s)

GROUNDS OF COMPLAINT

INTRODUCTION

1. The Claimant commenced employment with the First Respondent as production assistant on 17 April 2008.
2. The First Respondent is a manufacturing company producing bespoke packaging for cosmetics and perfumes.
3. The Claimant enjoyed a number of promotions such that at the time of writing she is the Senior Production Adviser.
4. The Claimant brings the following claims:

   (a) Direct disability discrimination contrary to section 13 of the Equality Act 2010 ('the Equality Act');
   (b) Disability related discrimination contrary to section 15 of the Equality Act;
   (c) Failure to make reasonable adjustments contrary to sections 20 and 21 of the Equality Act;
   (d) Harassment on grounds of disability contrary to section 26 of the Equality Act; and
   (e) Victimisation contrary to section 27 of the Equality Act.

THE CLAIMANT'S DISABILITY

5.   The Claimant suffers from dyslexia. She was diagnosed with dyslexia during her secondary school education in the late 1990s. The Claimant disclosed her dyslexia on her application form to the First Respondent.

BACKGROUND

6.   The Claimant's employment started well, with her receiving a number of promotions in the first few years.

7.   In 2010 the Claimant was assigned to a particularly demanding line producing packaging for celebrity scents, which resulted in a very high workload for the Claimant. Celebrity lines were often changed at short notice requiring substantial work within tight deadlines. Despite the difficulties of the task, the Claimant rose to the challenge and received very positive feedback in her appraisals in November 2010 and November 2011.

8.   In June 2012 the Claimant's line manager changed and her new line manager, the Second Respondent, wanted to introduce a paper-free office. One of the consequences of the Claimant's dyslexia is that she finds reading from a computer screen more difficult than reading from the printed page. In order to minimise this effect, the Claimant had developed a practice of printing the packaging proofs and using a coloured transparency provided by her doctor to manually check the hard copy. She then requested one of her juniors to make the electronic changes. Adopting this approach had ensured that in all the packaging runs the Claimant had managed there had never been any reported problems.

9.   Despite the Claimant explaining the reasons for her approach, the Second Respondent was not happy with the Claimant's insistence on printing the proofs. He removed the Claimant's printer and insisted that she check the documentation on screen.

10. On 2 July 2012 the Claimant requested a meeting with the Second Respondent and the First Respondent's HR manager, Mrs Moffett. In her email requesting the meeting the Claimant explained that due to her dyslexia she required assistance in particular tasks. She wanted to discuss these with the Second Respondent and Mrs Moffett to ensure adjustments could be made going forwards. The Claimant explained that the reason for requesting the meeting at this point in time was the Second Respondent's new requirement that all proofs had to be checked on screen, which the Claimant was finding difficult to comply with.

11. Despite the Claimant's request, no meeting took place. Instead the Second Respondent called a staff meeting of all the production assistants, production advisers and senior production advisers and said that the Claimant had complained about his instruction regarding checking the document on screen and he wanted to know whether anyone else had a problem with this approach or whether it was just the Claimant. The meeting took place on 6 July 2012.

12. The meeting was conducted in an aggressive and hostile manner and the Claimant felt humiliated in front of all of her colleagues. Many of her colleagues knew of the Claimant's dyslexia as she had discussed it with them during her employment. It was common knowledge within the team that the reason the Claimant printed out documentation was to assist her in managing her disability.

13. On 9 July 2012 the Claimant emailed Mrs Moffett to raise a formal grievance about the Second Respondent's conduct. She requested that the grievance was dealt with sensitively because she was anxious to avoid a repeat of the meeting of the previous week.

14. Mrs Moffett told the Claimant that since the Second Respondent was her line manager she would forward the grievance to him in the first instance. The Claimant was alarmed

by this and asked for someone else to deal with the grievance given that it was about the Second Respondent's conduct. Mrs Moffett said that if the Claimant did not like the outcome of the Second Respondent's grievance investigation then she could appeal to his manager.

15. In the circumstances the Claimant was left with no choice but to say to Mrs Moffett that she did not want to pursue her grievance. The Claimant feared that the process adopted would lead to further humiliation and bullying from the Second Respondent. Despite the Claimant indicating that she did not wish the grievance to go any further, Mrs Moffett forwarded a copy of the Claimant's grievance 'for reference' to the Second Respondent along with a note saying 'I have agreed with [the Claimant] that this will go no further and that she has no problem with you after all. It seems that she just got a bit upset over nothing, suggest you chat to her about dyslexia and show you understand. Perhaps arrange for someone else to proof her work as her spelling is unreliable'.

16. The Second Respondent met with the Claimant on 13 July 2012 and showed her the email exchange set out above. He told the Claimant that he did not take kindly to her going behind his back to Mrs Moffett and that in future he would view such conduct as gross misconduct. He said that if the Claimant could not spell properly she should not be doing the job and that he would like to monitor her performance for the next six months. The Second Respondent gave the Claimant a performance monitoring plan which he had completed. The Claimant was required to sign it there and then.

17. After the Claimant's meeting with the Second Respondent she read the performance monitoring plan and, although she disagreed with the content, she did not know how to raise a further complaint since each previous attempt had been unsuccessful. In order to try to comply with the Second Respondent's criteria the Claimant contacted IT to see whether her computer screen could be adjusted so that the colour contrast provided by her transparency could be applied to the screen. IT confirmed that they could do this but required a request form to be sent by the Claimant's line manager.

18. The Claimant emailed the Second Respondent with the completed request form and asked that he forward it to IT in order that they could make the necessary adjustment. The Claimant emailed the request to the Second Respondent on 20 July 2012 and reminded him on 27 July 2012, 3 August 2012 and 10 August 2012. The Second Respondent failed to action the form and on 13 August 2012 told the Claimant to stop contacting him about the issue.

19. Despite the Claimant's best efforts and seeking assistance from supportive colleagues, the Claimant was not able to effectively proof the packaging documentation on screen. As a result there was a mistake on one of the Claimant's product runs in September 2012. The mistake was small, the Claimant had missed an 'l' from 'millilitre', and the first one since the Claimant took on the role in 2010. Despite the relatively minor error, the Second Respondent came across to the Claimant on 14 September 2012 and shouted at her in front of the whole office. The First Respondent's offices are open plan. The Second Respondent shouted at the Claimant saying that she had to learn to spell, that she was stupid and that as a punishment she would have to write millilitre 20 times on the team white board. The Claimant was utterly humiliated by the Second Respondent's outburst and was crying throughout as she wrote on the board.

20. In October 2012 the Claimant had another small error on some product packaging. On this occasion the Second Respondent was away on annual leave at the time and the Claimant's colleague spotted the error and assisted her in correcting the production run so only a small number of products were affected.

21. In November 2012 the Claimant had her annual appraisal with the Second Respondent. He told her that since she had been on the performance monitoring plan she had made two fundamental mistakes in her work and therefore he was going to issue her with a formal written warning and continue to monitor her for the next six months. The Second Respondent informed the Claimant that a further mistake could lead to her dismissal.

The Second Respondent gave the Claimant a very poor appraisal, meaning that she did not qualify for her end-of-year bonus.

22. The Claimant fears further harassment and victimisation but having been unsuccessful in raising the matters within the Respondent she now brings claims to the employment tribunal.

THE CLAIMANT CLAIMS

Direct discrimination

23. The Claimant has suffered less favourable treatment from the Second Respondent and the First Respondent is also responsible for the same. Both Respondents were at all material times aware of the Claimant's disability. The less favourable treatment relied upon includes, without limitation:

    (a) the removal of her printer as set out in paragraph 9 above;
    (b) the failure to hold a private meeting as requested on 2 July 2012 and set out in paragraph 10 above;
    (c) being subjected to a humiliating team meeting as set out in paragraphs 11 and 12 above;
    (d) the failure to investigate, properly or at all, the Claimant's grievance as set out in paragraphs 13 to 15 above;
    (e) being subjected to derogatory comments in relation to her spelling by Mrs Moffett as set out in paragraph 15 above;
    (f) being placed on to a performance monitoring plan as set out in paragraphs 16 to 21 above;
    (g) the failure to complete the IT request form as set out in paragraphs 17 and 18 above;
    (h) being subjected to a humiliating public reprimand as set out in paragraph 19 above;
    (i) receiving a final written warning for minor mistakes as set out in paragraph 21 above;
    (j) being threatened with dismissal as set out in paragraph 21 above;
    (k) receiving a poor performance rating in her appraisal as set out in paragraph 21 above;
    (l) being prevented from obtaining her annual bonus as set out in paragraph 21 above;

24. The Claimant avers that her non-disabled colleagues were not treated in this manner nor would a hypothetical comparator have been. In the circumstances the Claimant has been subjected to a series of acts amounting individually and collectively to direct disability discrimination. For the avoidance of doubt, the Claimant avers that the conduct relied upon was part of a continuing act.

Discrimination arising from disability

25. Further or alternatively, it is averred that the conduct set out in the factual background and as summarised in paragraph 23 above amounts to unfavourable treatment relating to the Claimant's disability contrary to section 15 of the Equality Act.

26. Both the First and Second Respondent were aware of the Claimant's disability at all material times.

27. It is the Claimant's case that all of the matters set out above and the conduct of the Second Respondent in particular arises from her disability.

Failure to make reasonable adjustments

28. The Claimant avers that the Second Respondent's requirement that all documentation

was checked on screen rather than on hard copy was a provision, criterion or practice which places dyslexic people, including the Claimant, at a substantial disadvantage in accurately checking documentation.

29. It is averred that the Respondents failed to make reasonable adjustments which could remove the substantial disadvantage from the Claimant. Such adjustments include, without limitation:

    (a) permitting the Claimant to continue proofing documents in hard copy, including allowing her continued use of a printer;

    (b) permitting the Claimant to continue using a junior colleague to implement changes electronically;

    (c) authorising the alteration of the Claimant's screen contrast to assist with proofing documents on the screen; or

    (d) making adjustments to the performance monitoring and capability process to recognise the Claimant's disability.

Harassment

30. The Claimant relies on the matters set out in the factual background as demonstrating acts of harassment towards her. In particular, but without limitation, the Claimant relies on the matters summarised at paragraphs 23(c) to 23(l) above. Such conduct related to the Claimant's disability and had the purpose or effect of creating a humiliating, degrading, hostile, intimidating and offensive environment for her.

Victimisation

31. The Claimant relies on the email of 2 July 2012 and the complaint of 9 July 2012 as being protected acts within the meaning of subsection 27(2)(d) of the Equality Act.

32. As a result of the Claimant's protected acts, the Second Respondent subjected the Claimant to detrimental treatment. In particular the Claimant relies on the conduct summarised at 23(c) to 23(l) above as amounting to detrimental treatment because of her protected acts.

AND THE CLAIMANT CLAIMS:

    (a) direct disability discrimination;

    (b) disability related discrimination;

    (c) failure to make reasonable adjustments;

    (d) harassment on grounds of disability; and

    (e) victimisation.

33. The Claimant seeks a declaration that she has been discriminated against in the manner set out above.

34. The Claimant seeks compensation for the discrimination suffered.

1 December 2012

APPENDIX B2

Sample grounds of resistance

The information contained in this document may be provided to the tribunal at what is currently section 5.2 (Response) of Form ET3 or as a separate document as below. If a separate document is used, it must be submitted at the same time as Form ET3. Form ET3 is available from HM Courts and Tribunals Service website at **www.justice.gov.uk/ tribunals/employment.**

IN THE LONDON SOUTH EMPLOYMENT TRIBUNAL

CASE NO. 3112012/2012

BETWEEN

MRS ELEANOR TANG

Claimant

-and-

(1) PERFECT PACKAGING LIMITED

(2) MR IAN MORRIS

Respondents

GROUNDS OF RESISTANCE

INTRODUCTION

1. Unless otherwise stated references in this Grounds of Resistance to paragraph numbers are references to paragraphs in the Grounds of Complaint.
2. This Grounds of Resistance is provided on behalf of both Respondents.
3. Paragraphs 1 to 3 are admitted. The Claimant was promoted in both 2009 and 2010.
4. Paragraph 4 is noted. For the avoidance of doubt it is denied that the Respondents have discriminated against the Claimant in relation to her disability whether as set out in the Grounds of Complaint or otherwise.

THE CLAIMANT'S DISABILITY

5. As to paragraph 5, it is admitted that the Claimant informed the First Respondent of her dyslexia in her application form. The Respondents have no knowledge of when the Claimant was diagnosed with dyslexia, nor the extent of the condition. The Second Respondent had no knowledge until Mrs Moffett's email, addressed below.
6. The Claimant is required to prove that her alleged dyslexia amounts to a disability. The Respondents have not seen any medical evidence on which to consider the issue. The

remainder of this Grounds of Resistance is provided in the event that the Claimant is found to be disabled. No admissions are made in this regard.

JURISDICTION

7.   The Claimant relies on a number of alleged events that pre-date 2 September 2012. It is denied that the acts relied upon by the Claimant were part of a continuing act. The Respondent will submit that acts prior to 2 September 2012 are out of time and should not be heard by the Tribunal.

BACKGROUND

8.   Paragraph 6 is admitted. Details of the Claimant's employment history, to the extent that they are relevant, will be provided in disclosure and witness evidence.

9.   It is admitted that in 2010 the Claimant was assigned to the celebrity scents production line. It is denied that this is a particularly demanding line or that celebrity lines are different from any other line in relation to changes at short notice and last minute work. The Claimant received two 'satisfactory' appraisals in November 2010 and November 2011. Positive feedback was provided to the Claimant along with an indication of areas requiring improvement. For example, the Claimant was heavily dependent on her juniors and was informed in both appraisals that she needed to maintain responsibility for the final review of all packaging as the responsibility was with her alone. Except as set out above, the Claimant is required to prove the contents of paragraph 7.

10. It is admitted that the Second Respondent became the Claimant's line manager in June 2012 and that he, along with all area managers, was seeking to introduce a paper-free office. As for the remainder of paragraph 8, the Respondents were not aware of this practice if the Claimant in fact operated it. The First Respondent's practice was always to require documentation to be checked electronically and any changes were to be made personally by the Senior Production Adviser responsible. The Second Respondent did not change the First Respondent's existing practice in this regard.

11. As to paragraph 9, the Second Respondent does not recall any discussions with the Claimant in which she sought to explain why she needed to print documentation. The Second Respondent does recollect that the Claimant and a number of other employees said that they wanted to be able to print things out but no reason for this was given. The printer which the Claimant used was in fact the printer associated with the finance team. Shortly after the Second Respondent took up his post there was a reorganisation of the office involving the finance team moving upstairs. The printer was moved with the finance team.

12. As to paragraph 10, it is admitted that the Claimant sent an email on 2 July 2012 to the Second Respondent and Mrs Moffett. It is denied that the Claimant's summary is accurate and in fact the Respondent understood the email to be a generalised complaint that the Second Respondent had not explained the 'new' processes properly. The email's full contents will be relied upon at the tribunal hearing.

13. As a result of the Claimant's email the Second Respondent considered it necessary and appropriate to arrange a team meeting to see whether he could better understand the concerns being expressed and resolve any confusion within the team. Given that the Claimant's email had suggested that there were several members of the team who were confused, it was appropriate for the Second Respondent to conduct the meeting with the whole team. It is admitted that the meeting took place on 6 July 2012. In all other respects no admissions are made in relation to paragraph 11.

14. As to paragraph 12, it is denied that the meeting was conducted in an aggressive or

hostile manner. The Second Respondent was seeking to improve communications within the team and was at pains to answer any questions. Some employees did raise questions which the Second Respondent answered. In particular these related to the electronic filing of documents. No mention was made of the Claimant's alleged disability or any need to print documents to assist her to review them. The Respondents have no knowledge of the details of conversations between staff members.

15. It is admitted that the Claimant emailed Mrs Moffett on 9 July 2012. In her email the Claimant raised further questions in relation to the paper-free policy and said that she wanted to discuss these with someone other than the Second Respondent. It is denied that the Claimant's email was a formal grievance or was expressed to be as such.

16. Mrs Moffett explained to the Claimant that the appropriate person to answer her queries was the Second Respondent and that she would forward the email to him in the first instance. It is admitted that the Claimant called Mrs Moffett and asked her not to do so. The Claimant stressed to Mrs Moffett that she did not have any problem with the Second Respondent or the policy. She also said that she did not want to take it any further.

17. Mrs Moffett did inform the Claimant that if she was unhappy with the Second Respondent she could raise the issue with his superior. There was no discussion of this being by way of an appeal.

18. Following the conversation, Mrs Moffett emailed the Second Respondent with the Claimant's original email and comments of her own, relaying the conversations she had had with the Claimant. The reference to dyslexia was to a passing comment made by the Claimant that she was worried that she had dyslexia and may not be able to proof the packaging properly, especially with some of the ranges where celebrities liked to use French words to give it finesse. The comments were made to support the Claimant's concerns rather than by way of harassment or discrimination. Except as expressly admitted above, paragraphs 13 to 15 are denied.

19. It is admitted that the Second Respondent met with the Claimant on 13 July 2012 to discuss her concerns. The description of the meeting given by the Claimant is denied. The Second Respondent said that the Claimant should raise any concerns with him as he was here to support her. He reassured her that she would have every support necessary in proofing documents as did all members of the team.

20. It is admitted that the Second Respondent provided the Claimant with a performance monitoring plan at this meeting. This was a plan which the Second Respondent had inherited from the Claimant's former line manager and which had not been signed off. The Second Respondent discussed the contents of the plan with the Claimant and it became apparent that the actions had not been taken due to the change of line management. It was therefore agreed between the Claimant and the Second Respondent that the plan would commence from the date of the meeting and both parties signed it during the meeting. Except as expressly admitted, paragraphs 16 and 17 are denied.

21. As to paragraph 18, it is admitted that the Second Respondent received from the Claimant an IT request form by email on 20 July 2012. It is further admitted that the Claimant sent the reminder emails referred to in the Grounds of Complaint on the dates set out. The request form simply stated 'changes to screen as discussed with employee'. The Second Respondent informed the Claimant that without further information he was not able to complete the form or sign off the request. The Claimant did not provide that further information and therefore on 13 August 2012 the Second Respondent informed the Claimant that she should not raise the matter again.

22. It is admitted and averred that the Claimant made a mistake on one of the product runs that she managed in September 2012. It is admitted that the Second Respondent raised this with the Claimant in the open plan office on 14 September 2012. It is denied that the Second Respondent shouted at the Claimant. The Claimant did not take the feedback constructively and sarcastically suggested that she write the word 'millilitre' out 20 times on the whiteboard as if doing a detention. The Second Respondent decided to

diffuse the situation by leaving the office at this point. It is admitted that when the Second Respondent was locking up he saw the word written on the whiteboard 20 times followed by a smiley face. It is denied that the Second Respondent requested or required the Claimant to do this and it is not known who wrote on the board or why. No other admissions are made in relation to paragraph 19.

23. Paragraph 20 is admitted.

24. As to paragraph 21 it is admitted that the Claimant did not score well in her annual appraisal and was therefore not eligible for her annual performance bonus. It is also admitted that the Claimant received a formal written warning and that her performance monitoring plan was extended. It is denied that this related to the two mistakes pleaded. In fact the Claimant had failed to meet the objectives set in the performance monitoring plan and therefore it was appropriate to continue the process. It is denied that the Claimant was threatened with dismissal. The Claimant asked how the performance management process worked and the various stages were explained up to and including dismissal.

25. No admissions are made in relation to paragraph 22.

OUTLINE RESPONSE TO CLAIMS

Direct discrimination

26. It is denied that the Claimant has been subjected to direct discrimination as alleged or otherwise. It is denied that the matters set out in paragraph 23(a) to 23(l) amount to less favourable treatment. The Respondents rely on the explanations set out above to demonstrate that the alleged conduct did not take place or, alternatively, did not amount to less favourable treatment and was in any event not on the grounds of the Claimant's alleged disability which is not admitted.

27. It is denied that there is any discrimination and further denied that there was any continuing act. Accordingly paragraphs 23 and 24 are denied.

Discrimination arising from disability

28. Paragraphs 25 and 27 are also denied for the same reason as given above. The Respondents have at all times acted reasonably and fairly in managing the Claimant and it is denied that any of the events described arose from the alleged disability or were otherwise connected with it.

Failure to make reasonable adjustments

29. It is admitted that the pleaded PCP was in operation. The Claimant is required to prove that the PCP places dyslexic people, including herself, at a substantial disadvantage compared to non-disabled people.

30. It is denied that the Respondents failed to make reasonable adjustments whether as pleaded at paragraphs 28 and 29 or otherwise. In particular the Respondents were not aware of any difficulty and in the circumstances it was therefore not reasonable to make any adjustments. Furthermore, the Claimant is required to prove that the pleaded adjustments would have removed any substantial disadvantage.

31. The Respondents deny that there was any requirement to alter the performance monitoring process. There was no connection between the performance monitoring and the Claimant's alleged difficulties in reading documents on screen.

Harassment

32. It is denied that the Respondents, or either of them, have subjected the Claimant to harassment on grounds of her disability. The Respondents rely on the factual background set out previously. Paragraph 30 is denied. It is particularly denied that the Respondents' conduct was capable of having the prescribed effect.

Victimisation

33. Paragraphs 31 and 32 are denied. For the reasons set out above, it is denied that the email of 2 July 2012 or the complaint of 9 July 2012 amounts to a protected act within the meaning of subsection 27(2)(d) of the Equality Act. Furthermore, it is denied that any of the conduct relied upon amounts to a detriment.

SUMMARY

34. It is denied that the Claimant has been discriminated against whether as alleged or otherwise.
35. The Respondent has acted throughout with reasonable and proper motives and in the circumstances no declaration or compensation is appropriate.
36. Except as expressly admitted above, the Claimant's claims are denied in their entirety.

27 December 2012

APPENDIX B3

Impact statement

*In preparing this impact statement we have used the facts from the case study in **Part 2**. We have chosen these facts because the time that John had off work and the symptoms he experienced are familiar to many sufferers of depression. Unlike dyslexia, which has highly sophisticated diagnostic assessments, depression and anxiety are often difficult to assess and the oral evidence of the claimant is crucial.*

IN THE LEEDS EMPLOYMENT TRIBUNAL

CASE NO. 1111111/2012

MR JOHN DIXON

Claimant

-and-

XYZ INCORPORATED

Respondent

IMPACT STATEMENT OF CLAIMANT

I John Dixon of 18 Robin Lane, Amesbury, make this statement in relation to my disability.

1. I am severely dyslexic and suffer from rapid cycling bipolar disorder.
2. In relation to my dyslexia I have difficulties with reading and writing as well as processing information when it is provided to me orally. This means that I have made various adjustments to my life to allow me to accommodate my disability. For example, my laptop is adapted with ClaroRead software which improves my ability to write and present written information.
3. I use a dictaphone or digital recording device so that I can record instructions rather than writing them down. This helps me to process the instructions which I would otherwise find difficult to remember.
4. I also have adjustments to my computer screen to both reduce glare and change the colour of the background from white to green. This improves my ability to read and work on the screen. In order to ensure suitable written standards any computer which I work on needs to be fitted with ClaroRead or TextHelp.
5. I have previously been workplace assessed and these adjustments enable me to perform well. When I joined XYC Inc these adjustments were made for me by the Occupational Health nurse.
6. In relation to my bipolar, in the past when I have declared this I have found job offers rescinded so now I do not disclose it to prospective employers because of the stigma attached.
7. In order to combat my bipolar I am required to take lithium on a daily basis and to have regular blood tests to check the level of lithium in my blood. I tend to arrange my

working day so that I can address these requirements without telling anyone. I also have to ensure that I keep my salt and fluid levels steady in order to manage my bipolar.

8.   I usually suffer from four or more episodes of mania, hypomania and/or depression per year. Hypomania is a less severe form of mania which does not last as long as mania. Sometimes I suffer from a combination of mania, hypomania and depression. Recently I have learnt to manage my bipolar to the extent that I have not had any episodes which have required me to take time off work in the last six years.

9.   When I was younger I did not manage my bipolar and suffered from more regular episodes. My father has never accepted my disability and so I have found it difficult to come to terms with it. It has taken me a long time into my adult life to get it to a point where I can manage it and maintain a regular job.

Deterioration in my health

10.   Shortly after Bill became my manager he increased the number of reports which I had to produce and the pressure on all of the sales team. I began to feel quite stressed and starting taking work home to complete reports in the evenings. Some nights it took me until 2 am to complete the reports because of my dyslexia. This was adding to the stress which I was experiencing.

11.   I began submitting reports late because I was not able to keep up with the demands. Bill criticised me openly in front of the team which was humiliating and increased my feelings of stress.

12.   When my dictaphone broke and Bill refused to authorise a replacement I felt unable to cope. I could not face leaving the house and did not attend work the following day. I called my GP who signed me off with stress for two weeks. My GP also referred me to the local psychiatric hospital where I was admitted for treatment. I spent two months as an inpatient.

13.   I was diagnosed as having suffered a major depressive episode stemming from my bipolar and the stress I was under at work. In total I spent four months away from work during which time I saw my psychiatrist on a regular basis, both for one-on-one therapy and also as part of a group therapy course.

14.   During this period I struggled to cope with social interactions, for example failing to respond to phone calls, to answer emails or even answer the door. As a result of my irritability and inability to deal with social situations my relationship with my girlfriend deteriorated and we are both struggling to cope with the impact.

15.   Medication which I began taking during this period enabled me to begin considering a return to work. My psychiatrist advised a gradual phased return to work to allow me to avoid excessive hours and stress. My medication is likely to last for a year to 18 months at least. Alongside the medication I continue to have regular psychotherapy and group therapy.

16.   When I am experiencing a major depressive episode I am unable to sleep at night and find my motivation very low during the day. I spend a considerable amount of time lying in bed or on the sofa unable to sleep and staring at the ceiling. I usually enjoy my food but during an episode I have no appetite and, unless reminded to do so by friends, I can go days without eating. I have lost a lot of weight.

17.   My family does not give me any support so I am dependent on friends. A major depressive episode puts a huge pressure on these relationships, especially when I avoid socialising and find it difficult to reciprocate their kindness.

18.   The treatment and medication enable me to deal with day-to-day life. Without them I would not be able to function at all. I would not get up in the morning. I would not dress or cook. I would find it impossible to look after my health and hygiene or my financial affairs. Even with the medication it is a real struggle.

I confirm that the contents of this statement are true to the best of my knowledge, information and belief.

Signed..

JOHN DIXON

APPENDIX B4

Joint letter of instruction

A letter of instruction must be tailored to the particular circumstances of the case. What follows here is for illustrative purposes only. It is a sample which can be adapted for your purposes. In some cases a detailed summary of the law will not be required but it is always appropriate to include a summary of the expert's obligations in producing the report. Remember that the decision as to whether an employee is disabled is a legal decision to be made by the tribunal. The medical expert's opinion is intended to assist the tribunal making its determination.

*As with the impact statement (**Appendix B3**) we have used the facts from the case study in **Part 2** for the purposes of this letter. It is assumed that there is a dispute at tribunal in relation to Mr Dixon's depression and the major depressive episode which he suffered. It is this, rather than his dyslexia, which is the subject matter of the request to the medical expert.*

Dear Sir,

Case No: 11111111/2012

The Claimant in this claim which is before the Leeds Employment Tribunal is Mr Dixon. He is represented by Pendragon Solicitors. The Respondent, XYZ Inc, is represented by Burnes Solicitors.

This is a joint letter of instruction which has been agreed between the parties in respect of Mr Dixon. We confirm that Mr Dixon will attend an appointment with you on 15 August 2012 and we agree to meet your reasonable fees for the consultation and the report which is to be provided. Each party has been ordered to pay 50 per cent of your fees inclusive of VAT.

Background

Until his employment was terminated on or about 3 March 2012, Mr Dixon was a Senior Sales Executive of the Respondent.

Mr Dixon has issued Employment Tribunal proceedings against the Respondent on the basis that he has been unfairly dismissed and has been subjected to disability discrimination pursuant to the Equality Act 2010.

Mr Dixon is severely dyslexic, has rapid cycling bipolar disorder and suffers from depression and anxiety.

The Respondent disputes that the Claimant was disabled at the relevant time, i.e. between 12 November 2011 and 3 March 2012. The Respondent has seen the medical evidence provided by the Claimant's Consultant Psychiatrist and his GP.

Directions were issued on 17 July 2012 by Employment Judge Blackwell directing that the parties must appoint a joint expert and, no later than 30 October 2012, obtain a medical report on the Claimant.

Documents

By way of documentation we enclose at Appendices 1 and 2 Mr Dixon's ET1 claim form and Grounds of Resistance together with the Respondent's ET3 and Grounds of Response.

We also enclose a bundle of Mr Dixon's medical records in date order including (i) the Claimant's medical notes from his GP, Dr Raj; (ii) copy of Dr Raj's report to the Employment Tribunal on Mr Dixon; and (iii) copies of the notes from his Consultant Psychiatrist, Mr Baker.

We also attach a witness statement by Mr Dixon dated 7 May 2012 which details the impact on him of his illness and which was prepared and submitted to the Employment Tribunal at their request. That witness statement has not been tested by cross-examination and you should not treat the statements made in it as undisputed facts although its contents may assist you in preparation of the report.

We would ask that you read all the Tribunal documents, records and information provided in advance of your meeting with Mr Dixon. We thank you for agreeing to see Mr Dixon.

To assist the Tribunal in any questions they may have regarding Mr Dixon's health and questions surrounding this we would be grateful if you would prepare an expert report distinguishing between matters of fact and opinion in respect of the issues set out below. We would be grateful for your preparation of this report by 1 October 2012 or sooner if possible to allow discussion of this with our respective Counsel. You may also be required to attend as an expert witness at the Employment Tribunal hearing which will be listed later this year subject to availability. We will advise you in due course as to whether your attendance is required at the hearing and on which dates.

Once your report has been prepared you should be able and willing to answer any supplementary questions in writing about your report posed by either party.

If you will not be able to prepare your report by 1 October 2012 or if you have any connection with either party or their respective solicitors that would prevent you from providing a report for any reason (this includes regularly receiving instructions from either), please advise us both upon receipt of these instructions.

Content of the report

Your report may be used in Employment Tribunal proceedings to determine whether Mr Dixon is disabled within the meaning of section 6 of the Equality Act 2010 ('Equality Act'). Please bear in mind that the tribunal may not be familiar with certain medical concepts and phraseology and that your report should therefore be explicit and readily understandable.

General – overriding duties

When preparing your report, please bear in mind the following overriding duties:

- It is the duty of an expert to assist the tribunal on matters within his or her own expertise. This duty is paramount and overrides any obligation to the person from whom the expert has received instructions or by whom he or she is paid. In this instance you are jointly instructed and your fees will be borne in equal shares by the parties.
- Expert evidence should be the independent product of the expert, uninfluenced by the pressures of litigation.
- An expert should assist the tribunal by providing objective, unbiased opinion on matters within his or her own expertise and should not assume the role of an advocate.
- An expert should consider all material facts, including those which may detract from his or her opinion.
- An expert should make it clear when a question or issue falls outside his or her expertise and when he or she is not able to reach a definite opinion, for example due to insufficient information.

211

- If, after producing the report, an expert changes his or her view on any material matter, such change of view should be communicated to all parties without delay, including, when appropriate, the Tribunal.

Legal framework

The Equality Act 2010

The present claim is brought under the Equality Act and you should therefore have regard only to the current law.

Section 6 of the Equality Act provides that:

(1)   A person (P) has a disability if –

    (a)   P has a physical or mental impairment, and

    (b)   the impairment has a substantial and long-term adverse effect on P's ability to carry out normal day-to-day activities.

Assistance with the meanings of these terms may be found in Schedule 1, Part 1 to the Equality Act, as follows:

Substantial adverse effect

The requirement that an adverse effect on normal day-to-day activities should be a substantial one reflects the general understanding of disability as a limitation going beyond the normal differences in ability which may exist among people. A substantial effect is one that is greater than the effect which would be produced by the sort of physical or mental conditions experienced by many people which have only minor or trivial effects. Regard should be had to the time it takes to carry out an activity, the way in which an activity is carried out, the cumulative effects of an impairment, effects of behaviour and the effect of environment. A series of minor adverse effects are, however, capable of cumulatively amounting to a substantial effect. Please refer to the guidance as detailed below.

Long-term effects

(1)   The effect of an impairment is long-term if –

    (a)   it has lasted for at least 12 months,

    (b)   it is likely to last for at least 12 months, or

    (c)   it is likely to last for the rest of the life of the person affected.

(2)   If an impairment ceases to have a substantial adverse effect on a person's ability to carry out normal day-to-day activities, it is to be treated as continuing to have that effect if that effect is likely to recur.

The material time for assessing whether the impairment is long term is the time when the discrimination is alleged to have occurred. Further assistance is provided in the guidance – see below.

Please note that the word 'likely' should be interpreted as referring to an outcome that could well happen. Following *SCA Packaging* v. *Boyle* [2009] UKHL 37 this means that as long as there is some likelihood that it may happen, it does not have to be more than a 50 per cent chance.

Normal day-to-day activities

In order to determine an effect on normal day-to-day activities you should consider what the person can and cannot do and what he can do but only with difficulty. You are not confined to any specific categories of activities.

Effect of medical treatment

You should disregard or discount the effects of medical treatment. This includes medicines and also counselling, CBT, psychotherapy, etc. The issue is to determine, but for the treatment, how the person would be able to function and whether, but for the treatment, there would be an impact on their normal day-to-day activities. Refer to Schedule 1, paragraph 5 to the Equality Act:

(1)   An impairment is to be treated as having a substantial adverse effect on the ability of the person concerned to carry out normal day-to-day activities if –

    (a)   measures are being taken to treat or correct it, and

    (b)   but for that, it would be likely to have that effect.

(2)   'Measures' includes, in particular, medical treatment and the use of a prosthesis or other aid.

Where you discount medical treatment or other measures please make this clear in your report.

Excluded conditions

A number of conditions are excluded from the definition of disability in regulation 4 of the Equality Act 2010 (Disability) Regulations 2010 (SI 2010/2128). The exclusions apply only to freestanding conditions. If there is a second impairment arising from the excluded condition this may be covered by the Equality Act, provided the second impairment meet the section 6 definition. For example, if an alcoholic develops depression and anxiety, provided the depression and anxiety meets the test of having a long-term, substantial adverse effect on normal day-to-day activities, the second condition will render the person disabled, even though the first condition, alcoholism, is expressly excluded (*Power* v. *Panasonic UK Ltd* [2003] IRLR 151 (EAT)).

Guidance

The government has issued guidance to assist adjudicating bodies like courts and tribunals in deciding whether a person is a disabled person for the purposes of the Equality Act. Outline guidance can be found in the Equality Act 2010 Statutory Code of Practice on Employment (in particular Appendix 1 on the Definition of Disability) which can be found online at **www.equalityhumanrights.com/uploaded_files/EqualityAct/employercode.pdf**.

There is also more detailed guidance issued by the Government Office for Disability Issues which is entitled Equality Act 2010 Guidance on matters to be taken into account in determining questions relating to the definition of disability and which is also available online at **www.gov.uk/government/uploads/system/uploads/attachment_data/file/85038/disability-definition.pdf**.

Issues

We would be grateful if you would meet with Mr Dixon and prepare a report for the Tribunal hearing. In particular, we would be grateful if you would respond to the following questions:

1. What are and what have been Mr Dixon's conditions? Please provide a diagnosis with relevant dates.
2. Please give an account of the history of his medical condition(s), including their origins, history and any treatment and its effect.
3. When, in your opinion, did Mr Dixon's condition(s) commence?
4. Please give an account of the likely cause of Mr Dixon's condition(s).
5. What is the likely impact of Mr Dixon's condition(s) on his ability to carry out day-to-day activities?
6. At any stage did any condition which Mr Dixon has or had, have a substantial and long-term adverse effect on his ability to carry out normal day-to-day activities? If you conclude that there was a period during which such an impact was experienced, please specify the condition and the relevant time period.
7. Is there is a link between Mr Dixon's condition(s) and his conduct at work as set out in the Grounds of Complaint and Grounds of Resistance and to what extent did the condition(s) contribute to his conduct or performance?
8. Was Mr Dixon in November 2011 or at any time thereafter able to carry out his job of Senior Sales Executive or any job? If not, when might he be fit for work and what would be the nature of the job for which he will then be fit?

Conclusion

We must stress that in preparing your report, your overriding duty is to the Tribunal rather than to any party.

Please note in particular that the report must contain the following statement:

> I confirm that insofar as the facts stated in my report are not within my own knowledge I have made clear which they are and I believe them to be true, and that the opinions I have expressed represent my true and complete professional opinion.

Please include an appendix at the end of the report with a summary of your professional qualifications and experience to assist the Tribunal in assessing your suitability to give an opinion about Mr Dixon's condition.

Once you have completed your report, please forward a copy to the representatives of both parties. Should you have any queries concerning clarification of these instructions, please contact both representatives and copy in both parties on any correspondence to the other.

We look forward to hearing from you as soon as possible and thank you for your assistance in this matter.

Yours faithfully,

APPENDIX B5

Schedule of loss

*The schedule of loss below is based on the facts in ET1 and ET3 (**Appendices B1** and **B2**). On the facts the claimant remains an employee and her claims are therefore for declarations of discrimination, the loss of her bonus and an award for injury to feelings. Where an employee has lost his or her job, the schedule of loss needs to include loss of earnings and claims for basic award and compensation (**17.4**). Remember that the schedule of loss is provided by the claimant and therefore represents his or her best case scenario. Matters such as injury to feelings may well be disputed. The claimant should not overstate his or her case but is entitled to put it as high as is reasonably defensible.*

IN THE LONDON SOUTH EMPLOYMENT TRIBUNAL

CASE NO. 3112012/2012

BETWEEN

MRS ELEANOR TANG

Claimant

-and-

(1) PERFECT PACKAGING LIMITED

(2) MR IAN MORRIS

Respondents

SCHEDULE OF LOSS

KEY FIGURES

Claimant's bonus December 2008	£575
Claimant's bonus December 2009	£2,630
Claimant's bonus December 2010	£3,750
Claimant's bonus December 2011	£4,400

FINANCIAL LOSS

The Claimant claims that as a result of the discriminatory treatment to which she has been subjected she has been disqualified from earning her annual bonus. The annual bonus is based on the performance of the company and the performance of the individual.

The Claimant will say that the performance of the company matched the previous year or exceeded it and therefore a bonus is payable. As for the performance of the individual the Claimant will say that her annual appraisal rating ('poor') was an act of discrimination and that she should have been awarded 'satisfactory' or 'good', either of which would have qualified her for a bonus.

The Claimant claims the general pattern reflected a year-on-year increase in bonus. In the previous year she had only been performing her Senior Production Adviser role for six months so her bonus for a complete year in the role should be higher.

The Claimant will seek disclosure of the company performance figures and bonus amounts paid to other Senior Production Advisers.

At present the Claimant estimates that she would have earned a bonus of £5,000 but for the discriminatory acts set out in the claim form.

Estimated £5,000

INJURY TO FEELINGS

The Claimant seeks an award from the Tribunal to reflect the conduct of the Respondent including its failure to properly address her complaints of discrimination and the acts of victimisation from both her line manager and human resources. The Claimant leaves the sum to be assessed by the Tribunal but claims that it would be appropriate to recover a figure within the middle band of *Vento*.

Between £6,000 and £18,000

Estimated total claimed £11,000–£23,000

This schedule represents the Claimant's best estimate of loss as at December 2012. The Claimant reserves the right to amend this schedule of loss at any stage and will provide an up-to-date version for the Tribunal's use at the hearing.

APPENDIX B6

Scott Schedule

*This document is provided to demonstrate the layout of a Scott Schedule. The headings will vary depending on the case. The facts in the example are taken from the grounds of complaint and grounds of resistance at **Appendices B1** and **B2**. The Schedule will normally be prepared by the claimant and sent to the respondent to complete the last column. Sometimes a tribunal will order that this document be prepared. Sometimes parties choose to agree a schedule to identify what the issues in the case are and to expedite the proceedings. Please note that the example given does not deal with all of the claims and issues raised in the Grounds of Complaint. A completed Schedule would list all of the claims and issues.*

CASE NO. 3112012/2012

IN THE LONDON SOUTH EMPLOYMENT TRIBUNAL

BETWEEN

MRS ELEANOR TANG

Claimant

-and-

(1) PERFECT PACKAGING LIMITED

(2) MR IAN MORRIS

Respondents

SCOTT SCHEDULE

Issue	Date	Description of events	Discrimination claimed	Alleged comparator	Protected act	Respondent's response
1	During the last two weeks of June	The C's printer was removed as an act of less favourable treatment (see paragraph 9 of Grounds of Complaint)	Direct discrimination and/or discrimination arising from disability	Non-disabled colleagues or hypothetical comparator	N/A	The printer was not assigned to C. It was moved for non-discriminatory reasons (see paragraph 11 of Grounds of Resistance)

Issue	Date	Description of events	Discrimination claimed	Alleged comparator	Protected act	Respondent's response
2	Early July	R's failure to arrange a private meeting as requested in the email dated 2 July 2012 (see paragraph 10 of the Grounds of Complaint)	Direct discrimination and/or discrimination arising from disability	Non-disabled colleagues or hypothetical comparator	N/A	R acted reasonably and for reasons unconnected with C's disability (see paragraph 12 and 13 of the Grounds of Resistance)
3	6 July 2012	Being subjected to a humiliating team meeting as set out in paragraphs 11 and 12 of the Grounds of Complaint	Direct discrimination, discrimination arising from disability, harassment and/or victimisation	Non-disabled colleagues or hypothetical comparator	Email dated 2 July 2012	R denies the allegations for the reasons set out in paragraphs, 13 and 14 of the Grounds of Resistance
4	Mid July	Failure to investigate C's grievance as set out in paragraphs 13 to 15 of the Grounds of Complaint	Direct discrimination, discrimination arising from disability, harassment and/or victimisation	Non-disabled colleagues or hypothetical comparator	Email dated 2 July 2012 and/or email dated 9 July 2012	It is denied that there was any grievance raised or any failure to investigate for the reasons set out in paragraphs 15 to 18 of the Grounds of Resistance
5	Date unknown – believed to be mid-July	Derogatory comments from Mrs Moffett as set out in paragraph 15 of the Grounds of Complaint	Direct discrimination, discrimination arising from disability, harassment and/or victimisation	Non-disabled colleagues or hypothetical comparator	Email dated 2 July 2012 and/or email dated 9 July 2012	R denies the allegation for the reasons set in paragraph 18 of the Grounds of Resistance The comments were supportive not discriminatory

219

Statutory and guidance material

Equality Act 2010 (extracts)

PART 2   EQUALITY: KEY CONCEPTS

6   Disability

(1)   A person (P) has a disability if –

    (a)   P has a physical or mental impairment, and

    (b)   the impairment has a substantial and long-term adverse effect on P's ability to carry out normal day-to-day activities.

(2)   A reference to a disabled person is a reference to a person who has a disability.

(3)   In relation to the protected characteristic of disability –

    (a)   a reference to a person who has a particular protected characteristic is a reference to a person who has a particular disability;

    (b)   a reference to persons who share a protected characteristic is a reference to persons who have the same disability.

(4)   This Act (except Part 12 and section 190) applies in relation to a person who has had a disability as it applies in relation to a person who has the disability; accordingly (except in that Part and that section) –

    (a)   a reference (however expressed) to a person who has a disability includes a reference to a person who has had the disability, and

    (b)   a reference (however expressed) to a person who does not have a disability includes a reference to a person who has not had the disability.

(5)   A Minister of the Crown may issue guidance about matters to be taken into account in deciding any question for the purposes of subsection (1).

(6)   Schedule 1 (disability: supplementary provision) has effect.

13   Direct discrimination

(1)   A person (A) discriminates against another (B) if, because of a protected characteristic, A treats B less favourably than A treats or would treat others.

(2)   If the protected characteristic is age, A does not discriminate against B if A can show A's treatment of B to be a proportionate means of achieving a legitimate aim.

(3)   If the protected characteristic is disability, and B is not a disabled person, A does not discriminate against B only because A treats or would treat disabled persons more favourably than A treats B.

(4)   If the protected characteristic is marriage and civil partnership, this section applies to a contravention of Part 5 (work) only if the treatment is because it is B who is married or a civil partner.

(5)   If the protected characteristic is race, less favourable treatment includes segregating B from others.

(6)   If the protected characteristic is sex –

(a)   less favourable treatment of a woman includes less favourable treatment of her because she is breast-feeding;

(b)   in a case where B is a man, no account is to be taken of special treatment afforded to a woman in connection with pregnancy or childbirth.

(7)   Subsection (6)(a) does not apply for the purposes of Part 5 (work).

(8)   This section is subject to sections 17(6) and 18(7).

14   Combined discrimination: dual characteristics

(1)   A person (A) discriminates against another (B) if, because of a combination of two relevant protected characteristics, A treats B less favourably than A treats or would treat a person who does not share either of those characteristics.

(2)   The relevant protected characteristics are –

(a)   age;
(b)   disability;
(c)   gender reassignment;
(d)   race
(e)   religion or belief;
(f)   sex;
(g)   sexual orientation.

(3)   For the purposes of establishing a contravention of this Act by virtue of subsection (1), B need not show that A's treatment of B is direct discrimination because of each of the characteristics in the combination (taken separately).

(4)   But B cannot establish a contravention of this Act by virtue of subsection (1) if, in reliance on another provision of this Act or any other enactment, A shows that A's treatment of B is not direct discrimination because of either or both of the characteristics in the combination.

(5)   Subsection (1) does not apply to a combination of characteristics that includes disability in circumstances where, if a claim of direct discrimination because of disability were to be brought, it would come within section 116 (special educational needs).

(6)   A Minister of the Crown may by order amend this section so as to –

(a)   make further provision about circumstances in which B can, or in which B cannot, establish a contravention of this Act by virtue of subsection (1);

(b)   specify other circumstances in which subsection (1) does not apply.

(7)   The references to direct discrimination are to a contravention of this Act by virtue of section 13.

15   Discrimination arising from disability

(1)   A person (A) discriminates against a disabled person (B) if –

(a)   A treats B unfavourably because of something arising in consequence of B's disability, and

(b)   A cannot show that the treatment is a proportionate means of achieving a legitimate aim.

(2)   Subsection (1) does not apply if A shows that A did not know, and could not reasonably have been expected to know, that B had the disability.

19   Indirect discrimination

(1)   A person (A) discriminates against another (B) if A applies to B a provision, criterion or practice which is discriminatory in relation to a relevant protected characteristic of B's.

(2)   For the purposes of subsection (1), a provision, criterion or practice is discriminatory in relation to a relevant protected characteristic of B's if –

    (a)   A applies, or would apply, it to persons with whom B does not share the characteristic,

    (b)   it puts, or would put, persons with whom B shares the characteristic at a particular disadvantage when compared with persons with whom B does not share it,

    (c)   it puts, or would put, B at that disadvantage, and

    (d)   A cannot show it to be a proportionate means of achieving a legitimate aim.

(3)   The relevant protected characteristics are –

age;
disability;
gender reassignment;
marriage and civil partnership;
race;
religion or belief;
sex;
sexual orientation.

20   Duty to make adjustments

(1)   Where this Act imposes a duty to make reasonable adjustments on a person, this section, sections 21 and 22 and the applicable Schedule apply; and for those purposes, a person on whom the duty is imposed is referred to as A.

(2)   The duty comprises the following three requirements.

(3)   The first requirement is a requirement, where a provision, criterion or practice of A's puts a disabled person at a substantial disadvantage in relation to a relevant matter in comparison with persons who are not disabled, to take such steps as it is reasonable to have to take to avoid the disadvantage.

(4)   The second requirement is a requirement, where a physical feature puts a disabled person at a substantial disadvantage in relation to a relevant matter in comparison with persons who are not disabled, to take such steps as it is reasonable to have to take to avoid the disadvantage.

(5)   The third requirement is a requirement, where a disabled person would, but for the provision of an auxiliary aid, be put at a substantial disadvantage in relation to a relevant matter in comparison with persons who are not disabled, to take such steps as it is reasonable to have to take to provide the auxiliary aid.

(6)   Where the first or third requirement relates to the provision of information, the steps which it is reasonable for A to have to take include steps for ensuring that in the circumstances concerned the information is provided in an accessible format.

(7)   A person (A) who is subject to a duty to make reasonable adjustments is not (subject to express provision to the contrary) entitled to require a disabled person, in relation to whom A is required to comply with the duty, to pay to any extent A's costs of complying with the duty.

(8)   A reference in section 21 or 22 or an applicable Schedule to the first, second or third requirement is to be construed in accordance with this section.

(9)   In relation to the second requirement, a reference in this section or an applicable Schedule to avoiding a substantial disadvantage includes a reference to –

    (a)   removing the physical feature in question,
    (b)   altering it, or
    (c)   providing a reasonable means of avoiding it.

(10)   A reference in this section, section 21 or 22 or an applicable Schedule (apart from paragraphs 2 to 4 of Schedule 4) to a physical feature is a reference to –

    (a)   a feature arising from the design or construction of a building,
    (b)   a feature of an approach to, exit from or access to a building,
    (c)   a fixture or fitting, or furniture, furnishings, materials, equipment or other chattels, in or on premises, or
    (d)   any other physical element or quality.

(11)   A reference in this section, section 21 or 22 or an applicable Schedule to an auxiliary aid includes a reference to an auxiliary service.

(12)   A reference in this section or an applicable Schedule to chattels is to be read, in relation to Scotland, as a reference to moveable property.

(13)   The applicable Schedule is, in relation to the Part of this Act specified in the first column of the Table, the Schedule specified in the second column.

Part of this Act	Applicable Schedule
Part 3 (services and public functions)	Schedule 2
Part 4 (premises)	Schedule 4
Part 5 (work)	Schedule 8
Part 6 (education)	Schedule 13
Part 7 (associations)	Schedule 15
Each of the Parts mentioned above	Schedule 21

21   Failure to comply with duty

(1)   A failure to comply with the first, second or third requirement is a failure to comply with a duty to make reasonable adjustments.

(2)   A discriminates against a disabled person if A fails to comply with that duty in relation to that person.

(3)   A provision of an applicable Schedule which imposes a duty to comply with the first, second or third requirement applies only for the purpose of establishing whether A has contravened this Act by virtue of subsection (2); a failure to comply is, accordingly, not actionable by virtue of another provision of this Act or otherwise.

23   Comparison by reference to circumstances

(1)   On a comparison of cases for the purposes of section 13, 14, or 19 there must be no material difference between the circumstances relating to each case.

(2)   The circumstances relating to a case include a person's abilities if –

    (a)   on a comparison for the purposes of section 13, the protected characteristic is disability;
    (b)   on a comparison for the purposes of section 14, one of the protected characteristics in the combination is disability.

(3)   If the protected characteristic is sexual orientation, the fact that one person (whether or not the person referred to as B) is a civil partner while another is married is not a material difference between the circumstances relating to each case.

24   Irrelevance of alleged discriminator's characteristics

(1)   For the purpose of establishing a contravention of this Act by virtue of section 13(1), it does not matter whether A has the protected characteristic.

(2)   For the purpose of establishing a contravention of this Act by virtue of section 14(1), it does not matter –

    (a)   whether A has one of the protected characteristics in the combination;

    (b)   whether A has both.

26   Harassment

(1)   A person (A) harasses another (B) if –

    (a)   A engages in unwanted conduct related to a relevant protected characteristic, and

    (b)   the conduct has the purpose or effect of –

        (i)   violating B's dignity, or

        (ii)   creating an intimidating, hostile, degrading, humiliating or offensive environment for B.

(2)   A also harasses B if –

    (a)   A engages in unwanted conduct of a sexual nature, and

    (b)   the conduct has the purpose or effect referred to in subsection (1)(b).

(3)   A also harasses B if –

    (a)   A or another person engages in unwanted conduct of a sexual nature or that is related to gender reassignment or sex,

    (b)   the conduct has the purpose or effect referred to in subsection (1)(b), and

    (c)   because of B's rejection of or submission to the conduct, A treats B less favourably than A would treat B if B had not rejected or submitted to the conduct.

(4)   In deciding whether conduct has the effect referred to in subsection (1)(b), each of the following must be taken into account –

    (a)   the perception of B;

    (b)   the other circumstances of the case;

    (c)   whether it is reasonable for the conduct to have that effect.

(5)   The relevant protected characteristics are –

age;
disability;
gender reassignment;
race;
religion or belief;
sex;
sexual orientation.

27   Victimisation

(1)   A person (A) victimises another person (B) if A subjects B to a detriment because –

    (a)   B does a protected act, or

    (b)   A believes that B has done, or may do, a protected act.

(2)   Each of the following is a protected act –

    (a)   bringing proceedings under this Act;

    (b)   giving evidence or information in connection with proceedings under this Act;

    (c)   doing any other thing for the purposes of or in connection with this Act;

    (d)   making an allegation (whether or not express) that A or another person has contravened this Act.

(3)   Giving false evidence or information, or making a false allegation, is not a protected act if the evidence or information is given, or the allegation is made, in bad faith.

(4)   This section applies only where the person subjected to a detriment is an individual.

(5)   The reference to contravening this Act includes a reference to committing a breach of an equality clause or rule.

PART 5   WORK

39   Employees and applicants

(1)   An employer (A) must not discriminate against a person (B) –

    (a)   in the arrangements A makes for deciding to whom to offer employment;

    (b)   as to the terms on which A offers B employment;

    (c)   by not offering B employment.

(2)   An employer (A) must not discriminate against an employee of A's (B) –

    (a)   as to B's terms of employment;

    (b)   in the way A affords B access, or by not affording B access, to opportunities for promotion, transfer or training or for receiving any other benefit, facility or service;

    (c)   by dismissing B;

    (d)   by subjecting B to any other detriment.

(3)   An employer (A) must not victimise a person (B) –

    (a)   in the arrangements A makes for deciding to whom to offer employment;

    (b)   as to the terms on which A offers B employment;

    (c)   by not offering B employment.

(4)   An employer (A) must not victimise an employee of A's (B) –

    (a)   as to B's terms of employment;

    (b)   in the way A affords B access, or by not affording B access, to opportunities for promotion, transfer or training or for any other benefit, facility or service;

    (c)   by dismissing B;

    (d)   by subjecting B to any other detriment.

(5)   A duty to make reasonable adjustments applies to an employer.

(6)   Subsection (1)(b), so far as relating to sex or pregnancy and maternity, does not apply to a term that relates to pay –

    (a)   unless, were B to accept the offer, an equality clause or rule would have effect in relation to the term, or

(b)   if paragraph (a) does not apply, except in so far as making an offer on terms including that term amounts to a contravention of subsection (1)(b) by virtue of section 13, 14 or 18.

(7)   In subsections (2)(c) and (4)(c), the reference to dismissing B includes a reference to the termination of B's employment –

(a)   by the expiry of a period (including a period expiring by reference to an event or circumstance);

(b)   by an act of B's (including giving notice) in circumstances such that B is entitled, because of A's conduct, to terminate the employment without notice.

(8)   Subsection (7)(a) does not apply if, immediately after the termination, the employment is renewed on the same terms.

60   Enquiries about disability and health

(1)   A person (A) to whom an application for work is made must not ask about the health of the applicant (B) –

(a)   before offering work to B, or

(b)   where A is not in a position to offer work to B, before including B in a pool of applicants from whom A intends (when in a position to do so) to select a person to whom to offer work.

(2)   A contravention of subsection (1) (or a contravention of section 111 or 112 that relates to a contravention of subsection (1)) is enforceable as an unlawful act under Part 1 of the Equality Act 2006 (and, by virtue of section 120(8), is enforceable only by the Commission under that Part).

(3)   A does not contravene a relevant disability provision merely by asking about B's health; but A's conduct in reliance on information given in response may be a contravention of a relevant disability provision.

(4)   Subsection (5) applies if B brings proceedings before an employment tribunal on a complaint that A's conduct in reliance on information given in response to a question about B's health is a contravention of a relevant disability provision.

(5)   In the application of section 136 to the proceedings, the particulars of the complaint are to be treated for the purposes of subsection (2) of that section as facts from which the tribunal could decide that A contravened the provision.

(6)   This section does not apply to a question that A asks in so far as asking the question is necessary for the purpose of –

(a)   establishing whether B will be able to comply with a requirement to undergo an assessment or establishing whether a duty to make reasonable adjustments is or will be imposed on A in relation to B in connection with a requirement to undergo an assessment,

(b)   establishing whether B will be able to carry out a function that is intrinsic to the work concerned,

(c)   monitoring diversity in the range of persons applying to A for work,

(d)   taking action to which section 158 would apply if references in that section to persons who share (or do not share) a protected characteristic were references to disabled persons (or persons who are not disabled) and the reference to the characteristic were a reference to disability, or

(e)   if A applies in relation to the work a requirement to have a particular disability, establishing whether B has that disability.

(7)   In subsection (6)(b), where A reasonably believes that a duty to make reasonable

229

adjustments would be imposed on A in relation to B in connection with the work, the reference to a function that is intrinsic to the work is to be read as a reference to a function that would be intrinsic to the work once A complied with the duty.

(8)   Subsection (6)(e) applies only if A shows that, having regard to the nature or context of the work –

    (a)   the requirement is an occupational requirement, and

    (b)   the application of the requirement is a proportionate means of achieving a legitimate aim.

(9)   'Work' means employment, contract work, a position as a partner, a position as a member of an LLP, a pupillage or tenancy, being taken as a devil, membership of a stable, an appointment to a personal or public office, or the provision of an employment service; and the references in subsection (1) to offering a person work are, in relation to contract work, to be read as references to allowing a person to do the work.

(10)   A reference to offering work is a reference to making a conditional or unconditional offer of work (and, in relation to contract work, is a reference to allowing a person to do the work subject to fulfilment of one or more conditions).

(11)   The following, so far as relating to discrimination within section 13 because of disability, are relevant disability provisions –

    (a)   section 39(1)(a) or (c);

    (b)   section 41(1)(b);

    (c)   section 44(1)(a) or (c);

    (d)   section 45(1)(a) or (c);

    (e)   section 47(1)(a) or (c);

    (f)   section 48(1)(a) or (c);

    (g)   section 49(3)(a) or (c);

    (h)   section 50(3)(a) or (c);

    (i)   section 51(1);

    (j)   section 55(1)(a) or (c).

(12)   An assessment is an interview or other process designed to give an indication of a person's suitability for the work concerned.

(13)   For the purposes of this section, whether or not a person has a disability is to be regarded as an aspect of that person's health.

(14)   This section does not apply to anything done for the purpose of vetting applicants for work for reasons of national security.

PART 8   PROHIBITED CONDUCT: ANCILLARY

108   Relationships that have ended

(1)   A person (A) must not discriminate against another (B) if –

    (a)   the discrimination arises out of and is closely connected to a relationship which used to exist between them, and

    (b)   conduct of a description constituting the discrimination would, if it occurred during the relationship, contravene this Act.

(2)   A person (A) must not harass another (B) if –

    (a)   the harassment arises out of and is closely connected to a relationship which used to exist between them, and

(b)   conduct of a description constituting the harassment would, if it occurred during the relationship, contravene this Act.

(3)   It does not matter whether the relationship ends before or after the commencement of this section.

(4)   A duty to make reasonable adjustments applies to A if B is placed at a substantial disadvantage as mentioned in section 20.

(5)   For the purposes of subsection (4), sections 20, 21 and 22 and the applicable Schedules are to be construed as if the relationship had not ended.

(6)   For the purposes of Part 9 (enforcement), a contravention of this section relates to the Part of this Act that would have been contravened if the relationship had not ended.

(7)   But conduct is not a contravention of this section in so far as it also amounts to victimisation of B by A.

109 Liability of employers and principals

(1)   Anything done by a person (A) in the course of A's employment must be treated as also done by the employer.

(2)   Anything done by an agent for a principal, with the authority of the principal, must be treated as also done by the principal.

(3)   It does not matter whether that thing is done with the employer's or principal's knowledge or approval.

(4)   In proceedings against A's employer (B) in respect of anything alleged to have been done by A in the course of A's employment it is a defence for B to show that B took all reasonable steps to prevent A –

(a)   from doing that thing, or
(b)   from doing anything of that description.

(5)   This section does not apply to offences under this Act (other than offences under Part 12 (disabled persons: transport)).

110 Liability of employees and agents

(1)   A person (A) contravenes this section if –

(a)   A is an employee or agent,
(b)   A does something which, by virtue of section 109(1) or (2), is treated as having been done by A's employer or principal (as the case may be), and
(c)   the doing of that thing by A amounts to a contravention of this Act by the employer or principal (as the case may be).

(2)   It does not matter whether, in any proceedings, the employer is found not to have contravened this Act by virtue of section 109(4).

(3)   A does not contravene this section if –

(a)   A relies on a statement by the employer or principal that doing that thing is not a contravention of this Act, and
(b)   it is reasonable for A to do so.

(4)   A person (B) commits an offence if B knowingly or recklessly makes a statement mentioned in subsection (3)(a) which is false or misleading in a material respect.

(5)   A person guilty of an offence under subsection (4) is liable on summary conviction to a fine not exceeding level 5 on the standard scale.

(6)   Part 9 (enforcement) applies to a contravention of this section by A as if it were the contravention mentioned in subsection (1)(c).

(7)   The reference in subsection (1)(c) to a contravention of this Act does not include a reference to disability discrimination in contravention of Chapter 1 of Part 6 (schools).

111   Instructing, causing or inducing contraventions

(1)   A person (A) must not instruct another (B) to do in relation to a third person (C) anything which contravenes Part 3, 4, 5, 6 or 7 or section 108(1) or (2) or 112(1) (a basic contravention).

(2)   A person (A) must not cause another (B) to do in relation to a third person (C) anything which is a basic contravention.

(3)   A person (A) must not induce another (B) to do in relation to a third person (C) anything which is a basic contravention.

(4)   For the purposes of subsection (3), inducement may be direct or indirect.

(5)   Proceedings for a contravention of this section may be brought –

(a)   by B, if B is subjected to a detriment as a result of A's conduct;
(b)   by C, if C is subjected to a detriment as a result of A's conduct;
(c)   by the Commission.

(6)   For the purposes of subsection (5), it does not matter whether –

(a)   the basic contravention occurs;
(b)   any other proceedings are, or may be, brought in relation to A's conduct.

(7)   This section does not apply unless the relationship between A and B is such that A is in a position to commit a basic contravention in relation to B.

(8)   A reference in this section to causing or inducing a person to do something includes a reference to attempting to cause or induce the person to do it.

(9)   For the purposes of Part 9 (enforcement), a contravention of this section is to be treated as relating –

(a)   in a case within subsection (5)(a), to the Part of this Act which, because of the relationship between A and B, A is in a position to contravene in relation to B;
(b)   in a case within subsection (5)(b), to the Part of this Act which, because of the relationship between B and C, B is in a position to contravene in relation to C.

112   Aiding contraventions

(1)   A person (A) must not knowingly help another (B) to do anything which contravenes Part 3, 4, 5, 6 or 7 or section 108(1) or (2) or 111 (a basic contravention).

(2)   It is not a contravention of subsection (1) if –

(a)   A relies on a statement by B that the act for which the help is given does not contravene this Act, and
(b)   it is reasonable for A to do so.

(3)   B commits an offence if B knowingly or recklessly makes a statement mentioned in subsection (2)(a) which is false or misleading in a material respect.

(4)   A person guilty of an offence under subsection (3) is liable on summary conviction to a fine not exceeding level 5 on the standard scale.

(5)   For the purposes of Part 9 (enforcement), a contravention of this section is to be treated as relating to the provision of this Act to which the basic contravention relates.

(6)   The reference in subsection (1) to a basic contravention does not include a reference to disability discrimination in contravention of Chapter 1 of Part 6 (schools).

PART 9 ENFORCEMENT

123 Time limits

(1) Subject to section 140A, proceedings on a complaint within section 120 may not be brought after the end of –

    (a) the period of 3 months starting with the date of the act to which the complaint relates, or

    (b) such other period as the employment tribunal thinks just and equitable.

(2) Proceedings may not be brought in reliance on section 121(1) after the end of –

    (a) the period of 6 months starting with the date of the act to which the proceedings relate, or

    (b) such other period as the employment tribunal thinks just and equitable.

(3) For the purposes of this section –

    (a) conduct extending over a period is to be treated as done at the end of the period;

    (b) failure to do something is to be treated as occurring when the person in question decided on it.

(4) In the absence of evidence to the contrary, a person (P) is to be taken to decide on failure to do something –

    (a) when P does an act inconsistent with doing it, or

    (b) if P does no inconsistent act, on the expiry of the period in which P might reasonably have been expected to do it.

124 Remedies: general

(1) This section applies if an employment tribunal finds that there has been a contravention of a provision referred to in section 120(1).

(2) The tribunal may –

    (a) make a declaration as to the rights of the complainant and the respondent in relation to the matters to which the proceedings relate;

    (b) order the respondent to pay compensation to the complainant;

    (c) make an appropriate recommendation.

(3) An appropriate recommendation is a recommendation that within a specified period the respondent takes specified steps for the purpose of obviating or reducing the adverse effect of any matter to which the proceedings relate –

    (a) on the complainant;

    (b) on any other person.

(4) Subsection (5) applies if the tribunal –

    (a) finds that a contravention is established by virtue of section 19, but

    (b) is satisfied that the provision, criterion or practice was not applied with the intention of discriminating against the complainant.

(5) It must not make an order under subsection (2)(b) unless it first considers whether to act under subsection (2)(a) or (c).

(6) The amount of compensation which may be awarded under subsection (2)(b) corresponds to the amount which could be awarded by a county court or the sheriff under section 119.

(7)   If a respondent fails, without reasonable excuse, to comply with an appropriate recommendation in so far as it relates to the complainant, the tribunal may –

  (a)   if an order was made under subsection (2)(b), increase the amount of compensation to be paid;
  (b)   if no such order was made, make one.

SCHEDULE 1   DISABILITY: SUPPLEMENTARY PROVISION

Section 6

PART 1   DETERMINATION OF DISABILITY

Impairment

1   Regulations may make provision for a condition of a prescribed description to be, or not to be, an impairment.

Long-term effects

2   (1)   The effect of an impairment is long-term if –

  (a)   it has lasted for at least 12 months,
  (b)   it is likely to last for at least 12 months, or
  (c)   it is likely to last for the rest of the life of the person affected.

  (2)   If an impairment ceases to have a substantial adverse effect on a person's ability to carry out normal day-to-day activities, it is to be treated as continuing to have that effect if that effect is likely to recur.
  (3)   For the purposes of sub-paragraph (2), the likelihood of an effect recurring is to be disregarded in such circumstances as may be prescribed.
  (4)   Regulations may prescribe circumstances in which, despite sub-paragraph (1), an effect is to be treated as being, or as not being, long-term.

Severe disfigurement

3   (1)   An impairment which consists of a severe disfigurement is to be treated as having a substantial adverse effect on the ability of the person concerned to carry out normal day-to-day activities.
  (2)   Regulations may provide that in prescribed circumstances a severe disfigurement is not to be treated as having that effect.
  (3)   The regulations may, in particular, make provision in relation to deliberately acquired disfigurement.

Substantial adverse effects

4   Regulations may make provision for an effect of a prescribed description on the ability of a person to carry out normal day-to-day activities to be treated as being, or as not being, a substantial adverse effect.

Effect of medical treatment

5   (1)   An impairment is to be treated as having a substantial adverse effect on the ability of the person concerned to carry out normal day-to-day activities if –

        (a)   measures are being taken to treat or correct it, and
        (b)   but for that, it would be likely to have that effect.

    (2)   'Measures' includes, in particular, medical treatment and the use of a prosthesis or other aid.

    (3)   Sub-paragraph (1) does not apply –

        (a)   in relation to the impairment of a person's sight, to the extent that the impairment is, in the person's case, correctable by spectacles or contact lenses or in such other ways as may be prescribed;
        (b)   in relation to such other impairments as may be prescribed, in such circumstances as are prescribed.

Certain medical conditions

6   (1)   Cancer, HIV infection and multiple sclerosis are each a disability.

    (2)   HIV infection is infection by a virus capable of causing the Acquired Immune Deficiency Syndrome.

Deemed disability

7   (1)   Regulations may provide for persons of prescribed descriptions to be treated as having disabilities.

    (2)   The regulations may prescribe circumstances in which a person who has a disability is to be treated as no longer having the disability.

    (3)   This paragraph does not affect the other provisions of this Schedule.

Progressive conditions

8   (1)   This paragraph applies to a person (P) if –

        (a)   P has a progressive condition,
        (b)   as a result of that condition P has an impairment which has (or had) an effect on P's ability to carry out normal day-to-day activities, but
        (c)   the effect is not (or was not) a substantial adverse effect.

    (2)   P is to be taken to have an impairment which has a substantial adverse effect if the condition is likely to result in P having such an impairment.

    (3)   Regulations may make provision for a condition of a prescribed description to be treated as being, or as not being, progressive.

Past disabilities

9   (1)   A question as to whether a person had a disability at a particular time ('the relevant time') is to be determined, for the purposes of section 6, as if the provisions of, or made under, this Act were in force when the act complained of was done had been in force at the relevant time.

(2)   The relevant time may be a time before the coming into force of the provision of this Act to which the question relates.

PART 2   GUIDANCE

Preliminary

10   This Part of this Schedule applies in relation to guidance referred to in section 6(5).

Examples

11   The guidance may give examples of –

(a)   effects which it would, or would not, be reasonable, in relation to particular activities, to regard as substantial adverse effects;

(b)   substantial adverse effects which it would, or would not, be reasonable to regard as long-term.

Adjudicating bodies

12   (1)   In determining whether a person is a disabled person, an adjudicating body must take account of such guidance as it thinks is relevant.

(2)   An adjudicating body is –

(a)   a court;

(b)   a tribunal;

(c)   a person (other than a court or tribunal) who may decide a claim relating to a contravention of Part 6 (education).

Representations

13   Before issuing the guidance, the Minister must –

(a)   publish a draft of it;

(b)   consider any representations made to the Minister about the draft;

(c)   make such modifications as the Minister thinks appropriate in the light of the representations.

Parliamentary procedure

14   (1)   If the Minister decides to proceed with proposed guidance, a draft of it must be laid before Parliament.

(2)   If, before the end of the 40-day period, either House resolves not to approve the draft, the Minister must take no further steps in relation to the proposed guidance.

(3)   If no such resolution is made before the end of that period, the Minister must issue the guidance in the form of the draft.

(4)   Sub-paragraph (2) does not prevent a new draft of proposed guidance being laid before Parliament.

(5)   The 40-day period –

(a) begins on the date on which the draft is laid before both Houses (or, if laid before each House on a different date, on the later date);

(b) does not include a period during which Parliament is prorogued or dissolved;

(c) does not include a period during which both Houses are adjourned for more than 4 days.

Commencement

15 The guidance comes into force on the day appointed by order by the Minister.

Revision and revocation

16 (1) The Minister may –

(a) revise the whole or part of guidance and re-issue it;

(b) by order revoke guidance.

(2) A reference to guidance includes a reference to guidance which has been revised and re-issued.

SCHEDULE 8   WORK: REASONABLE ADJUSTMENTS

PART 3   LIMITATIONS ON THE DUTY

Lack of knowledge of disability, etc.

20 (1) A is not subject to a duty to make reasonable adjustments if A does not know, and could not reasonably be expected to know –

(a) in the case of an applicant or potential applicant, that an interested disabled person is or may be an applicant for the work in question;

(b) in any case referred to in Part 2 of this Schedule, that an interested disabled person has a disability and is likely to be placed at the disadvantage referred to in the first, second or third requirement.

(2) An applicant is, in relation to the description of A specified in the first column of the table, a person of a description specified in the second column (and the reference to a potential applicant is to be construed accordingly).

Description of A	Applicant
An employer	An applicant for employment
A firm or proposed firm	A candidate for a position as a partner
An LLP or proposed LLP	A candidate for a position as a member
A barrister or barrister's clerk	An applicant for a pupillage or tenancy
An advocate or advocate's clerk	An applicant for being taken as an advocate's devil or for becoming a member of a stable

APPENDIX C1

Description of A	Applicant
A relevant person in relation to a personal or public office	A person who is seeking appointment to, or recommendation or approval for appointment to, the office
A qualifications body	An applicant for the conferment of a relevant qualification
An employment service-provider	An applicant for the provision of an employment service
A trade organisation	An applicant for membership

(3)   If the duty to make reasonable adjustments is imposed on A by section 55, this paragraph applies only in so far as the employment service which A provides is vocational training within the meaning given by section 56(6)(b).

APPENDIX C2

Equality and Human Rights Commission: Equality Act 2010 Code of Practice (extracts)

EMPLOYMENT STATUTORY CODE OF PRACTICE[1]

CHAPTER 4: INDIRECT DISCRIMINATION

What is a disadvantage?

4.9 'Disadvantage' is not defined by the Act. It could include denial of an opportunity or choice, deterrence, rejection or exclusion. The courts have found that 'detriment', a similar concept, is something that a reasonable person would complain about – so an unjustified sense of grievance would not qualify. A disadvantage does not have to be quantifiable and the worker does not have to experience actual loss (economic or otherwise). It is enough that the worker can reasonably say that they would have preferred to be treated differently.

4.10 Sometimes, a provision, criterion or practice is intrinsically liable to disadvantage a group with a particular protected characteristic.

Example:

At the end of the year, an employer decides to invite seasonal workers employed during the previous summer to claim a bonus within a 30 day time limit. By writing to these workers at their last known address, the employer is liable to disadvantage migrant workers. This is because these workers normally return to their home country during the winter months, and so they are unlikely to apply for the bonus within the specified period. This could amount to indirect race discrimination, unless the practice can be objectively justified.

4.11 In some situations, the link between the protected characteristic and the disadvantage might be obvious; for example, dress codes create a disadvantage for some workers with particular religious beliefs. In other situations it will be less obvious how people sharing a protected characteristic are put (or would be put) at a disadvantage, in which case statistics or personal testimony may help to demonstrate that a disadvantage exists.

---

[1] © Equality and Human Rights Commission 2011. The full text of this Code of Practice can be found at **www.equalityhumanrights.com/uploaded_files/EqualityAct/employercode.pdf**.

239

Example:

A hairdresser refuses to employ stylists who cover their hair, believing it is important for them to exhibit their flamboyant haircuts. It is clear that this criterion puts at a particular disadvantage both Muslim women and Sikh men who cover their hair. This may amount to indirect discrimination unless the criterion can be objectively justified.

Example:

A consultancy firm reviews the use of psychometric tests in their recruitment procedures and discovers that men tend to score lower than women. If a man complains that the test is indirectly discriminatory, he would not need to explain the reason for the lower scores or how the lower scores are connected to his sex to show that men have been put at a disadvantage; it is sufficient for him to rely on the statistical information.

4.12 Statistics can provide an insight into the link between the provision, criterion or practice and the disadvantage that it causes. Statistics relating to the workplace in question can be obtained through the questions procedure (see paragraphs 15.5 to 15.10). It may also be possible to use national or regional statistics to throw light on the nature and extent of the particular disadvantage.

4.13 However, a statistical analysis may not always be appropriate or practicable, especially when there is inadequate or unreliable information, or the numbers of people are too small to allow for a statistically significant comparison. In this situation, the Employment Tribunal may find it helpful for an expert to provide evidence as to whether there is any disadvantage and, if so, the nature of it.

4.14 There are other cases where it may be useful to have evidence (including, if appropriate, from an expert) to help the Employment Tribunal to understand the nature of the protected characteristic or the behaviour of the group sharing the characteristic – for example, evidence about the principles of a particular religious belief.

Example:

A Muslim man who works for a small manufacturing company wishes to undertake the Hajj. However, his employer only allows their staff to take annual leave during designated shutdown periods in August and December. The worker considers that he has been subjected to indirect religious discrimination. In assessing the case, the Employment Tribunal may benefit from expert evidence from a Muslim cleric or an expert in Islam on the timing of the Hajj and whether it is of significance.

The comparative approach

4.15 Once it is clear that there is a provision, criterion or practice which puts (or would put) people sharing a protected characteristic at a particular disadvantage, then the next stage is to consider a comparison between workers with the protected characteristic and those without it. The circumstances of the two groups must be sufficiently similar for a comparison to be made and there must be no material differences in circumstances.

4.16   It is important to be clear which protected characteristic is relevant. In relation to disability, this would not be disabled people as a whole but people with a particular disability – for example, with an equivalent level of visual impairment. For race, it could be all Africans or only Somalis, for example. For age, it is important to identify the age group that is disadvantaged by the provision, criterion or practice.

Example:

If an employer were to advertise a position requiring at least five GCSEs at grades A to C without permitting any equivalent qualifications, this criterion would put at a particular disadvantage everyone born before 1971, as they are more likely to have taken O level examinations rather than GCSEs. This might be indirect age discrimination if the criterion could not be objectively justified.

The 'pool for comparison'

4.17   The people used in the comparative exercise are usually referred to as the 'pool for comparison'.

4.18   In general, the pool should consist of the group which the provision, criterion or practice affects (or would affect) either positively or negatively, while excluding workers who are not affected by it, either positively or negatively. In most situations, there is likely to be only one appropriate pool, but there may be circumstances where there is more than one. If this is the case, the Employment Tribunal will decide which of the pools to consider.

Example:

A marketing company employs 45 women, 10 of whom are part-timers, and 55 men who all work full-time. One female receptionist works Mondays, Wednesdays and Thursdays. The annual leave policy requires that all workers take time off on public holidays, at least half of which fall on a Monday every year. The receptionist argues that the policy is indirectly discriminatory against women and that it puts her at a personal disadvantage because she has proportionately less control over when she can take her annual leave. The appropriate pool for comparison is all the workers affected by the annual leave policy. The pool is not all receptionists or all part-time workers, because the policy does not only affect these groups.

Making the comparison

4.19   Looking at the pool, a comparison must be made between the impact of the provision, criterion or practice on people without the relevant protected characteristic, and its impact on people with the protected characteristic.

4.20   The way that the comparison is carried out will depend on the circumstances, including the protected characteristic concerned. It may in some circumstances be necessary to carry out a formal comparative exercise using statistical evidence.

Carrying out a formal comparative exercise

4.21   If the Employment Tribunal is asked to undertake a formal comparative exercise to decide an indirect discrimination claim, it can do this in a number of ways. One established approach involves the Employment Tribunal asking these questions:

- What proportion of the pool has the particular protected characteristic?
- Within the pool, does the provision, criterion or practice affect workers without the protected characteristic?
- How many of these workers are (or would be) disadvantaged by it? How is this expressed as a proportion ('x')?
- Within the pool, how does the provision, criterion or practice affect people who share the protected characteristic?
- How many of these workers are (or would be) put at a disadvantage by it? How is this expressed as a proportion ('y')?

4.22   Using this approach, the Employment Tribunal will then compare (x) with (y). It can then decide whether the group with the protected characteristic experiences a 'particular disadvantage' in comparison with others. Whether a difference is significant will depend on the context, such as the size of the pool and the numbers behind the proportions. It is not necessary to show that that the majority of those within the pool who share the protected characteristic are placed at a disadvantage.

Example:

A single mother of two young children is forced to resign from her job as a train driver when she cannot comply with her employer's new shift system.

The shift system is a provision, criterion or practice which causes particular disadvantage to this single mother. In an indirect discrimination claim, an Employment Tribunal must carry out a comparative exercise to decide whether the shift system puts (or would put) workers who share her protected characteristic of sex at a particular disadvantage when compared with men.

The Employment Tribunal decides to use as a pool for comparison all the train drivers working for the same employer. There are 20 female train drivers, while 2,000 are men.

It is accepted as common knowledge that men are far less likely than women to be single parents with childcare responsibilities.

- Of the 2,000 male drivers, two are unable to comply with the new shift system. This is expressed as a proportion of 0.001
- Of the 20 female train drivers, five are unable to comply with the new shift system. This is expressed as a proportion of 0.25

It is clear that a higher proportion of female drivers (0.25) than male drivers (0.001) are unable to comply with the shift system.

Taking all this into account, the Employment Tribunal decides that female train drivers – in comparison to their male counterparts – are put at a particular disadvantage by the shift system.

Is the worker concerned put at that disadvantage?

4.23   It is not enough that the provision, criterion or practice puts (or would put) at a particular disadvantage a group of people who share a protected characteristic. It must also have that effect (or be capable of having it) on the individual worker concerned. So it is not enough for a worker merely to establish that they are a member of the relevant group. They must also show they have personally suffered (or could suffer) the particular disadvantage as an individual.

Example:

An airline operates a dress code which forbids workers in customer-facing roles from displaying any item of jewellery. A Sikh cabin steward complains that this policy indirectly discriminates against Sikhs by preventing them from wearing the Kara bracelet. However, because he no longer observes the Sikh articles of faith, the steward is not put at a particular disadvantage by this policy and could not bring a claim for indirect discrimination.

The intention behind the provision, criterion or practice is irrelevant

4.24   Indirect discrimination is unlawful, even where the discriminatory effect of the provision, criterion or practice is not intentional, unless it can be objectively justified. If an employer applies the provision, criterion or practice without the intention of discriminating against the worker, the Employment Tribunal may decide not to order a payment of compensation (see paragraph 15.44).

Example:

An employer starts an induction session for new staff with an ice-breaker designed to introduce everyone in the room to the others. Each worker is required to provide a picture of themselves as a toddler. One worker is a transsexual woman who does not wish her colleagues to know that she was brought up as a boy. When she does not bring in her photo, the employer criticises her in front of the group for not joining in. It would be no defence that it did not occur to the employer that this worker may feel disadvantaged by the requirement to disclose such information.

CHAPTER 5: DISCRIMINATION ARISING FROM DISABILITY

Introduction

5.1   This chapter explains the duty of employers not to treat disabled people unfavourably because of something connected with their disability. Protection from this type of discrimination, which is known as 'discrimination arising from disability', only applies to disabled people.

What the Act says

5.2   The Act says that treatment of a disabled person amounts to discrimination where:

- an employer treats the disabled person unfavourably;
- this treatment is because of something arising in consequence of the disabled person's disability; and
- the employer cannot show that this treatment is a proportionate means of achieving a legitimate aim,

unless the employer does not know, and could not reasonably be expected to know, that the person has the disability.

How does it differ from direct discrimination?

5.3 Direct discrimination occurs when the employer treats someone less favourably because of disability itself (see Chapter 3). By contrast, in discrimination arising from disability, the question is whether the disabled person has been treated unfavourably because of something arising in consequence of their disability.

Example:

An employer dismisses a worker because she has had three months' sick leave. The employer is aware that the worker has multiple sclerosis and most of her sick leave is disability-related. The employer's decision to dismiss is not because of the worker's disability itself. However, the worker has been treated unfavourably because of something arising in consequence of her disability (namely, the need to take a period of disability-related sick leave).

How does it differ from indirect discrimination?

5.4 Indirect discrimination occurs when a disabled person is (or would be) disadvantaged by an unjustifiable provision, criterion or practice applied to everyone, which puts (or would put) people sharing the disabled person's disability at a particular disadvantage compared to others, and puts (or would put) the disabled person at that disadvantage (see Chapter 4).

5.5 In contrast, discrimination arising from disability only requires the disabled person to show they have experienced unfavourable treatment because of something connected with their disability. If the employer can show that they did not know and could not reasonably have been expected to know that the disabled person had the disability, it will not be discrimination arising from disability (see paragraphs 5.13 to 5.19). However, as with indirect discrimination, the employer may avoid discrimination arising from disability if the treatment can be objectively justified as a proportionate means of achieving a legitimate aim (see paragraph 5.11)

Is a comparator required?

5.6 Both direct and indirect discrimination require a comparative exercise. But in considering discrimination arising from disability, there is no need to compare a disabled person's treatment with that of another person. It is only necessary to demonstrate that the unfavourable treatment is because of something arising in consequence of the disability.

Example:

In considering whether the example of the disabled worker dismissed for disability-related sickness absence (see paragraph 5.3) amounts to discrimination arising from disability, it is irrelevant whether or not other workers would have been dismissed for having the same or similar length of absence. It is not necessary to compare the treatment of the disabled worker with that of her colleagues or any hypothetical comparator. The decision to dismiss her will be discrimination arising from disability if the employer cannot objectively justify it.

What is 'unfavourable treatment'?

5.7   For discrimination arising from disability to occur, a disabled person must have been treated 'unfavourably'. This means that he or she must have been put at a disadvantage. Often, the disadvantage will be obvious and it will be clear that the treatment has been unfavourable; for example, a person may have been refused a job, denied a work opportunity or dismissed from their employment. But sometimes unfavourable treatment may be less obvious. Even if an employer thinks that they are acting in the best interests of a disabled person, they may still treat that person unfavourably.

What does 'something arising in consequence of disability' mean?

5.8   The unfavourable treatment must be because of something that arises in consequence of the disability. This means that there must be a connection between whatever led to the unfavourable treatment and the disability.

5.9   The consequences of a disability include anything which is the result, effect or outcome of a disabled person's disability. The consequences will be varied, and will depend on the individual effect upon a disabled person of their disability. Some consequences may be obvious, such as an inability to walk unaided or inability to use certain work equipment. Others may not be obvious, for example, having to follow a restricted diet.

Example:

A woman is disciplined for losing her temper at work. However, this behaviour was out of character and is a result of severe pain caused by cancer, of which her employer is aware. The disciplinary action is unfavourable treatment. This treatment is because of something which arises in consequence of the worker's disability, namely her loss of temper. There is a connection between the 'something' (that is, the loss of temper) that led to the treatment and her disability. It will be discrimination arising from disability if the employer cannot objectively justify the decision to discipline the worker.

5.10   So long as the unfavourable treatment is because of something arising in consequence of the disability, it will be unlawful unless it can be objectively justified, or unless the employer did not know or could not reasonably have been expected to know that the person was disabled (see paragraph 5.13).

When can discrimination arising from disability be justified?

5.11   Unfavourable treatment will not amount to discrimination arising from disability if the employer can show that the treatment is a 'proportionate means of achieving a legitimate aim'. This 'objective justification' test is explained in detail in paragraphs 4.25 to 4.32.

5.12   It is for the employer to justify the treatment. They must produce evidence to support their assertion that it is justified and not rely on mere generalisations.

What if the employer does not know that the person is disabled?

5.13   If the employer can show that they:

- did not know that the disabled person had the disability in question; and
- could not reasonably have been expected to know that the disabled person had the disability,

then the unfavourable treatment does not amount to discrimination arising from disability.

5.14   It is not enough for the employer to show that they did not know that the disabled person had the disability. They must also show that they could not reasonably have been expected to know about it. Employers should consider whether a worker has a disability even where one has not been formally disclosed, as, for example, not all workers who meet the definition of disability may think of themselves as a 'disabled person'.

5.15   An employer must do all they can reasonably be expected to do to find out if a worker has a disability. What is reasonable will depend on the circumstances. This is an objective assessment. When making enquiries about disability, employers should consider issues of dignity and privacy and ensure that personal information is dealt with confidentially.

Example:

A disabled man who has depression has been at a particular workplace for two years. He has a good attendance and performance record. In recent weeks, however, he has become emotional and upset at work for no apparent reason. He has also been repeatedly late for work and has made some mistakes in his work. The worker is disciplined without being given any opportunity to explain that his difficulties at work arise from a disability and that recently the effects of his depression have worsened.

The sudden deterioration in the worker's time-keeping and performance and the change in his behaviour at work should have alerted the employer to the possibility that that these were connected to a disability. It is likely to be reasonable to expect the employer to explore with the worker the reason for these changes and whether the difficulties are because of something arising in consequence of a disability.

5.16   However, employers should note that the Act imposes restrictions on the types of health or disability-related enquiries that can be made prior to making someone a job offer or including someone in a pool of successful candidates to be offered a job when one becomes available (see paragraphs 10.25 to 10.43).

When can an employer be assumed to know about disability?

5.17   If an employer's agent or employee (such as an occupational health adviser or a HR officer) knows, in that capacity, of a worker's or applicant's or potential applicant's disability, the employer will not usually be able to claim that they do not know of the disability, and that they cannot therefore have subjected a disabled person to discrimination arising from disability.

5.18   Therefore, where information about disabled people may come through different channels, employers need to ensure that there is a means – suitably confidential and subject to the disabled person's consent – for bringing that information together to make it easier for the employer to fulfil their duties under the Act.

Example:

An occupational health (OH) adviser is engaged by a large employer to provide them with information about their workers' health. The OH adviser becomes aware of a worker's disability that is relevant to his work, and the worker consents to this information being disclosed to the employer. However, the OH adviser does not pass that information on to Human Resources or to the worker's line manager. As the OH adviser is acting as the employer's agent, it is not a defence for the employer to claim that they did not know about the worker's disability. This is because the information gained by the adviser on the employer's behalf is attributed to the employer.

5.19   Information will not be attributed ('imputed') to the employer if it is gained by a person providing services to workers independently of the employer. This is the case even if the employer has arranged for those services to be provided.

Example:

An employer contracts with an agency to provide an independent counselling service to workers. The contract states that the counsellors are not acting on the employer's behalf while in the counselling role. Any information obtained by a counsellor during such counselling would not be attributed to the employer.

Relevance of reasonable adjustments

5.20   Employers can often prevent unfavourable treatment which would amount to discrimination arising from disability by taking prompt action to identify and implement reasonable adjustments (see Chapter 6).

5.21   If an employer has failed to make a reasonable adjustment which would have prevented or minimised the unfavourable treatment, it will be very difficult for them to show that the treatment was objectively justified.

5.22   Even where an employer has complied with a duty to make reasonable adjustments in relation to the disabled person, they may still subject a disabled person to unlawful discrimination arising from disability. This is likely to apply where, for example, the adjustment is unrelated to the particular treatment complained of.

Example:

The employer in the example at paragraph 5.3 made a reasonable adjustment for the worker who has multiple sclerosis. They adjusted her working hours so that she started work at 9.30am instead of 9am.

However, this adjustment is not relevant to the unfavourable treatment – namely, her dismissal for disability-related sickness absence – which her claim concerns. And so, despite the fact that reasonable adjustments were made, there will still be discrimination arising from disability unless the treatment is justified.

CHAPTER 6: DUTY TO MAKE REASONABLE ADJUSTMENTS

Introduction

6.1 This chapter describes the principles and application of the duty to make reasonable adjustments for disabled people in employment.

6.2 The duty to make reasonable adjustments is a cornerstone of the Act and requires employers to take positive steps to ensure that disabled people can access and progress in employment. This goes beyond simply avoiding treating disabled workers, job applicants and potential job applicants unfavourably and means taking additional steps to which non-disabled workers and applicants are not entitled.

6.3 The duty to make reasonable adjustments applies to employers of all sizes, but the question of what is reasonable may vary according to the circumstances of the employer. Part 2 of the Code has more information about good practice in making reasonable adjustments in different work situations, such as in recruitment or during employment.

What the Act says

6.4 Discrimination against a disabled person occurs where an employer fails to comply with a duty to make reasonable adjustments imposed on them in relation to that disabled person.

What is the duty to make reasonable adjustments?

6.5 The duty to make reasonable adjustments comprises three requirements. Employers are required to take reasonable steps to:

- Avoid the substantial disadvantage where a provision, criterion or practice applied by or on behalf of the employer puts a disabled person at a substantial disadvantage compared to those who are not disabled.
- Remove or alter a physical feature or provide a reasonable means of avoiding such a feature where it puts a disabled person at a substantial disadvantage compared to those who are not disabled.
- Provide an auxiliary aid (which includes an auxiliary service – see paragraph 6.13)

where a disabled person would, but for the provision of that auxiliary aid, be put at a substantial disadvantage compared to those who are not disabled.

Accessible information

6.6   The Act states that where the provision, criterion or practice or the need for an auxiliary aid relates to the provision of information, the steps which it is reasonable for the employer to take include steps to ensure that the information is provided in an accessible format; for example, providing letters, training materials or recruitment forms in Braille or on audio-tape.

Avoiding substantial disadvantages caused by physical features

6.7   The Act says that avoiding a substantial disadvantage caused by a physical feature includes:

- removing the physical feature in question;
- altering it; or
- providing a reasonable means of avoiding it.

Which disabled people does the duty protect?

6.8   The duty to make reasonable adjustments applies in recruitment and during all stages of employment, including dismissal. It may also apply after employment has ended. The duty relates to all disabled workers of an employer and to any disabled applicant for employment. The duty also applies in respect of any disabled person who has notified the employer that they may be an applicant for work.

6.9   In order to avoid discrimination, it would be sensible for employers not to attempt to make a fine judgment as to whether a particular individual falls within the statutory definition of disability, but to focus instead on meeting the needs of each worker and job applicant.

What is a provision, criterion or practice?

6.10   The phrase 'provision, criterion or practice' is not defined by the Act but should be construed widely so as to include, for example, any formal or informal policies, rules, practices, arrangements or qualifications including one-off decisions and actions (see also paragraph 4.5).

Example:

An employer has a policy that designated car parking spaces are only offered to senior managers. A worker who is not a manager, but has a mobility impairment and needs to park very close to the office, is given a designated car parking space. This is likely to be a reasonable adjustment to the employer's car parking policy.

What is a 'physical feature'?

6.11   The Act says that the following are to be treated as a physical feature of the premises occupied by the employer:

* any feature of the design or construction of a building;
* any feature of an approach to, exit from or entrance to a building;
* a fixture or fitting, or furniture, furnishings, materials, equipment or other chattels (moveable property in Scotland) in or on the premises;
* any other physical element or quality of the premises.

All these features are covered, whether temporary or permanent.

6.12   Physical features will include steps, stairways, kerbs, exterior surfaces and paving, parking areas, building entrances and exits (including emergency escape routes), internal and external doors, gates, toilet and washing facilities, lighting and ventilation, lifts and escalators, floor coverings, signs, furniture and temporary or moveable items. This is not an exhaustive list.

Example:

Clear glass doors at the end of a corridor in a particular workplace present a hazard for a visually impaired worker. This is a substantial disadvantage caused by the physical features of the workplace.

What is an 'auxiliary aid'?

6.13   An auxiliary aid is something which provides support or assistance to a disabled person. It can include provision of a specialist piece of equipment such as an adapted keyboard or text to speech software. Auxiliary aids include auxiliary services; for example, provision of a sign language interpreter or a support worker for a disabled worker.

What disadvantage gives rise to the duty?

6.14   The duty to make adjustments arises where a provision, criterion, or practice, any physical feature of work premises or the absence of an auxiliary aid puts a disabled person at a substantial disadvantage compared with people who are not disabled.

6.15   The Act says that a substantial disadvantage is one which is more than minor or trivial. Whether such a disadvantage exists in a particular case is a question of fact, and is assessed on an objective basis.

6.16   The purpose of the comparison with people who are not disabled is to establish whether it is because of disability that a particular provision, criterion, practice or physical feature or the absence of an auxiliary aid disadvantages the disabled person in question. Accordingly – and unlike direct or indirect discrimination – under the duty to make adjustments there is no requirement to identify a comparator or comparator group whose circumstances are the same or nearly the same as the disabled person's.

What if the employer does not know that a disabled person is an actual or potential job applicant?

6.17 An employer only has a duty to make an adjustment if they know, or could reasonably be expected to know, that a disabled person is, or may be, an applicant for work.

6.18 There are restrictions on when health or disability-related enquiries can be made prior to making a job offer or including someone in a pool of people to be offered a job. However, questions are permitted to determine whether reasonable adjustments need to be made in relation to an assessment, such as an interview or other process designed to give an indication of a person's suitability for the work concerned. These provisions are explained in detail in paragraphs 10.25 to 10.43.

What if the employer does not know the worker is disabled?

6.19 For disabled workers already in employment, an employer only has a duty to make an adjustment if they know, or could reasonably be expected to know, that a worker has a disability and is, or is likely to be, placed at a substantial disadvantage. The employer must, however, do all they can reasonably be expected to do to find out whether this is the case. What is reasonable will depend on the circumstances. This is an objective assessment. When making enquiries about disability, employers should consider issues of dignity and privacy and ensure that personal information is dealt with confidentially.

Example:

A worker who deals with customers by phone at a call centre has depression which sometimes causes her to cry at work. She has difficulty dealing with customer enquiries when the symptoms of her depression are severe. It is likely to be reasonable for the employer to discuss with the worker whether her crying is connected to a disability and whether a reasonable adjustment could be made to her working arrangements.

6.20 The Act does not prevent a disabled person keeping a disability confidential from an employer. But keeping a disability confidential is likely to mean that unless the employer could reasonably be expected to know about it anyway, the employer will not be under a duty to make a reasonable adjustment. If a disabled person expects an employer to make a reasonable adjustment, they will need to provide the employer – or someone acting on their behalf – with sufficient information to carry out that adjustment.

When can an employer be assumed to know about disability?

6.21 If an employer's agent or employee (such as an occupational health adviser, a HR officer or a recruitment agent) knows, in that capacity, of a worker's or applicant's or potential applicant's disability, the employer will not usually be able to claim that they do not know of the disability and that they therefore have no obligation to make a reasonable adjustment. Employers therefore need to ensure that where information about disabled people may come through different channels, there is a means – suitably confidential and subject to the disabled person's consent – for bringing that information together to make it easier for the employer to fulfil their duties under the Act.

Example:

In the example in paragraph 5.18, if the employer's working arrangements put the worker at a substantial disadvantage because of the effects of his disability and he claims that a reasonable adjustment should have been made, it will not be a defence for the employer to claim that they were unaware of the worker's disability. Because the information gained by the OH adviser on the employer's behalf is assumed to be shared with the employer, the OH adviser's knowledge means that the employer's duty under the Act applies.

6.22 Information will not be 'imputed' or attributed to the employer if it is gained by a person providing services to employees independently of the employer. This is the case even if the employer has arranged for those services to be provided.

What is meant by 'reasonable steps'?

6.23 The duty to make adjustments requires employers to take such steps as it is reasonable to have to take, in all the circumstances of the case, in order to make adjustments. The Act does not specify any particular factors that should be taken into account. What is a reasonable step for an employer to take will depend on all the circumstances of each individual case.

6.24 There is no onus on the disabled worker to suggest what adjustments should be made (although it is good practice for employers to ask). However, where the disabled person does so, the employer should consider whether such adjustments would help overcome the substantial disadvantage, and whether they are reasonable.

6.25 Effective and practicable adjustments for disabled workers often involve little or no cost or disruption and are therefore very likely to be reasonable for an employer to have to make. Even if an adjustment has a significant cost associated with it, it may still be cost-effective in overall terms – for example, compared with the costs of recruiting and training a new member of staff – and so may still be a reasonable adjustment to have to make.

6.26 Many adjustments do not involve making physical changes to premises. However, where such changes need to be made and an employer occupies premises under a lease or other binding obligation, the employer may have to obtain consent to the making of reasonable adjustments. These provisions are explained in Appendix 3.

6.27 If making a particular adjustment would increase the risk to health and safety of any person (including the disabled worker in question) then this is a relevant factor in deciding whether it is reasonable to make that adjustment. Suitable and sufficient risk assessments should be used to help determine whether such risk is likely to arise.

6.28 The following are some of the factors which might be taken into account when deciding what is a reasonable step for an employer to have to take:

- whether taking any particular steps would be effective in preventing the substantial disadvantage;
- the practicability of the step;
- the financial and other costs of making the adjustment and the extent of any disruption caused;
- the extent of the employer's financial or other resources;

- the availability to the employer of financial or other assistance to help make an adjustment (such as advice through Access to Work); and
- the type and size of the employer.

6.29   Ultimately the test of the 'reasonableness' of any step an employer may have to take is an objective one and will depend on the circumstances of the case.

Can failure to make a reasonable adjustment ever be justified?

6.30   The Act does not permit an employer to justify a failure to comply with a duty to make a reasonable adjustment. However, an employer will only breach such a duty if the adjustment in question is one which it is reasonable for the employer to have to make. So, where the duty applies, it is the question of 'reasonableness' which alone determines whether the adjustment has to be made.

What happens if the duty is not complied with?

6.31   If an employer does not comply with the duty to make reasonable adjustments they will be committing an act of unlawful discrimination. A disabled worker will have the right to take a claim to the Employment Tribunal based on this.

Reasonable adjustments in practice

6.32   It is a good starting point for an employer to conduct a proper assessment, in consultation with the disabled person concerned, of what reasonable adjustments may be required. Any necessary adjustments should be implemented in a timely fashion, and it may also be necessary for an employer to make more than one adjustment. It is advisable to agree any proposed adjustments with the disabled worker in question before they are made.

6.33   Examples of steps it might be reasonable for employers to have to take include:

Making adjustments to premises

Example:

An employer makes structural or other physical changes such as widening a doorway, providing a ramp or moving furniture for a wheelchair user.

Providing information in accessible formats

Example:

The format of instructions and manuals might need to be modified for some disabled workers (for example, produced in Braille or on audio tape) and instructions for people with learning disabilities might need to be conveyed orally with individual demonstration or in Easy Read. Employers may also need to arrange for recruitment materials to be provided in alternative formats.

Allocating some of the disabled person's duties to another worker

---

Example:

An employer reallocates minor or subsidiary duties to another worker as a disabled worker has difficulty doing them because of his disability. For example, the job involves occasionally going onto the open roof of a building but the employer transfers this work away from a worker whose disability involves severe vertigo.

Transferring the disabled worker to fill an existing vacancy

Example:

An employer should consider whether a suitable alternative post is available for a worker who becomes disabled (or whose disability worsens), where no reasonable adjustment would enable the worker to continue doing the current job. Such a post might also involve retraining or other reasonable adjustments such as equipment for the new post or transfer to a position on a higher grade.

Altering the disabled worker's hours of work or training

Example:

An employer allows a disabled person to work flexible hours to enable him to have additional breaks to overcome fatigue arising from his disability. It could also include permitting part-time working or different working hours to avoid the need to travel in the rush hour if this creates a problem related to an impairment. A phased return to work with a gradual build-up of hours might also be appropriate in some circumstances.

Assigning the disabled worker to a different place of work or training or arranging home working

---

Example:

An employer relocates the workstation of a newly disabled worker (who now uses a wheelchair) from an inaccessible third floor office to an accessible one on the ground floor. It may be reasonable to move his place of work to other premises of the same employer if the first building is inaccessible. Allowing the worker to work from home might also be a reasonable adjustment for the employer to make.

Allowing the disabled worker to be absent during working or training hours for rehabilitation, assessment or treatment

---

Example:

An employer allows a person who has become disabled more time off work than would be allowed to non-disabled workers to enable him to have rehabilitation training. A similar adjustment may be appropriate if a disability worsens or if a disabled person needs occasional treatment anyway.

Giving, or arranging for, training or mentoring (whether for the disabled person or any other worker)

This could be training in particular pieces of equipment which the disabled person uses, or an alteration to the standard workplace training to reflect the worker's particular disability.

Example:

All workers are trained in the use of a particular machine but an employer provides slightly different or longer training for a worker with restricted hand or arm movements. An employer might also provide training in additional software for a visually impaired worker so that he can use a computer with speech output.

Acquiring or modifying equipment

Example:

An employer might have to provide special equipment such as an adapted keyboard for someone with arthritis, a large screen for a visually impaired worker, or an adapted telephone for someone with a hearing impairment, or other modified equipment for disabled workers (such as longer handles on a machine).

There is no requirement to provide or modify equipment for personal purposes unconnected with a worker's job, such as providing a wheelchair if a person needs one in any event but does not have one. The disadvantages in such a case do not flow from the employer's arrangements or premises.

Modifying procedures for testing or assessment

Example:

A worker with restricted manual dexterity would be disadvantaged by a written test, so the employer gives that person an oral test instead.

Providing a reader or interpreter

Example:

An employer arranges for a colleague to read mail to a worker with a visual impairment at particular times during the working day. Alternatively, the employer might hire a reader.

Providing supervision or other support

Example:

An employer provides a support worker or arranges help from a colleague, in appropriate circumstances, for someone whose disability leads to uncertainty or lack of confidence in unfamiliar situations, such as on a training course.

Allowing a disabled worker to take a period of disability leave

---

Example:

A worker who has cancer needs to undergo treatment and rehabilitation. His employer allows a period of disability leave and permits him to return to his job at the end of this period.

Participating in supported employment schemes, such as Workstep

---

Example:

A man applies for a job as an office assistant after several years of not working because of depression. He has been participating in a supported employment scheme where he saw the post advertised. He asks the employer to let him make private phone calls during the working day to a support worker at the scheme and the employer allows him to do so as a reasonable adjustment.

Employing a support worker to assist a disabled worker

Example:

An adviser with a visual impairment is sometimes required to make home visits to clients. The employer employs a support worker to assist her on these visits.

Modifying disciplinary or grievance procedures for a disabled worker

Example:

A worker with a learning disability is allowed to take a friend (who does not work with her) to act as an advocate at a meeting with her employer about a grievance. The employer also ensures that the meeting is conducted in a way that does not disadvantage or patronise the disabled worker.

Adjusting redundancy selection criteria for a disabled worker

Example:

Because of his condition, a man with an autoimmune disease has taken several short periods of absence during the year. When his employer is taking the absences into account as a criterion for selecting people for redundancy, they discount these periods of disability-related absence.

Modifying performance-related pay arrangements for a disabled worker

Example:

A disabled worker who is paid purely on her output needs frequent short additional breaks during her working day – something her employer agrees to as a reasonable adjustment. It may be a reasonable adjustment for her employer to pay her at an agreed rate (for example, her average hourly rate) for these breaks.

6.34 It may sometimes be necessary for an employer to take a combination of steps.

Example:

A worker who is blind is given a new job with her employer in an unfamiliar part of the building. The employer:

- arranges facilities for her assistance dog in the new area;
- arranges for her new instructions to be in Braille; and

257

- provides disability equality training to all staff.

6.35   In some cases, a reasonable adjustment will not succeed without the cooperation of other workers. Colleagues as well as managers may therefore have an important role in helping ensure that a reasonable adjustment is carried out in practice. Subject to considerations about confidentiality, employers must ensure that this happens. It is unlikely to be a valid defence to a claim under the Act to argue that an adjustment was unreasonable because staff were obstructive or unhelpful when the employer tried to implement it. An employer would at least need to be able to show that they took such behaviour seriously and dealt with it appropriately. Employers will be more likely to be able to do this if they establish and implement the type of policies and practices described in Chapter 18.

Example:

An employer ensures that a worker with autism has a structured working day as a reasonable adjustment. As part of this adjustment, it is the responsibility of the employer to ensure that other workers co-operate with this arrangement.

The Access to Work scheme

6.36   The Access to Work scheme may assist an employer to decide what steps to take. If financial assistance is available from the scheme, it may also make it reasonable for an employer to take certain steps which would otherwise be unreasonably expensive.

6.37   However, Access to Work does not diminish any of an employer's duties under the Act. In particular:

- The legal responsibility for making a reasonable adjustment remains with the employer – even where Access to Work is involved in the provision of advice or funding in relation to the adjustment.
- it is likely to be a reasonable step for the employer to help a disabled person in making an application for assistance from Access to Work and to provide on-going administrative support (by completing claim forms, for example).

6.38   It may be unreasonable for an employer to decide not to make an adjustment based on its cost before finding out whether financial assistance for the adjustment is available from Access to Work or another source.

6.39   More information about the Access to Work scheme is available from: http://www.direct.gov.uk/en/DisabledPeople/Employmentsupport/WorkSchemesAndProgrammes/DG_4000347

CHAPTER 7: HARASSMENT

7.7   Unwanted conduct covers a wide range of behaviour, including spoken or written words or abuse, imagery, graffiti, physical gestures, facial expressions, mimicry, jokes, pranks, acts affecting a person's surroundings or other physical behaviour.

7.8 The word 'unwanted' means essentially the same as 'unwelcome' or 'uninvited'. 'Unwanted' does not mean that express objection must be made to the conduct before it is deemed to be unwanted. A serious one-off incident can also amount to harassment.

Example:

In front of her male colleagues, a female electrician is told by her supervisor that her work is below standard and that, as a woman, she will never be competent to carry it out. The supervisor goes on to suggest that she should instead stay at home to cook and clean for her husband. This could amount to harassment related to sex as such a statement would be self-evidently unwanted and the electrician would not have to object to it before it was deemed to be unlawful harassment.

7.10 Protection from harassment also applies where a person is generally abusive to other workers but, in relation to a particular worker, the form of the unwanted conduct is determined by that worker's protected characteristic.

Example:

During a training session attended by both male and female workers, a male trainer directs a number of remarks of a sexual nature to the group as a whole. A female worker finds the comments offensive and humiliating to her as a woman. She would be able to make a claim for harassment, even though the remarks were not specifically directed at her.

b) Where there is any connection with a protected characteristic.

Protection is provided because the conduct is dictated by a relevant protected characteristic, whether or not the worker has that characteristic themselves. This means that protection against unwanted conduct is provided where the worker does not have the relevant protected characteristic, including where the employer knows that the worker does not have the relevant characteristic. Connection with a protected characteristic may arise in several situations:

- The worker may be associated with someone who has a protected characteristic.

Example:

A worker has a son with a severe disfigurement. His work colleagues make offensive remarks to him about his son's disability. The worker could have a claim for harassment related to disability.

- The worker may be wrongly perceived as having a particular protected characteristic.

Example:

A Sikh worker wears a turban to work. His manager wrongly assumes he is Muslim and subjects him to Islamaphobic abuse. The worker could have a claim for harassment related to religion or belief because of his manager's perception of his religion.

- The worker is known not to have the protected characteristic but nevertheless is subjected to harassment related to that characteristic.

Example:

A worker is subjected to homophobic banter and name calling, even though his colleagues know he is not gay. Because the form of the abuse relates to sexual orientation, this could amount to harassment related to sexual orientation.

- The unwanted conduct related to a protected characteristic is not directed at the particular worker but at another person or no one in particular.

Example:

A manager racially abuses a black worker. As a result of the racial abuse, the black worker's white colleague is offended and could bring a claim of racial harassment.

- The unwanted conduct is related to the protected characteristic, but does not take place because of the protected characteristic.

Example:

A female worker has a relationship with her male manager. On seeing her with another male colleague, the manager suspects she is having an affair. As a result, the manager makes her working life difficult by continually criticising her work in an offensive manner. The behaviour is not because of the sex of the female worker, but because of the suspected affair which is related to her sex. This could amount to harassment related to sex.

9.18 An inducement may amount to no more than persuasion and need not involve a benefit or loss. Nor does the inducement have to be applied directly: it may be indirect. It is enough if it is applied in such a way that the other person is likely to come to know about the inducement.

Example:

The managing partner of an accountancy firm is aware that the head of the administrative team is planning to engage a senior receptionist with a physical disability. The managing partner does not issue any direct instruction but suggests to the head of administration that to do this would reflect poorly on his judgement and so affect his future with the firm. This is likely to amount to causing or attempting to cause the head of administration to act unlawfully.

CHAPTER 10: OBLIGATIONS AND LIABILITIES UNDER THE ACT

Harassment of job applicants and employees

10.24   Depending on the size and resources of an employer, reasonably practical steps might include:

- having a policy on harassment;
- notifying third parties that harassment of employees is unlawful and will not be tolerated, for example by the display of a public notice;
- inclusion of a term in all contracts with third parties notifying them of the employer's policy on harassment and requiring them to adhere to it;
- encouraging employees to report any acts of harassment by third parties to enable the employer to support the employee and take appropriate action;
- taking action on every complaint of harassment by a third party.

10.31   It is lawful to ask questions about disability or health that are needed to establish whether a person (whether disabled or not) can undertake an assessment as part of the recruitment process, including questions about reasonable adjustments for this purpose.

APPENDIX 1: THE MEANING OF DISABILITY

1.   This Appendix is included to aid understanding about who is covered by the Act. Government guidance on determining questions relating to the definition of disability is also available from the Office of Disability Issues: http://www.officefordisability.gov.uk/docs/wor/new/ea-guide.pdf

When is a person disabled?

2.   A person has a disability if they have a physical or mental impairment, which has a substantial and long-term adverse effect on their ability to carry out normal day-to-day activities.

3.   However, special rules apply to people with some conditions such as progressive conditions (see paragraph 19 of this Appendix) and some people are automatically deemed disabled for the purposes of the Act (see paragraph 18).

What about people who have recovered from a disability?

4.   People who have had a disability within the definition are protected from discrimination even if they have since recovered, although those with past disabilities are not covered in relation to Part 12 (transport) and section 190 (improvements to let dwelling houses).

What does 'impairment' cover?

5.   It covers physical or mental impairments. This includes sensory impairments, such as those affecting sight or hearing.

Are all mental impairments covered?

6. The term 'mental impairment' is intended to cover a wide range of impairments relating to mental functioning, including what are often known as learning disabilities.

What if a person has no medical diagnosis?

7. There is no need for a person to establish a medically diagnosed cause for their impairment. What it is important to consider is the effect of the impairment, not the cause.

What is a 'substantial' adverse effect?

8. A substantial adverse effect is something which is more than a minor or trivial effect. The requirement that an effect must be substantial reflects the general understanding of disability as a limitation going beyond the normal differences in ability which might exist among people.

9. Account should also be taken of where a person avoids doing things which, for example, cause pain, fatigue or substantial social embarrassment; or because of a loss of energy and motivation.

10. An impairment may not directly prevent someone from carrying out one or more normal day-to-day activities, but it may still have a substantial adverse long-term effect on how they carry out those activities. For example, where an impairment causes pain or fatigue in performing normal day-to-day activities, the person may have the capacity to do something but suffer pain in doing so; or the impairment might make the activity more than usually fatiguing so that the person might not be able to repeat the task over a sustained period of time.

What is a 'long-term' effect?

11. A long-term effect of an impairment is one:

    - which has lasted at least 12 months; or
    - where the total period for which it lasts is likely to be at least 12 months; or
    - which is likely to last for the rest of the life of the person affected.

12. Effects which are not long-term would therefore include loss of mobility due to a broken limb which is likely to heal within 12 months, and the effects of temporary infections, from which a person would be likely to recover within 12 months.

What if the effects come and go over a period of time?

13. If an impairment has had a substantial adverse effect on normal day-to-day activities but that effect ceases, the substantial effect is treated as continuing if it is likely to recur; that is, if it might well recur.

What are 'normal day-to-day activities'?

14. They are activities which are carried out by most men or women on a fairly regular and frequent basis. The term is not intended to include activities which are normal only for a particular person or group of people, such as playing a musical instrument, or participating in a sport to a professional standard, or performing a skilled or specialised task at work. However, someone who is affected in such a specialised way but is also affected in normal day-to-day activities would be covered by this part of the definition.

15. Day-to-day activities thus include – but are not limited to –activities such as walking, driving, using public transport, cooking, eating, lifting and carrying everyday objects, typing, writing (and taking exams), going to the toilet, talking, listening to conversations or music, reading, taking part in normal social interaction or forming social relationships, nourishing and caring for one's self. Normal day-to-day activities also encompass the activities which are relevant to working life.

What about treatment?

16. Someone with an impairment may be receiving medical or other treatment which alleviates or removes the effects (though not the impairment). In such cases, the treatment is ignored and the impairment is taken to have the effect it would have had without such treatment. This does not apply if substantial adverse effects are not likely to recur even if the treatment stops (that is, the impairment has been cured).

Does this include people who wear spectacles?

17. No. The sole exception to the rule about ignoring the effects of treatment is the wearing of spectacles or contact lenses. In this case, the effect while the person is wearing spectacles or contact lenses should be considered.

Are people who have disfigurements covered?

18. People with severe disfigurements are covered by the Act. They do not need to demonstrate that the impairment has a substantial adverse effect on their ability to carry out normal day-to-day activities. However, they do need to meet the long-term requirement.

Are there any other people who are automatically treated as disabled under the Act?

19. Anyone who has HIV, cancer or multiple sclerosis is automatically treated as disabled under the Act. In some circumstances, people who have a sight impairment are automatically treated as disabled under Regulations made under the Act.

What about people who know their condition is going to get worse over time?

20. Progressive conditions are conditions which are likely to change and develop over time. Where a person has a progressive condition they will be covered by the Act from the moment the condition leads to an impairment which has some effect on ability to carry out normal day-to-day activities, even though not a substantial effect, if that impairment might well have a substantial adverse effect on such ability in the future. This applies provided that the effect meets the long-term requirement of the definition.

APPENDIX C3

Office for Disability Issues: Equality Act 2010 Guidance (extracts)

EQUALITY ACT 2010: GUIDANCE ON MATTERS TO BE TAKEN
INTO ACCOUNT IN DETERMINING QUESTIONS RELATING TO
THE DEFINITION OF DISABILITY[1]

SECTION B: SUBSTANTIAL

This section should not be read in isolation but must be considered together with sections A, C and D. Whether a person satisfies the definition of a disabled person for the purposes of the Act will depend upon the full circumstances of the case. That is, whether the adverse effect of the person's impairment on the carrying out of normal day-to-day activities is substantial and long term.

Meaning of 'substantial adverse effect'

B1. The requirement that an adverse effect on normal day-to-day activities should be a substantial one reflects the general understanding of disability as a limitation going beyond the normal differences in ability which may exist among people. A substantial effect is one that is more than a minor or trivial effect. This is stated in the **Act at S212(1)**. This section looks in more detail at what 'substantial' means. **It should be read in conjunction with Section D which considers what is meant by 'normal day-to-day activities'.**

The time taken to carry out an activity

B2. The time taken by a person with an impairment to carry out a normal day-to-day activity should be considered when assessing whether the effect of that impairment is substantial. It should be compared with the time it might take a person who did not have the impairment to complete an activity.

A ten-year-old child has cerebral palsy. The effects include muscle stiffness, poor balance and unco-ordinated movements. The child is still able to do most things for himself, but he gets tired very easily and it is harder for him to accomplish tasks like eating and drinking, washing, and getting dressed. He has the ability to carry out everyday activities such as these,

---

[1]   © Crown Copyright 2011. Last issued by the Office for Disability Issues, May 2011. The full text of this guidance can be found at **www.gov.uk/government/uploads/system/uploads/ attachment_data/file/85038/disability-definition.pdf**.

264

but everything takes much longer compared to a child of a similar age who does not have cerebral palsy. This amounts to a substantial adverse effect.

The way in which an activity is carried out

B3.   Another factor to be considered when assessing whether the effect of an impairment is substantial is the way in which a person with that impairment carries out a normal day-to-day activity. The comparison should be with the way that the person might be expected to carry out the activity compared with someone who does not have the impairment.

A person who has obsessive compulsive disorder (OCD) constantly checks and rechecks that electrical appliances are switched off and that the doors are locked when leaving home. A person without the disorder would not normally carry out these frequent checks. The need to constantly check and recheck has a substantial adverse effect.

Cumulative effects of an impairment

B4.   An impairment might not have a substantial adverse effect on a person's ability to undertake a particular day-to-day activity in isolation. However, it is important to consider whether its effects on more than one activity, when taken together, could result in an overall substantial adverse effect.

B5.   For example, a person whose impairment causes breathing difficulties may, as a result, experience minor effects on the ability to carry out a number of activities such as getting washed and dressed, going for a walk or travelling on public transport. But taken together, the cumulative result would amount to a substantial adverse effect on his or her ability to carry out these normal day-to-day activities.

A man with depression experiences a range of symptoms that include a loss of energy and motivation that makes even the simplest of tasks or decisions seem quite difficult. He finds it difficult to get up in the morning, get washed and dressed, and prepare breakfast. He is forgetful and cannot plan ahead. As a result he has often run out of food before he thinks of going shopping again. Household tasks are frequently left undone, or take much longer to complete than normal. Together, the effects amount to the impairment having a substantial adverse effect on carrying out normal day-to-day activities.

B6.   A person may have more than one impairment, any one of which alone would not have a substantial effect. In such a case, account should be taken of whether the impairments together have a substantial effect overall on the person's ability to carry out normal day-to-day activities. For example, a minor impairment which affects physical co-ordination and an irreversible but minor injury to a leg which affects mobility, when taken together, might have a substantial effect on the person's ability to carry out certain normal day-to-day activities. The cumulative effect of more than one impairment should also be taken into account when determining whether the effect is long-term, **see Section C**.

A person has mild learning disability. This means that his assimilation of information is slightly slower than that of somebody without the impairment. He also has a mild speech impairment that slightly affects his ability to form certain words. Neither impairment on its own has a substantial adverse effect, but the effects of the impairments taken together have a substantial adverse effect on his ability to converse.

Effects of behaviour

B7. Account should be taken of how far a person can **reasonably** be expected to modify his or her behaviour, for example by use of a coping or avoidance strategy, to prevent or reduce the effects of an impairment on normal day-to-day activities. In some instances, a coping or avoidance strategy might alter the effects of the impairment to the extent that they are no longer substantial and the person would no longer meet the definition of disability. In other instances, even with the coping or avoidance strategy, there is still an adverse effect on the carrying out of normal day-to-day activities.

For example, a person who needs to avoid certain substances because of allergies may find the day-to-day activity of eating substantially affected. Account should be taken of the degree to which a person can reasonably be expected to behave in such a way that the impairment ceases to have a substantial adverse effect on his or her ability to carry out normal day-to-day activities. (**See also paragraph B12.**)

When considering modification of behaviour, it would be reasonable to expect a person who has chronic back pain to avoid extreme activities such as skiing. It would not be reasonable to expect the person to give up, or modify, more normal activities that might exacerbate the symptoms; such as shopping, or using public transport.

B8. Similarly, it would be reasonable to expect a person with a phobia to avoid extreme activities or situations that would aggravate their condition. It would not be reasonable to expect him or her to give up, or modify, normal activities that might exacerbate the symptoms.

A person with acrophobia (extreme fear of heights which can induce panic attacks) might reasonably be expected to avoid the top of extremely high buildings, such as the Eiffel Tower, but not to avoid all multi-storey buildings.

B9. Account should also be taken of where a person avoids doing things which, for example, cause pain, fatigue or substantial social embarrassment, or avoids doing things because of a loss of energy and motivation. It would **not** be reasonable to conclude that a person who employed an avoidance strategy was not a disabled person. In determining a question as to whether a person meets the definition of disability **it is important to consider the things that a person cannot do, or can only do with difficulty**.

In order to manage her mental health condition, a woman who experiences panic attacks finds that she can manage daily tasks, such as going to work, if she can avoid the stress of travelling in the rush hour.

In determining whether she meets the definition of disability, consideration should be given to the extent to which it is reasonable to expect her to place such restrictions on her working and personal life.

B10.   In some cases, people have coping or avoidance strategies which cease to work in certain circumstances (for example, where someone who has dyslexia is placed under stress). If it is possible that a person's ability to manage the effects of an impairment will break down so that effects will sometimes still occur, this possibility must be taken into account when assessing the effects of the impairment.

See also paragraphs B12 to B17 (effects of treatment), paragraphs C9 to C11 (likelihood of recurrence) and paragraph D22 (indirect effects).)

Effects of treatment

B16.   Account should be taken of where the effect of the continuing medical treatment is to create a permanent improvement rather than a temporary improvement. It is necessary to consider whether, as a consequence of the treatment, the impairment would cease to have a substantial adverse effect. For example, a person who develops pneumonia may be admitted to hospital for treatment including a course of antibiotics. This cures the impairment and no substantial effects remain. **(See also paragraph C11, regarding medical or other treatment that permanently reduces or removes the effects of an impairment.)**

B17.   However, if a person receives treatment which cures a condition that would otherwise meet the definition of a disability, the person would be protected by the Act as a person who had a disability in the past. **(See paragraph A16.)**

Progressive conditions

B18.   Progressive conditions, which are conditions that have effects which increase in severity over time, are subject to the special provisions set out in **Sch1, Para 8**. These provisions provide that a person with a progressive condition is to be regarded as having an impairment which has a substantial adverse effect on his or her ability to carry out normal day-to-day activities **before** it actually has that effect.

B19.   A person who has a progressive condition, will be treated as having an impairment which has a **substantial** adverse effect from the moment any impairment resulting from that condition first has some adverse effect on his or her ability to carry out normal day-to-day activities, provided that in the future the adverse effect is **likely** to become substantial. Medical prognosis of the likely impact of the condition will be the normal route to establishing protection under this provision. The effect need not be continuous and need not be substantial. **(See also paragraphs C5 to C8 on recurring or fluctuating effects)**. The person will still need to show that the impairment meets the long-term condition of the definition. **(Sch1, Para 2)**

B20.   Examples of progressive conditions to which the special provisions apply include systemic lupus erythematosis (SLE), various types of dementia, and motor neurone disease. This list, however, is not exhaustive.

A young boy aged 8 has been experiencing muscle cramps and some weakness. The effects are quite minor at present, but he has been diagnosed as having muscular dystrophy.

Eventually it is expected that the resulting muscle weakness will cause substantial adverse effects on his ability to walk, run and climb stairs. Although there is no substantial adverse effect at present, muscular dystrophy is a progressive condition, and this child will still be entitled to the protection of the Act under the special provisions in Sch1, Para 8 of the Act if it can be shown that the effects are likely to become substantial.

A woman has been diagnosed with systemic lupus erythematosis (SLE) following complaints to her GP that she is experiencing mild aches and pains in her joints. She has also been feeling generally unwell, with some flu-like symptoms. The initial symptoms do not have a substantial adverse effect on her ability to carry out normal day-to-day activities. However, SLE is a progressive condition, with fluctuating effects. She has been advised that the condition may come and go over many years, and in the future the effects may become substantial, including severe joint pain, inflammation, stiffness, and skin rashes. Providing it can be shown that the effects are likely to become substantial, she will be covered by the special provisions relating to progressive conditions. She will also need to meet the 'long-term' condition of the definition in order to be protected by the Act.

SECTION C: LONG-TERM

This section should not be read in isolation but must be considered together with sections A, C and D. Whether a person satisfies the definition of a disabled person for the purposes of the Act will depend upon the full circumstances of the case. That is, whether the adverse effect of the person's impairment on the carrying out of normal day-to-day activities is substantial and long term.

Recurring or fluctuating effects

C5. **The Act states** that, if an impairment has had a substantial adverse effect on a person's ability to carry out normal day-to-day activities but that effect ceases, the substantial effect is treated as continuing if it is likely to recur. (In deciding whether a person has had a disability in the past, the question is whether a substantial adverse effect has in fact recurred.) Conditions with effects which recur only sporadically or for short periods can still qualify as impairments for the purposes of the Act, in respect of the meaning of 'long-term' (**Sch1, Para 2(2), see also paragraphs C3 to C4 (meaning of likely).**)

C6. For example, a person with rheumatoid arthritis may experience substantial adverse effects for a few weeks after the first occurrence and then have a period of remission. **See also example at paragraph B11**. If the substantial adverse effects are likely to recur, they are to be treated as if they were continuing. If the effects are likely to recur beyond 12 months after the first occurrence, they are to be treated as long-term. Other impairments with effects which can recur beyond 12 months, or where effects can be sporadic, include Menières Disease and epilepsy as well as mental health conditions such as schizophrenia, bipolar affective disorder, and certain types of depression, though this is not an exhaustive list. Some impairments with recurring or fluctuating effects may be less obvious in their impact on the individual concerned than is the case with other impairments where the effects are more constant.

A young man has bipolar affective disorder, a recurring form of depression. The first episode occurred in months one and two of a 13-month period. The second episode took place in month 13. This man will satisfy the requirements of the definition in respect of the meaning of long-term, because the adverse effects have recurred beyond 12 months after the first occurrence and are therefore treated as having continued for the whole period (in this case, a period of 13 months).

In contrast, a woman has two discrete episodes of depression within a ten-month period. In month one she loses her job and has a period of depression lasting six weeks. In month nine she experiences a bereavement and has a further episode of depression lasting eight weeks. Even though she has experienced two episodes of depression she will not be covered by the Act. This is because, as at this stage, the effects of her impairment have not yet lasted more than 12 months after the first occurrence, and there is no evidence that these episodes are part of an underlying condition of depression which is likely to recur beyond the 12-month period.

However, if there was evidence to show that the two episodes did arise from an underlying condition of depression, the effects of which are likely to recur beyond the 12-month period, she would satisfy the long term requirement.

C7. It is not necessary for the effect to be the same throughout the period which is being considered in relation to determining whether the 'long-term' element of the definition is met. A person may still satisfy the long-term element of the definition even if the effect is not the same throughout the period. It may change: for example activities which are initially very difficult may become possible to a much greater extent. The effect might even disappear temporarily. Or other effects on the ability to carry out normal day-to-day activities may develop and the initial effect may disappear altogether.

A person has Menières Disease. This results in his experiencing mild tinnitus at times, which does not adversely affect his ability to carry out normal day-to-day activities. However, it also causes temporary periods of significant hearing loss every few months. The hearing loss substantially and adversely affects his ability to conduct conversations or listen to the radio or television. Although his condition does not continually have this adverse effect, it satisfies the long-term requirement because it has substantial adverse effects that are likely to recur beyond 12 months after he developed the impairment.

C8. Regulations specifically exclude seasonal allergic rhinitis (e.g. hayfever) except where it aggravates the effects of an existing condition8. For example, this may occur in some cases of asthma. (**See also paragraphs A12 to A15 (exclusions).**)

APPENDIX

*An illustrative and non-exhaustive list of factors which, if they are experienced by a person, **it would be reasonable** to regard as having a substantial adverse effect on normal day-to-day activities.*

Whether a person satisfies the definition of a disabled person for the purposes of the Act will depend upon the full circumstances of the case. That is, whether the substantial adverse effect of the impairment on normal day-to-day activities is long term.

In the following examples, the effect described should be thought of as if it were the **only** effect of the impairment.

- Difficulty in getting dressed, for example, because of physical restrictions, a lack of understanding of the concept, or low motivation;
- Difficulty carrying out activities associated with toileting, or caused by frequent minor incontinence;

- Difficulty preparing a meal, for example, because of restricted ability to do things like open cans or packages, or because of an inability to understand and follow a simple recipe;
- Difficulty eating; for example, because of an inability to co-ordinate the use of a knife and fork, a need for assistance, or the effect of an eating disorder;
- Difficulty going out of doors unaccompanied, for example, because the person has a phobia, a physical restriction, or a learning disability;
- Difficulty waiting or queuing, for example, because of a lack of understanding of the concept, or because of pain or fatigue when standing for prolonged periods;
- Difficulty using transport; for example, because of physical restrictions, pain or fatigue, a frequent need for a lavatory or as a result of a mental impairment or learning disability;
- Difficulty in going up or down steps, stairs or gradients; for example, because movements are painful, fatiguing or restricted in some way;
- A total inability to walk, or an ability to walk only a short distance without difficulty; for example because of physical restrictions, pain or fatigue;
- Difficulty entering or staying in environments that the person perceives as strange or frightening;
- Behaviour which challenges people around the person, making it difficult for the person to be accepted in public places;
- Persistent difficulty crossing a road safely, for example, because of physical restrictions or a failure to understand and manage the risk;
- Persistent general low motivation or loss of interest in everyday activities;
- Difficulty accessing and moving around buildings; for example because of inability to open doors, grip handrails on steps or gradients, or an inability to follow directions;
- Difficulty operating a computer, for example, because of physical restrictions in using a keyboard, a visual impairment or a learning disability;
- Difficulty picking up and carrying objects of moderate weight, such as a bag of shopping or a small piece of luggage, with one hand;
- Inability to converse, or give instructions orally, in the person's native spoken language;
- Difficulty understanding or following simple verbal instructions;
- Difficulty hearing and understanding another person speaking clearly over the voice telephone (where the telephone is not affected by bad reception);
- Persistent and significant difficulty in reading or understanding written material where this is in the person's native written language, for example because of a mental impairment, or learning disability, or a visual impairment (except where that is corrected by glasses or contact lenses);
- Intermittent loss of consciousness;
- Frequent confused behaviour, intrusive thoughts, feelings of being controlled, or delusions;
- Persistently wanting to avoid people or significant difficulty taking part in normal social interaction or forming social relationships, for example because of a mental health condition or disorder;
- Persistent difficulty in recognising, or remembering the names of, familiar people such as family or friends;
- Persistent distractibility or difficulty concentrating;
- Compulsive activities or behaviour, or difficulty in adapting after a reasonable period to minor changes in a routine.

*An illustrative and non-exhaustive list of factors which, if they are experienced by a person, **it would not be reasonable** to regard as having a substantial adverse effect on normal day-to-day activities.*

Whether a person satisfies the definition of a disabled person for the purposes of the Act will depend upon the full circumstances of the case. That is, whether the substantial adverse effect of the impairment on normal day-to-day activities is long term.

- Inability to move heavy objects without assistance or a mechanical aid, such as moving a large suitcase or heavy piece of furniture without a trolley;
- Experiencing some discomfort as a result of travelling, for example by car or plane, for a journey lasting more than two hours;
- Experiencing some tiredness or minor discomfort as a result of walking unaided for a distance of about 1.5 kilometres or one mile;
- Minor problems with writing or spelling;
- Inability to reach typing speeds standardised for secretarial work;
- Inability to read very small or indistinct print without the aid of a magnifying glass;
- Inability to fill in a long, detailed, technical document, which is in the person's native language, without assistance;
- Inability to speak in front of an audience simply as a result of nervousness;
- Some shyness and timidity;
- Inability to articulate certain sounds due to a lisp;
- Inability to be understood because of having a strong accent;
- Inability to converse orally in a language which is not the speaker's native spoken language;
- Inability to hold a conversation in a very noisy place, such as a factory floor, a pop concert, sporting event or alongside a busy main road;
- Inability to sing in tune;
- Inability to distinguish a known person across a substantial distance (e.g. across the width of a football pitch);
- Occasionally forgetting the name of a familiar person, such as a colleague;
- Inability to concentrate on a task requiring application over several hours;
- Occasional apprehension about significant heights;
- A person consciously taking a higher than normal risk on their own initiative, such as persistently crossing a road when the signals are adverse, or driving fast on highways for own pleasure;
- Simple inability to distinguish between red and green, which is not accompanied by any other effect such as blurring of vision;
- Infrequent minor incontinence;
- Inability to undertake activities requiring delicate hand movements, such as threading a small needle or picking up a pin.

Access to Medical Reports Act 1988

1 Right of access

It shall be the right of an individual to have access, in accordance with the provisions of this Act, to any medical report relating to the individual which is to be, or has been, supplied by a medical practitioner for employment purposes or insurance purposes.

2 Interpretation

(1)   In this Act –

'the applicant' means the person referred to in section 3(1) below;

'care' includes examination, investigation or diagnosis for the purposes of, or in connection with, any form of medical treatment;

'employment purposes', in the case of any individual, means the purposes in relation to the individual of any person by whom he is or has been, or is seeking to be, employed (whether under a contract of service or otherwise);

'health professional' has the same meaning as in the Data Protection Act 1998;

'insurance purposes', in a case of any individual who has entered into, or is seeking to enter into, a contract of insurance with an insurer, means the purposes of that insurer in relation to that individual;

'insurer' means –

(a)   a person who has permission under Part 4 of the Financial Services and Markets Act 2000 to effect or carry out contracts of insurance;

(b)   an EEA firm of the kind mentioned in paragraph 5(d) of Schedule 3 to that Act, which has permission under paragraph 15 of that Schedule (as a result of qualifying for authorisation under paragraph 12 of that Schedule) to effect or carry out relevant contracts of insurance;

'medical practitioner' means a person registered under the Medical Act 1983;

'medical report', in the case of an individual, means a report relating to the physical or mental health of the individual prepared by a medical practitioner who is or has been responsible for the clinical care of the individual.

(1A)   The definitions of 'insurance purposes' and 'insurer' in subsection (1) must be read with –

(a)   section 22 of the Financial Services and Markets Act 2000;

(b)   any relevant order under that section; and

(c)   Schedule 2 to that Act.

(2)   Any reference in this Act to the supply of a medical report for employment or insurance purposes shall be construed –

(a) as a reference to the supply of such a report for employment or insurance purposes which are purposes of the person who is seeking to be supplied with it; or

(b) (in the case of a report that has already been supplied) as a reference to the supply of such a report for employment or insurance purposes which, at the time of its being supplied, were purposes of the person to whom it was supplied.

3 Consent to applications for medical reports for employment or insurance purposes

(1) A person shall not apply to a medical practitioner for a medical report relating to any individual to be supplied to him for employment or insurance purposes unless –

(a) that person ('the applicant') has notified the individual that he proposes to make the application; and

(b) the individual has notified the applicant that he consents to the making of the application.

(2) Any notification given under subsection (1)(a) above must inform the individual of his right to withhold his consent to the making of the application, and of the following rights under this Act, namely –

(a) the rights arising under sections 4(1) to (3) and 6(2) below with respect to access to the report before or after it is supplied,

(b) the right to withhold consent under subsection (1) of section 5 below, and

(c) the right to request the amendment of the report under subsection (2) of that section,

as well as of the effect of section 7 below.

4 Access to reports before they are supplied

(1) An individual who gives his consent under section 3 above to the making of an application shall be entitled, when giving his consent, to state that he wishes to have access to the report to be supplied in response to the application before it is so supplied; and, if he does so, the applicant shall –

(a) notify the medical practitioner of that fact at the time when the application is made, and

(b) at the same time notify the individual of the making of the application;

and each such notification shall contain a statement of the effect of subsection (2) below.

(2) Where a medical practitioner is notified by the applicant under subsection (1) above that the individual in question wishes to have access to the report before it is supplied, the practitioner shall not supply the report unless –

(a) he has given the individual access to it and any requirements of section 5 below have been complied with, or

(b) the period of 21 days beginning with the date of the making of the application has elapsed without his having received any communication from the individual concerning arrangements for the individual to have access to it.

(3) Where a medical practitioner –

(a) receives an application for a medical report to be supplied for employment or insurance purposes without being notified by the applicant as mentioned in subsection (1) above, but

(b)   before supplying the report receives a notification from the individual that he wishes to have access to the report before it is supplied,

the practitioner shall not supply the report unless –

(i)   he has given the individual access to it and any requirements of section 5 below have been complied with, or

(ii)   the period of 21 days beginning with the date of that notification has elapsed without his having received (either with that notification or otherwise) any communication from the individual concerning arrangements for the individual to have access to it.

(4)   References in this section and section 5 below to giving an individual access to a medical report are references to –

(a)   making the report or a copy of it available for his inspection; or

(b)   supplying him with a copy of it;

and where a copy is supplied at the request, or otherwise with the consent, of the individual the practitioner may charge a reasonable fee to cover the costs of supplying it.

5   Consent to supplying of report and correction of errors

(1)   Where an individual has been given access to a report under section 4 above the report shall not be supplied in response to the application in question unless the individual has notified the medical practitioner that he consents to its being so supplied.

(2)   The individual shall be entitled, before giving his consent under subsection (1) above, to request the medical practitioner to amend any part of the report which the individual considers to be incorrect or misleading; and, if the individual does so, the practitioner –

(a)   if he is to any extent prepared to accede to the individual's request, shall amend the report accordingly;

(b)   if he is to any extent not prepared to accede to it but the individual requests him to attach to the report a statement of the individual's views in respect of any part of the report which he is declining to amend, shall attach such a statement to the report.

(3)   Any request made by an individual under subsection (2) above shall be made in writing.

6   Retention of reports

(1)   A copy of any medical report which a medical practitioner has supplied for employment or insurance purposes shall be retained by him for at least six months from the date on which it was supplied.

(2)   A medical practitioner shall, if so requested by an individual, give the individual access to any medical report relating to him which the practitioner has supplied for employment or insurance purposes in the previous six months.

(3)   The reference in subsection (2) above to giving an individual access to a medical report is a reference to –

(a)   making a copy of the report available for his inspection; or

(b)   supplying him with a copy of it;

and where a copy is supplied at the request, or otherwise with the consent, of the individual the practitioner may charge a reasonable fee to cover the costs of supplying it.

7   Exemptions

(1)   A medical practitioner shall not be obliged to give an individual access, in accordance with the provisions of section 4(4) or 6(3) above, to any part of a medical report whose disclosure would in the opinion of the practitioner be likely to cause serious harm to the physical or mental health of the individual or others or would indicate the intentions of the practitioner in respect of the individual.

(2)   A medical practitioner shall not be obliged to give an individual access, in accordance with those provisions, to any part of a medical report whose disclosure would be likely to reveal information about another person, or to reveal the identity of another person who has supplied information to the practitioner about the individual, unless –

(a)   that person has consented; or
(b)   that person is a health professional who has been involved in the care of the individual and the information relates to or has been provided by the professional in that capacity.

(3)   Where it appears to a medical practitioner that subsection (1) or (2) above is applicable to any part (but not the whole) of a medical report –

(a)   he shall notify the individual of that fact; and
(b)   references in the preceding sections of this Act to the individual being given access to the report shall be construed as references to his being given access to the remainder of it;

and other references to the report in sections 4(4), 5(2) and 6(3) above shall similarly be construed as references to the remainder of the report.

(4)   Where it appears to a medical practitioner that subsection (1) or (2) above is applicable to the whole of a medical report –

(a)   he shall notify the individual of that fact; but
(b)   he shall not supply the report unless he is notified by the individual that the individual consents to its being supplied;

and accordingly, if he is so notified by the individual, the restrictions imposed by section 4(2) and (3) above on the supply of the report shall not have effect in relation to it.

8   Application to the court

(1)   If a court is satisfied on the application of an individual that any person, in connection with a medical report relating to that individual, has failed or is likely to fail to comply with any requirement of this Act, the court may order that person to comply with that requirement.

(2)   The jurisdiction conferred by this section shall be exercisable by a county court or, in Scotland, by the sheriff.

9   Notifications under this Act

Any notification required or authorised to be given under this Act –

(a)   shall be given in writing; and

(b)   may be given by post.

10   Short title, commencement and extent

(1)   This Act may be cited as the Access to Medical Reports Act 1988.

(2)   This Act shall come into force on 1st January 1989.

(3)   Nothing in this Act applies to a medical report prepared before the coming into force of this Act.

(4)   This Act does not extend to Northern Ireland.

Employment Rights Act 1996 (extracts)

PART IX TERMINATION OF EMPLOYMENT

Minimum period of notice

86 Rights of employer and employee to minimum notice

(1)   The notice required to be given by an employer to terminate the contract of employment of a person who has been continuously employed for one month or more –

    (a)   is not less than one week's notice if his period of continuous employment is less than two years,

    (b)   is not less than one week's notice for each year of continuous employment if his period of continuous employment is two years or more but less than twelve years, and

    (c)   is not less than twelve weeks' notice if his period of continuous employment is twelve years or more.

(2)   The notice required to be given by an employee who has been continuously employed for one month or more to terminate his contract of employment is not less than one week.

(3)   Any provision for shorter notice in any contract of employment with a person who has been continuously employed for one month or more has effect subject to subsections (1) and (2); but this section does not prevent either party from waiving his right to notice on any occasion or from accepting a payment in lieu of notice.

(4)   Any contract of employment of a person who has been continuously employed for three months or more which is a contract for a term certain of one month or less shall have effect as if it were for an indefinite period; and, accordingly, subsections (1) and (2) apply to the contract.

(5)   *[Repealed]*

(6)   This section does not affect any right of either party to a contract of employment to treat the contract as terminable without notice by reason of the conduct of the other party.

87 Rights of employee in period of notice

(1)   If an employer gives notice to terminate the contract of employment of a person who has been continuously employed for one month or more, the provisions of sections 88 to 91 have effect as respects the liability of the employer for the period of notice required by section 86(1).

(2)   If an employee who has been continuously employed for one month or more gives notice to terminate his contract of employment, the provisions of sections 88 to 91 have effect as respects the liability of the employer for the period of notice required by section 86(2).

(3)   In sections 88 to 91 'period of notice' means –

    (a)   where notice is given by an employer, the period of notice required by section 86(1), and

    (b)   where notice is given by an employee, the period of notice required by section 86(2).

(4)   This section does not apply in relation to a notice given by the employer or the employee if the notice to be given by the employer to terminate the contract must be at least one week more than the notice required by section 86(1).

88 Employments with normal working hours

(1)   If an employee has normal working hours under the contract of employment in force during the period of notice and during any part of those normal working hours –

    (a)   the employee is ready and willing to work but no work is provided for him by his employer,

    (b)   the employee is incapable of work because of sickness or injury,

    (c)   the employee is absent from work wholly or partly because of pregnancy or childbirth or on adoption leave, parental leave or ordinary or additional paternity leave, or

    (d)   the employee is absent from work in accordance with the terms of his employment relating to holidays,

the employer is liable to pay the employee for the part of normal working hours covered by any of paragraphs (a), (b), (c) and (d) a sum not less than the amount of remuneration for that part of normal working hours calculated at the average hourly rate of remuneration produced by dividing a week's pay by the number of normal working hours.

(2)   Any payments made to the employee by his employer in respect of the relevant part of the period of notice (whether by way of sick pay, statutory sick pay, maternity pay, statutory maternity pay, paternity pay, ordinary statutory paternity pay, additional statutory paternity pay, adoption pay, statutory adoption pay, holiday pay or otherwise) go towards meeting the employer's liability under this section.

(3)   Where notice was given by the employee, the employer's liability under this section does not arise unless and until the employee leaves the service of the employer in pursuance of the notice.

89 Employments without normal working hours

(1)   If an employee does not have normal working hours under the contract of employment in force in the period of notice, the employer is liable to pay the employee for each week of the period of notice a sum not less than a week's pay.

(2)   The employer's liability under this section is conditional on the employee being ready and willing to do work of a reasonable nature and amount to earn a week's pay.

(3)   Subsection (2) does not apply –

    (a)   in respect of any period during which the employee is incapable of work because of sickness or injury,

    (b)   in respect of any period during which the employee is absent from work wholly or partly because of pregnancy or childbirth or on adoption leave, parental leave or ordinary or additional paternity leave, or

    (c)   in respect of any period during which the employee is absent from work in accordance with the terms of his employment relating to holidays.

(4)   Any payment made to an employee by his employer in respect of a period within subsection (3) (whether by way of sick pay, statutory sick pay, maternity pay, statutory maternity pay, paternity pay, ordinary statutory paternity pay, additional statutory paternity pay, adoption pay, statutory adoption pay, holiday pay or otherwise) shall be taken into account for the purposes of this section as if it were remuneration paid by the employer in respect of that period.

(5)   Where notice was given by the employee, the employer's liability under this section does not arise unless and until the employee leaves the service of the employer in pursuance of the notice.

90 Short-term incapacity benefit, contributory employment and support allowance and industrial injury benefit

(1)   This section has effect where the arrangements in force relating to the employment are such that –

(a)   payments by way of sick pay are made by the employer to employees to whom the arrangements apply, in cases where any such employees are incapable of work because of sickness or injury, and

(b)   in calculating any payment so made to any such employee an amount representing, or treated as representing, short-term incapacity benefit, contributory employment and support allowance or industrial injury benefit is taken into account, whether by way of deduction or by way of calculating the payment as a supplement to that amount.

(2)   If –

(a)   during any part of the period of notice the employee is incapable of work because of sickness or injury,

(b)   one or more payments by way of sick pay are made to him by the employer in respect of that part of the period of notice, and

(c)   in calculating any such payment such an amount as is referred to in paragraph (b) of subsection (1) is taken into account as mentioned in that paragraph,

for the purposes of section 88 or 89 the amount so taken into account shall be treated as having been paid by the employer to the employee by way of sick pay in respect of that part of that period, and shall go towards meeting the liability of the employer under that section accordingly.

91 Supplementary

(1)   An employer is not liable under section 88 or 89 to make any payment in respect of a period during which an employee is absent from work with the leave of the employer granted at the request of the employee, including any period of time off taken in accordance with –

(a)   Part VI of this Act, or

(b)   section 168 or 170 of the Trade Union and Labour Relations (Consolidation) Act 1992 (trade union duties and activities).

(2)   No payment is due under section 88 or 89 in consequence of a notice to terminate a contract given by an employee if, after the notice is given and on or before the termination of the contract, the employee takes part in a strike of employees of the employer.

(3)   If, during the period of notice, the employer breaks the contract of employment, payments received under section 88 or 89 in respect of the part of the period after the

breach go towards mitigating the damages recoverable by the employee for loss of earnings in that part of the period of notice.

(4)   If, during the period of notice, the employee breaks the contract and the employer rightfully treats the breach as terminating the contract, no payment is due to the employee under section 88 or 89 in respect of the part of the period falling after the termination of the contract.

(5)   If an employer fails to give the notice required by section 86, the rights conferred by sections 87 to 90 and this section shall be taken into account in assessing his liability for breach of the contract.

(6)   Sections 86 to 90 and this section apply in relation to a contract all or any of the terms of which are terms which take effect by virtue of any provision contained in or having effect under an Act (whether public or local) as in relation to any other contract; and the reference in this subsection to an Act includes, subject to any express provision to the contrary, an Act passed after this Act.

98 General

(1)   In determining for the purposes of this Part whether the dismissal of an employee is fair or unfair, it is for the employer to show –

(a)   the reason (or, if more than one, the principal reason) for the dismissal, and

(b)   that it is either a reason falling within subsection (2) or some other substantial reason of a kind such as to justify the dismissal of an employee holding the position which the employee held.

(2)   A reason falls within this subsection if it –

(a)   relates to the capability or qualifications of the employee for performing work of the kind which he was employed by the employer to do,

(b)   relates to the conduct of the employee,

(c)   is that the employee was redundant, or

(d)   is that the employee could not continue to work in the position which he held without contravention (either on his part or on that of his employer) of a duty or restriction imposed by or under an enactment.

(3)   In subsection (2)(a) –

(a)   'capability', in relation to an employee, means his capability assessed by reference to skill, aptitude, health or any other physical or mental quality, and

(b)   'qualifications', in relation to an employee, means any degree, diploma or other academic, technical or professional qualification relevant to the position which he held.

(4)   Where the employer has fulfilled the requirements of subsection (1), the determination of the question whether the dismissal is fair or unfair (having regard to the reason shown by the employer) –

(a)   depends on whether in the circumstances (including the size and administrative resources of the employer's undertaking) the employer acted reasonably or unreasonably in treating it as a sufficient reason for dismissing the employee, and

(b)   shall be determined in accordance with equity and the substantial merits of the case.

(5)   [Repealed]

(6)   Subsection (4) is subject to –

(a)   sections 98A to 107 of this Act, and

(b)   sections 152, 153, 238 and 238A of the Trade Union and Labour Relations (Consolidation) Act 1992 (dismissal on ground of trade union membership or activities or in connection with industrial action).

118   General

(1)   Where a tribunal makes an award of compensation for unfair dismissal under section 112(4) or 117(3)(a) the award shall consist of –

    (a)   a basic award (calculated in accordance with sections 119 to 122 and 126), and

    (b)   a compensatory award (calculated in accordance with sections 123, 124, 124A and 126).

(2)   *[Repealed]*

(3)   *[Repealed]*

(4)   *[Repealed]*

119   Basic award

(1)   Subject to the provisions of this section, sections 120 to 122 and section 126, the amount of the basic award shall be calculated by –

    (a)   determining the period, ending with the effective date of termination, during which the employee has been continuously employed,

    (b)   reckoning backwards from the end of that period the number of years of employment falling within that period, and

    (c)   allowing the appropriate amount for each of those years of employment.

(2)   In subsection (1)(c) 'the appropriate amount' means –

    (a)   one and a half weeks' pay for a year of employment in which the employee was not below the age of forty-one,

    (b)   one week's pay for a year of employment (not within paragraph (a)) in which he was not below the age of twenty-two, and

    (c)   half a week's pay for a year of employment not within paragraph (a) or (b).

(3)   Where twenty years of employment have been reckoned under subsection (1), no account shall be taken under that subsection of any year of employment earlier than those twenty years.

(4)   *[Repealed]*

(5)   *[Repealed]*

(6)   *[Repealed]*

120   Basic award: minimum in certain cases

(1)   The amount of the basic award (before any reduction under section 122) shall not be less than £5,000 where the reason (or, if more than one, the principal reason) –

    (a)   in a redundancy case, for selecting the employee for dismissal, or

    (b)   otherwise, for the dismissal,

    is one of those specified in section 100(1)(a) and (b), 101A(d), 102(1) or 103.

(1A)   Where –

(a)   an employee is regarded as unfairly dismissed by virtue of section 98ZG (whether or not his dismissal is unfair or regarded as unfair for any other reason),

(b)   an award of compensation falls to be made under section 112(4), and

(c)   the amount of the award under section 118(1)(a), before any reduction under section 122(3A) or (4), is less than the amount of four weeks' pay,

the employment tribunal shall, subject to subsection (1B), increase the award under section 118(1)(a) to the amount of four weeks' pay.

(1B)   An employment tribunal shall not be required by subsection (1A) to increase the amount of an award if it considers that the increase would result in injustice to the employer.

(1C)   Where an employee is regarded as unfairly dismissed by virtue of section 104F (blacklists) (whether or not the dismissal is unfair or regarded as unfair for any other reason), the amount of the basic award of compensation (before any reduction is made under section 122) shall not be less than £5,000.

(2)   [*Repealed*]

121   Basic award of two weeks' pay in certain cases

The amount of the basic award shall be two weeks' pay where the tribunal finds that the reason (or, where there is more than one, the principal reason) for the dismissal of the employee is that he was redundant and the employee –

(a)   by virtue of section 138 is not regarded as dismissed for the purposes of Part XI, or

(b)   by virtue of section 141 is not, or (if he were otherwise entitled) would not be, entitled to a redundancy payment.

122   Basic award: reductions

(1)   Where the tribunal finds that the complainant has unreasonably refused an offer by the employer which (if accepted) would have the effect of reinstating the complainant in his employment in all respects as if he had not been dismissed, the tribunal shall reduce or further reduce the amount of the basic award to such extent as it considers just and equitable having regard to that finding.

(2)   Where the tribunal considers that any conduct of the complainant before the dismissal (or, where the dismissal was with notice, before the notice was given) was such that it would be just and equitable to reduce or further reduce the amount of the basic award to any extent, the tribunal shall reduce or further reduce that amount accordingly.

(3)   Subsection (2) does not apply in a redundancy case unless the reason for selecting the employee for dismissal was one of those specified in section 100(1)(a) and (b), 101A(d), 102(1) or 103; and in such a case subsection (2) applies only to so much of the basic award as is payable because of section 120.

(3A)   Where the complainant has been awarded any amount in respect of the dismissal under a designated dismissal procedures agreement, the tribunal shall reduce or further reduce the amount of the basic award to such extent as it considers just and equitable having regard to that award.

(4)   The amount of the basic award shall be reduced or further reduced by the amount of –

(a)   any redundancy payment awarded by the tribunal under Part XI in respect of the same dismissal, or

(b)   any payment made by the employer to the employee on the ground that the dismissal was by reason of redundancy (whether in pursuance of Part XI or otherwise).

(5)   Where a dismissal is regarded as unfair by virtue of section 104F (blacklists), the amount of the basic award shall be reduced or further reduced by the amount of any basic award in respect of the same dismissal under section 156 of the Trade Union and Labour Relations (Consolidation) Act 1992 (minimum basic award in case of dismissal on grounds related to trade union membership or activities).]

123   Compensatory award

(1)   Subject to the provisions of this section and sections 124, 124A and 126, the amount of the compensatory award shall be such amount as the tribunal considers just and equitable in all the circumstances having regard to the loss sustained by the complainant in consequence of the dismissal in so far as that loss is attributable to action taken by the employer.

(2)   The loss referred to in subsection (1) shall be taken to include –

(a)   any expenses reasonably incurred by the complainant in consequence of the dismissal, and

(b)   subject to subsection (3), loss of any benefit which he might reasonably be expected to have had but for the dismissal.

(3)   The loss referred to in subsection (1) shall be taken to include in respect of any loss of –

(a)   any entitlement or potential entitlement to a payment on account of dismissal by reason of redundancy (whether in pursuance of Part XI or otherwise), or

(b)   any expectation of such a payment,

only the loss referable to the amount (if any) by which the amount of that payment would have exceeded the amount of a basic award (apart from any reduction under section 122) in respect of the same dismissal.

(4)   In ascertaining the loss referred to in subsection (1) the tribunal shall apply the same rule concerning the duty of a person to mitigate his loss as applies to damages recoverable under the common law of England and Wales or (as the case may be) Scotland.

(5)   In determining, for the purposes of subsection (1), how far any loss sustained by the complainant was attributable to action taken by the employer, no account shall be taken of any pressure which by –

(a)   calling, organising, procuring or financing a strike or other industrial action, or

(b)   threatening to do so,

was exercised on the employer to dismiss the employee; and that question shall be determined as if no such pressure had been exercised.

(6)   Where the tribunal finds that the dismissal was to any extent caused or contributed to by any action of the complainant, it shall reduce the amount of the compensatory award by such proportion as it considers just and equitable having regard to that finding.

(7)   If the amount of any payment made by the employer to the employee on the ground that the dismissal was by reason of redundancy (whether in pursuance of Part XI or otherwise) exceeds the amount of the basic award which would be payable but for section 122(4), that excess goes to reduce the amount of the compensatory award.

(8)   Where the amount of the compensatory award falls to be calculated for the purposes

of an award under section 117(3)(a), there shall be deducted from the compensatory award any award made under section 112(5) at the time of the order under section 113.

124 Limit of compensatory award etc.

(1)   The amount of –

(a)   any compensation awarded to a person under section 117(1) and (2), or

(b)   a compensatory award to a person calculated in accordance with section 123,

shall not exceed £68,400.

(1A)   Subsection (1) shall not apply to compensation awarded, or a compensatory award made, to a person in a case where he is regarded as unfairly dismissed by virtue of section 100, 103A, 105(3) or 105(6A).

(2)   [*Repealed*]

(3)   In the case of compensation awarded to a person under section 117(1) and (2), the limit imposed by this section may be exceeded to the extent necessary to enable the award fully to reflect the amount specified as payable under section 114(2)(a) or section 115(2)(d).

(4)   Where –

(a)   a compensatory award is an award under paragraph (a) of subsection (3) of section 117, and

(b)   an additional award falls to be made under paragraph (b) of that subsection,

the limit imposed by this section on the compensatory award may be exceeded to the extent necessary to enable the aggregate of the compensatory and additional awards fully to reflect the amount specified as payable under section 114(2)(a) or section 115(2)(d).

(5)   The limit imposed by this section applies to the amount which the employment tribunal would, apart from this section, award in respect of the subject matter of the complaint after taking into account –

(a)   any payment made by the respondent to the complainant in respect of that matter, and

(b)   any reduction in the amount of the award required by any enactment or rule of law.

124A Adjustments under the Employment Act 2002

Where an award of compensation for unfair dismissal falls to be –

(a)   reduced or increased under section 207A of the Trade Union and Labour Relations (Consolidation) Act 1992 (effect of failure to comply with Code: adjustment of awards), or

(b)   increased under section 38 of that Act (failure to give statement of employment particulars),

the adjustment shall be in the amount awarded under section 118(1)(b) and shall be applied immediately before any reduction under section 123(6) or (7).

125

[*Repealed*]

126 Acts which are both unfair dismissal and discrimination

(1)   This section applies where compensation falls to be awarded in respect of any act both under –

    (a)   the provisions of this Act relating to unfair dismissal, and

    (b)   the Equality Act 2010.

(2)   An employment tribunal shall not award compensation under either of those Acts in respect of any loss or other matter which is or has been taken into account under the other by the tribunal (or another employment tribunal) in awarding compensation on the same or another complaint in respect of that act.

Income Tax (Earnings and Pensions) Act 2003 (extracts)

403   Charge on payment or other benefit

(1)   The amount of a payment or benefit to which this Chapter applies counts as employment income of the employee or former employee for the relevant tax year if and to the extent that it exceeds the £30,000 threshold.

(2)   In this section 'the relevant tax year' means the tax year in which the payment or other benefit is received.

(3)   For the purposes of this Chapter –

   (a)   a cash benefit is treated as received –

      (i)   when it is paid or a payment is made on account of it, or
      (ii)   when the recipient becomes entitled to require payment of or on account of it, and

   (b)   a non-cash benefit is treated as received when it is used or enjoyed.

(4)   For the purposes of this Chapter the amount of a payment or benefit in respect of an employee or former employee exceeds the £30,000 threshold if and to the extent that, when it is aggregated with other such payments or benefits to which this Chapter applies, it exceeds £30,000 according to the rules in section 404 (how the £30,000 threshold applies).

(5)   If it is received after the death of the employee or former employee –

   (a)   the amount of a payment or benefit to which this Chapter applies counts as the employment income of the personal representatives for the relevant year if or to the extent that it exceeds £30,000 according to the rules in section 404, and

   (b)   the tax is accordingly to be assessed and charged on them and is a debt due from and payable out of the estate.

(6)   In this Chapter references to the taxable person are to the person in relation to whom subsection (1) or (5) provides for an amount to count as employment income.

404   How the £30,000 threshold applies

(1)   For the purpose of the £30,000 threshold in section 403(4) and (5), the payments and other benefits provided in respect of an employee or former employee which are to be aggregated are those provided –

   (a)   in respect of the same employment,
   (b)   in respect of different employments with the same employer, and
   (c)   in respect of employments with employers who are associated.

(2)   For this purpose employers are 'associated' if on a termination or change date –

(a)   one of them is under the control of the other, or

(b)   one of them is under the control of a third person who on that termination or change date or another such date controls or is under the control of the other.

(3)   In subsection (2) –

(a)   references to an employer, or to a person controlling or controlled by an employer, include the successors of the employer or person, and

(b)   'termination or change date' means a date on which a termination or change occurs in connection with which a payment or other benefit to which this Chapter applies is received in respect of the employee or former employee.

(4)   If payments and other benefits are received in different tax years, the £30,000 is set against the amount of payments and other benefits received in earlier years before those received in later years.

(5)   If more than one payment or other benefit is received in a tax year in which the threshold is exceeded –

(a)   the £30,000 (or the balance of it) is set against the amounts of cash benefits as they are received, and

(b)   any balance at the end of the year is set against the aggregate amount of non-cash benefits received in the year.

404A   Amounts charged to be treated as highest part of total income

(1)   A payment or other benefit which counts as a person's employment income as a result of section 403 is treated as the highest part of the person's total income.

(2)   Subsection (1) has effect for all income tax purposes except the purposes of sections 535 to 537 of ITTOIA 2005 (gains from contracts for life insurance etc: top slicing relief).

(3)   See section 1012 of ITA 2007 (relationship between highest part rules) for the relationship between –

(a)   the rule in subsection (1), and

(b)   other rules requiring particular income to be treated as the highest part of a person's total income.

405   Exception for certain payments exempted when received as earnings

(1)   This Chapter does not apply to any payment received in connection with the termination of a person's employment which, were it received for the performance of the duties of the employment, would fall within section 308 (exemption of contributions to approved personal pension arrangements).

(2)   This Chapter does not apply to any payment received in connection with any change in the duties of, or earnings from, a person's employment to the extent that, were it received for the performance of the duties of the employment, it would fall within section 271(1) (limited exemption of removal benefits and expenses).

406   Exception for death or disability payments and benefits

This Chapter does not apply to a payment or other benefit provided –

(a)   in connection with the termination of employment by the death of an employee, or

(b)   on account of injury to, or disability of, an employee.

Other reference material

APPENDIX D1

Online resource list

RESOURCES REFERRED TO IN THIS BOOK WHICH ARE AVAILABLE ONLINE

ACAS Guide to Discipline and Grievances at Work, Appendix 4 'Dealing with absence' (ACAS, 2011)
www.acas.org.uk/media/pdf/s/o/Acas-Guide-on-discipline-and-grievances_at_work_(April_11)-accessible-version-may-2012.pdf

Council Directive 2000/78/EC of 27 November 2000 establishing a general framework for equal treatment in employment and occupation
eur-lex.europa.eu/LexUriServ/LexUriServ.do?uri=CELEX:32000L0078:en:HTML

The Equality Act 2010 (Disability) Regulations 2010, SI 2010/2128
www.legislation.gov.uk/uksi/2010/2128/part/2/made

Equality Act 2010 Guidance – Guidance on matters to be taken into account in determining questions relating to the definition of disability (ODI, 2010)
www.gov.uk/government/uploads/system/uploads/attachment_data/file/85038/disability-definition.pdf

The Equality Act 2010 Statutory Code of Practice on Employment
www.equalityhumanrights.com/uploaded_files/EqualityAct/employercode.pdf

Explanatory Notes to the Equality Act 2010
www.legislation.gov.uk/ukpga/2010/15/notes/contents

Cases

For full transcripts of cases referred to and which are free to download online go to BAILII.
www.bailii.org/form/search_cases.html

HM Courts and Tribunals Service

Information on employment tribunals and the EAT, together with forms and guidance are available to view and download at:
www.justice.gov.uk/tribunals/employment

To appeal an employment tribunal decision refer to the website of the EAT.
www.justice.gov.uk/tribunals/employment-appeals

For further information on the rules that govern employment tribunals see:
www.justice.gov.uk/tribunals/employment/rules-and-legislation#rules

Statutory sick pay

Further information on statutory sick pay is available on the government website and HMRC's website.
www.gov.uk/statutory-sick-pay-ssp/overview
www.hmrc.gov.uk/paye/employees/statutory-pay/ssp-overview.htm

OTHER USEFUL RESOURCES AROUND DISABILITY EQUALITY AND MENTAL HEALTH DISABILITIES

Business Disability Forum

This employer-focused organisation considers the impact of disability as it affects business. Its stated aim is to enable businesses to become disability confident.
businessdisabilityforum.org.uk

The Equality and Human Rights Commission

A wealth of information on disability equality is available on the EHRC website.
www.equalityhumanrights.com/advice-and-guidance/your-rights/disability

Government Equalities Office

The discrimination questionnaire forms (until they are repealed) can be found at:
www.gov.uk/government/publications/process-for-complaints-under-the-equality-act-2010

The Mental Health Foundation

MHF carries out research and publishes pertinent information which can assist employers in understanding mental health disabilities.
www.mentalhealth.org.uk

Mindful Employer

By employers, for employers, this initiative promotes awareness of mental health at work. It also provides support for businesses in recruiting and retaining staff with mental health disabilities.
www.mindfulemployer.net

Rethink Mental Illness

Rethink offers information and advice on all issues relating to mental health disability.
www.rethink.org

Index

Access to medical records 7.2,
10.5, App.A1
    employee consent 7.2.2, App.A2,
    App.A3
Addictions 1.2.2
Adjournments 17.3
**Advisory, Conciliation and
Arbitration Service
(ACAS)** 14.3
Agents
    vicarious liability 6.3.1
Aggravated damages 17.4.3.9
Aiding discrimination 6.3.4
Aids *see* Auxiliary aids
AIDS/HIV
    automatic disability 1.2.1
Alcoholism 1.2.2
**Alternative dispute resolution
(ADR)** *see* Settlement out of
court
Anxiety and stress *see* Stress
Appeal process 17.6
Assessment
    material time for assessing
    disability 1.6
    see also Medical examination
Associative discrimination 2.2
Asthma 1.3.1
**Attitudes to mental health
disabilities** 9.1.1
Automatic disabilities 1.2.1
Auxiliary aids 4.7.2.1
    reasonable adjustments duty and
    4.3.3

Bad faith
    victimisation and 6.2.4.3
Benefits *see* Employment
benefits
**Bonus payments during
sickness absence** 7.5.5

Bringing a claim *see* ET1
form
Bundle
    contents 16.5.1
    costs 16.5.4
    index 16.5.2
    preparation 16.5.3

Cancer
    automatic disability 1.2.1
Capability
    dismissal and 8.4
Career advancement 7.1.3
Career breaks 4.11
**Case management discussion
(CMD)** 16.1, 16.2
Case study
    dismissal 10.11
    harassment 10.10
    knowledge of disability 10.3
    managing a return to work 10.8
    medical evidence 10.7
    new management 10.4
    obtaining medical records 10.5
    reasonable adjustments duty 10.2
    recruitment and interview 10.1
    sick pay 10.6
    vicarious liability 10.9
Cast list 16.7.4
Cause of impairment 1.1.1
    contributory causes 17.4.3.7
Causing discrimination 6.3.3
**Characteristics of alleged
discriminator** 2.4.3
Chronology 16.7.3
Closing submissions 17.1.4
**Code of Practice on
Employment, Equality Act
2010** Intro, 1.1, 3.2.4, 3.5, 4.3.1,
5.2.5, 6.1.3, App.C3

Combined (dual) discrimination 2.4.4

Communication

mental health disabilities and 9.1.2

Comparators

direct disability discrimination 2.1.3

no comparator for section 15 discrimination arising from disability 3.2.2

reasonable adjustments duty and comparison with non-disabled people 4.6

victimisation 6.2.4.1

Compensation 17.4.3

Compromise agreement 14.2

Consecutive impairments 1.3.3

Consent

access to medical records and 7.2.2, App.A2, App.A3

attending medical assessment App.A5

Consent order 14.6

Consultation

reasonable adjustments duty and employer duty to consult 4.9

Contractors

vicarious liability 6.3.1

Contractual provisions around sickness and disability 7.4

Contributory causes 17.4.3.7

Costs

preparation of bundle 16.5.4

seeking new employment 17.4.3.5

tribunals 17.7

Cross-examination 17.1.3.2

Cumulative conditions 1.3.3

Cured conditions 1.3.1

Customers

third party harassment 6.1.7

Damages

aggravated 17.4.3.9

exemplary 17.4.3.8

Date of disability 12.5.3

Deduced effect 1.5

Defences to discrimination claim 2.1.5

section 15 discrimination arising from disability 3.2.6

Definition of disability 1.1, 1.7, 2.3

automatic disabilities 1.2.1

cumulative conditions 1.3.3

effect of medical treatment and prostheses 1.5

excluded conditions 1.2.2

long term 1.1.3

material time for assessing disability 1.6

normal day-to-day activities 1.1.4

past disabilities 1.4

physical or mental impairment 1.1.1

progressive conditions 1.3.2

recurring or fluctuating conditions 1.3.1

specified conditions 1.2

substantial adverse effect 1.1.2

variable conditions 1.3

Definition of disability discrimination

direct disability discrimination s.13 definition 2.1.1

indirect disability discrimination s.19 definition 5.2

section 15 discrimination arising from disability 3.2.1

Definition of harassment 6.1.2

Definition of victimisation 6.2.1

Delays in tribunal process 9.2.3.3

Deliberations 17.1.5

Depression 1.2.2, 1.3.3, 3.2.3, 9.1.1

Determination of disability 15.1

documentary evidence 15.3.3

impact statement 15.2, App.B3

medical evidence *see* Medical evidence

statement from respondent 15.3.2

supporting statement for claimant 15.3.1

Detriment

victimisation and 6.2.3

Direct disability discrimination 2.5

alleged discriminator's characteristics and 2.4.3

'because of' disability 2.1.2

comparators 2.1.3

dual discrimination 2.4.4

effective or substantial reasons 2.1.4

elements of claim 12.5.5.1, 13.5.6.1

justification and defences 2.1.5

knowledge of disability   2.1.6
motive   2.1.7
occupational requirements   2.4.2
positive discrimination   2.4.1
proof   2.1.8
response to claim brought   13.5.6.1
s.13 definition   2.1.1
Disadvantage
group disadvantage   5.2.3
indirect disability discrimination
and   5.2.2
particular disadvantage   5.2.5
reasonable adjustments duty and
substantial disadvantage   4.5
shared disability and   5.2.4
Disciplinary procedures   3.2.3
adjustments to policies during
employment   7.3.1
Disclosure   16.4
Discretion
sick pay and   7.5.1
Disfigurement
automatic disability   1.2.1
Dismissal
Burchell test   8.4.2
capability and   8.4
case study   10.11
discriminatory   8.2
fairness of procedure   8.4.1
reasonable adjustments duty and
4.12, 8.1
unfair dismissal   8.2, 12.6
Doctors *see* Medical advisers
Documents
documentary evidence of disability
15.3.3
preparation of bundle   16.5
reading time   17.1.1
Dual discrimination   2.4.4

Earnings *see* Pay arrangements
**Effective reasons for
discrimination**   2.1.4
Employee handbooks
contractual provisions around
sickness and disability   7.4
**Employment Appeal Tribunal
(EAT)**   17.6
Employment benefits
claim for loss of   17.4.3.3
permanent health insurance (PHI)
7.5.3
Employment contracts

contractual provisions around
sickness and disability   7.4
Epilepsy   1.3.1
ET1 form   12.3, 12.6
content   12.5
details of alleged disability   12.5.3
grounds of complaint   12.3, 12.6,
App.B1
heading for rider   12.4
introduction of parties   12.5.1
matters relied upon in relation to
each element of claim   12.5.5
purpose of   12.1
relevant factual background   12.5.4
summary of legal complaints
brought   12.5.2
timing of   12.2
ET3 form   13.3, 13.6
admission or denial of disability
and/or employer's knowledge of
it   13.5.4
content   13.5
grounds of resistance   13.3, 13.4, 13.6,
App.B2
heading   13.4
introduction to parties   13.5.1
jurisdictional issues   13.5.3
purpose   13.1
relevant factual background   13.5.5
response to claims brought   13.5.6
summary of response to legal
complaints brought   13.5.2
timing of   13.2
**Evidence in relation to
remedies**   17.4.2
Evidence of disability
documentary evidence   15.3.3
hearings   17.1.3
impact statement   15.2, App.B3
medical *see* Medical evidence
statement from respondent   15.3.2
supporting statement for the
claimant   15.3.1
witness statements   16.6
Evidence of discrimination
8.4.6
Excluded conditions   1.2.2
Exemplary damages   17.4.3.8
Expert evidence   15.4
agreeing choice of medical expert
15.4.3.1
calling expert at tribunal   15.4.4
choice of medical expert   15.4.2

Expert evidence – *continued*
  instruction of medical expert 15.4.3
  joint letter of instruction 15.4.3.2,
    App.B4

Families
  associative discrimination 2.2
Feelings
  injury to 17.4.3.2
Financial compensation 17.4.3
  aggravated damages 17.4.3.9
  costs of seeking new employment
    17.4.3.5
  exemplary damages 17.4.3.8
  injury to feelings 17.4.3.2
  loss of earnings claim 17.4.3.1
  loss of employment benefits 17.4.3.3
  loss of statutory rights 17.4.3.6
  pension loss 17.4.3.4
  personal injury 17.4.3.7
Fluctuating conditions 1.3.1

Grievance procedures
  adjustments before tribunal process
    11.3
  adjustments to policies during
    employment 7.3.2
Grounds of complaint 12.3,
  12.6, App.B1
Grounds of resistance 13.3,
  13.4, 13.6, App.B2
Group disadvantage 5.2.3

Harassment 6.5
  background 6.1.1
  case study 10.10
  definition 6.1.2
  elements of claim 12.5.5.5, 13.5.6.5
  factors to be taken into account 6.1.6
  no justification for 6.1.8
  purpose or effect of violating dignity
    or creating a hostile environment
    6.1.5
  'related to' disability 6.1.4
  response to claim brought 13.5.6.5
  third party harassment 6.1.7
  unwanted conduct 6.1.3
Hayfever 1.3.1
Health questions
  pre-employment 7.1.1
Hearings
  adjournments 17.3

  adjustments during litigation 9.2.2,
    17.2
  closing submissions 17.1.4
  deliberation and reserved
    judgments 17.1.5
  evidence 17.1.3
  opening the case 17.1.2
  preparation for *see* Preparation for
    hearing
  running order 17.1
HIV/AIDS
  automatic disability 1.2.1
**Holiday pay during sickness
  absence** 7.5.4

Impact statement 15.2, App.B3
Impairment 1.7
  affecting normal day-to-day
    activities 1.1.4
  automatic disability 1.2.1
  cumulative conditions 1.3.3
  effect of medical treatment and
    prostheses 1.5
  excluded conditions 1.2.2
  long term 1.1.3
  material time for assessing
    disability 1.6
  past disabilities 1.4
  physical or mental impairment 1.1.1
  progressive conditions 1.3.2
  recurring or fluctuating conditions
    1.3.1
  specified conditions 1.2
  substantial adverse effect 1.1.2
Independent mediation 14.5
**Indirect disability
  discrimination** 5.3
  background 5.1.1
  disadvantage 5.2.2
  elements of claim 12.5.5.3, 13.5.6.3
  group disadvantage 5.2.3
  justification 5.2.6
  knowledge and 5.2.7
  particular disadvantage 5.2.5
  provision, criteria or practices (PCP)
    and 5.2.1
  relationship with section 15
    discrimination arising from
    disability 3.4
  response to claim brought 13.5.6.3
  s.19 definition 5.2
  shared disability 5.2.4

Individual liability for discriminatory acts 6.3.2
Inducing discrimination 6.3.3
Information
online resource list App.D1
provision of further information
16.7.1
Injury to feelings 17.4.3.2
Instructing discrimination
6.3.3
Interviewing
case study 10.1

Joint letter of instruction
15.4.3.2, App.B4
Judgments
reserved 17.1.5
Judicial mediation 14.4
Jurisdictional issues
ET3 form 13.5.3
Justification for discrimination 2.1.5
indirect disability discrimination
5.2.6
no justification for harassment 6.1.8
no justification for victimisation
6.2.6
proportionate means of achieving
legitimate aim 3.2.5

Knowledge of disability
case study 10.3
direct disability discrimination and
2.1.6
indirect disability discrimination
and 5.2.7
reasonable adjustments duty and 4.8
section 15 discrimination arising
from disability 3.2.6

Leave
disability leave 4.11
Legislation extracts
Access to Medical Reports Act
1988 App.C4
Employment Rights Act 1996
App.C5
Equality Act 2012 App.C1
Income Taxes (Earnings and
Pensions) Act 2003 App.C4
Liability for discriminatory acts
aiding discrimination 6.3.4

individual liability 6.3.2
instructing, causing, inducing
discrimination 6.3.3
vicarious liability 6.3.1
Long term
definition of disability and 1.1.3

Material time for assessing disability 1.6
Mediation
independent 14.5
judicial 14.4
Medical advisers
letter to medical adviser requesting
assessment App.A6
writing to 7.2.3
Medical assessment *see*
Medical examination
Medical evidence 2.1.1, 15.4,
15.5
agreeing choice of medical expert
15.4.3.1
case study 10.7
choice of medical expert 15.4.2
disciplinary proceedings 7.3.1
instruction of medical expert 15.4.3
joint letter of instruction 15.4.3.2,
App.B4
mental health disabilities 9.2.1
personal injury claims 17.4.3.7
refusal to provide 7.4
use of 15.4.1
see also Medical records
Medical examination 2.1.6
consent to attending medical
assessment App.A5
letter to employee requesting
assessment App.A4
letter to medical adviser requesting
assessment App.A6
permanent health insurance (PHI)
and 7.5.3
Medical records 7.2, 10.5,
App.A1
employee consent for access to
7.2.2, App.A2, App.A3
Medical treatment 1.5
Mental health disabilities 9.3
adjustments during litigation 9.2.2
communicating with care 9.1.2
establishing disability 9.2.1
managing stress of litigation 9.2.3
personal injury claims 17.4.3.7

Mental health disabilities – *continued*
prevailing attitudes 9.1.1
Motive for discrimination
2.1.7
Multiple sclerosis
automatic disability 1.2.1

New employment
costs of seeking 17.4.3.5
Non-financial remedies 17.4.4
reinstatement or re-engagement
17.4.4.2
tribunal recommendations 17.4.4.1
Normal day-to-day activities
definition of disability and 1.1.4
**Notice pay for sick
employees** 7.5.6

Occupational requirements
2.4.2
**Office for Disability Issues
(ODI) guidance** Intro, 1.1, 1.3,
1.7, App.C3
Online resource list App.D1
Opening the case 17.1.2
Out of court settlement *see*
Settlement out of court

Particular disadvantage 5.2.5
Past disabilities 1.4
Pay arrangements
bonus payments during sickness
absence 7.5.5
holiday pay during sickness
absence 7.5.4
loss of earnings claim 17.4.3.1
notice pay for sick employees 7.5.6
permanent health insurance (PHI)
7.5.3
reasonable adjustments duty and
7.5.2
sick pay 4.10, 7.5.1
termination of employment and
payments on account of
disability 8.6
Pension loss 17.4.3.4
Perception discrimination 2.3
**Performance improvement
plans (PIPs)** 3.2.3
**Permanent health insurance
(PHI)** 7.5.3
Personal injury claims 17.4.3.7
Phased return to work 4.7.2.1

Physical features
reasonable adjustments duty and
4.3.2
Policies
adjustments to policies during
employment 7.3
Positive discrimination 2.4.1
**Post-termination
victimisation** 6.2.5
**Pre-employment health
questions** 7.1.1
Preparation for hearing 16.8
case management discussion
(CMD) 16.1, 16.2
cast list 16.7.4
chronology 16.7.3
disclosure 16.4
preparation of bundle 16.5
process overview 16.1
provision of further information
16.7.1
schedule of loss 16.3, App.B5
Scott Schedules 16.7.2, App.B6
witness statements 16.6
Progressive conditions 1.3.2
Promotion 7.1.3
Proof
direct disability discrimination 2.1.8
substantial adverse effect 1.1.2
Prostheses 1.5
**Provision, criteria or practices
(PCP)**
indirect disability discrimination
and 5.2.1
Psychiatric injury claims
17.4.3.7

Racial discrimination 2.1.7
Reading time 17.1.1
Reasonable adjustments
duty 4.1, 4.14
adjustments before tribunal process
11.3
adjustments during litigation 9.2.2,
17.2
adjustments to policies during
employment 7.3
adjustments which may be
reasonable 4.7.2.1
adjustments which might not be
reasonable 4.7.2.2
auxiliary aids 4.3.3
breadth of the duty 4.2

burden on claimant 4.7.1
case study 10.2
comparison with non-disabled
  people 4.6
disability leave 4.11
disciplinary procedures 7.3.1
dismissals and 4.12, 8.1
elements of claim of failure to make
  reasonable adjustments 12.5.5.4,
  13.5.6.4
employer duty to consult 4.9
flexibility in policies 7.3.3
grievance procedures 7.3.2
knowledge and 4.8
no justification for failure to make
  reasonable adjustments 4.13
pay and 7.5.2
physical features 4.3.2
provision, criteria or practices
  (PCP) 4.3.1
question of reasonableness 4.7.2
recruitment process and 7.1.2
required steps 4.4
response to claim brought 13.5.6.4
section 15 discrimination arising
  from disability and 3.5
sick pay and 4.10
substantial disadvantage 4.5
termination of employment and 8.1
three requirements 4.3
Reasons for discrimination
2.1.4, 2.1.7
Recruitment
case study 10.1
medical records 7.2, 10.5
pre-employment health questions
  7.1.1
reasonable adjustments duty and
  7.1.2
vicarious liability of recruitment
  consultants 6.3.1
Recurring conditions 1.3.1
Redundancy 8.3
**Reinstatement or
re-engagement** 17.4.4.2
Remedies 17.4
determination of 17.4.1
evidence in relation to 17.4.2
financial claims 17.4.3
non-financial 17.4.4
Reserved judgments 17.1.5
Resource list App.D1

Responding to claim *see* ET3
  form
Retirement 8.5
Return to work
case study 10.8
Review process 17.5
Running order 17.1
reading time 17.1.1

Salary *see* Pay arrangements
Schedule of loss 16.3, App.B5
Scott Schedules 16.7.2, App.B6
**Section 15 discrimination
arising from disability** 3.6
arising in consequence of disability
  3.2.4
brief background 3.1
comparison of old and new regimes
  3.1.4
definition 3.2.1
elements of claim 12.5.5.2, 13.5.6.2
knowledge defence 3.2.6
Malcolm case 3.1.2, 3.1.3
no comparator 3.2.2
overlap with reasonable adjustments
  duty 3.5
proportionate means of achieving
  legitimate aim 3.2.5
relationship with indirect
  discrimination 3.4
response to claim brought 13.5.6.2
some early cases 3.3
unfavourable treatment 3.2.3
Settlement out of court 14.7
ACAS and 14.3
benefits 14.1
compromise agreement 14.2
consent order 14.6
judicial mediation 14.4
Shared disability 5.2.4
Sick pay 4.10
case study 10.6
reasonable adjustments duty and
  4.10
Sickness
bonus payments during sickness
  absence 7.5.5
capability and dismissal 8.4
contractual provisions around
  sickness and disability 7.4
employer responsibility for 8.4.4
holiday pay during sickness
  absence 7.5.4

Sickness – *continued*
   mental illness *see* Mental health
      disabilities
   notice pay for sick employees 7.5.6
Small companies
   reasonable adjustments duty and
      4.7.2.2
Statutory rights
   loss of 17.4.3.6
Statutory sick pay (SSP) 7.5.1
Stigma 9.1.1
Stress
   managing stress of litigation 9.2.3
   psychiatric injury claims 17.4.3.7
Strict liability
   direct disability discrimination and
      2.1.5
   harassment 6.1.8
Substantial disadvantage
   reasonable adjustments duty and 4.5
**Substantial reasons for
   discrimination** 2.1.4
Suppliers
   third party harassment 6.1.7
Support workers 4.7.2.1

Termination of employment
   8.7
   dismissal *see* Dismissal
   payments on account of disability
      8.6
   reasonable adjustments duty and 8.1
   redundancy 8.3
   retirement 8.5
Third parties
   harassment and 6.1.7
   instructing, causing, inducing
      discrimination 6.3.3
   vicarious liability 6.3.1
Time limits 11.3
   victimisation 6.2.4.2
Training 7.1.3
Tribunals 11.1, 11.4
   adjustments before tribunal process
      11.3

adjustments during litigation 9.2.2,
   17.2
appeal process 17.6
bringing a claim *see* ET1 form
calling expert 15.4.4
costs 17.7
hearings *see* Hearings
managing stress of litigation 9.2.3
physical needs for time at tribunal
   9.2.3.4
preparation for *see* Preparation for
   hearing
remedies *see* Remedies
responding to claim *see* ET3 form
review process 17.5
steps before tribunal process 11.2

Unfair dismissal 8.2, 12.6
Unfavourable treatment
   section 15 discrimination arising
      from disability 3.2.3
Unwanted conduct
   harassment and 6.1.3

Vicarious liability 6.3.1, 6.5
   case study 10.9
Victimisation
   bad faith 6.2.4.3
   comparators 6.2.4.1
   definition 6.2.1
   detriment 6.2.3
   elements of claim 12.5.5.6, 13.5.6.6
   no justification for 6.2.6
   post-termination 6.2.5
   protected acts 6.2.2
   response to claim brought 13.5.6.6
   time limits 6.2.4.2

**'Without prejudice'
   discussions** 14.2
Witnesses
   expert *see* Expert evidence
   impact statement 15.2, App.B3
   statements 16.6